THE
GUIDEPOSTS
ANTHOLOGY

THE
GUIDEPOSTS ANTHOLOGY

Edited by
Norman Vincent Peale

GUIDEPOSTS ASSOCIATES, INC.
PAWLING, NEW YORK

To Our Authors

PERHAPS NEVER IN THE HISTORY of publishing have such a galaxy of celebrities in government, business, industry, science, the Armed Forces, and the world of entertainment been represented, first as authors in the Magazine *Guideposts,* and now in The Guideposts Anthology.

We dedicate this volume to these men and women. We are grateful to them not only for the inspiration their personal experiences have brought to others, but also for donating their articles to *Guideposts*. They have, in effect, tithed their time, as well as potential income, a return gift to Him who gave us our time and talent.

RAYMOND THORNBURG
Publisher

Foreword

WHAT IS THE almost incredible Power and greatness in human beings that changes defeat into victory—a failure into success—and enables people to climb stairways to the stars?

Extraordinary things are happening to peoples' lives every day. As minister, counselor and writer for the past 25 years, I have been a student of human nature and can state that just as there has been great scientific progress in material things, so too, are people learning to live more effectively through the science of creative spiritual living.

The stories in this Guideposts Anthology are by some of the greatest personalities of this age—and also by just plain folks, like your aunt Martha in Toledo. These authors represent the three major faiths in America—Protestant, Catholic, and Jewish —and are from all walks of life. They have found in their religion very practical and workable techniques that, when applied to specific situations, change people, events and even history.

When you think of the most famous comebacks by people in recent years, you automatically think of people like Ben Hogan, the golfer, and Jane Froman, the singer.

Everybody knows that these people have deep inner resources. What are they?

In the Guideposts Anthology you will read the private victories of these individuals and many others; you will discover the spiritual techniques that helped make Fritz Kreisler a great violinist, Arthur Godfrey a human, lovable television personality and Eddie Rickenbacker one of the great Americans of our time. Most of these people arose from humble circumstances through a spirit and faith characteristic of Americans.

In this book are answers to almost every major problem that ever existed in human living. If it is sorrow, fear, guilt, physical handicap or illness, worry, frustration—whatever the problem there have been many other people who have the answers. A bus driver, a housewife, a construction worker and a proofreader have found solutions in a deep personal faith just as have President Eisenhower, James Farley, Bob Hope, Jimmy Doolittle and many other prominent Americans.

The important word in this volume is *how*. It isn't enough today for people to say "I believe—I pray—and I go to church," as important as these are. People want to know *why* you do these things and *how*. When Jane Froman shows how one of Christ's parables helped her as she lay in the hospital crippled and near death, it gives other shut-ins and hospitalized patients a clarifying illumination as to how they too can rise above their difficulty.

Somewhere in this volume is a message or an experience or an idea that will drive to the core of your problem, or the problem of someone close to you.

The Guideposts movement is a thrilling adventure and I only wish there was space to pay tribute to all the employees and friends who are helping in the creation and development of this dynamic, inspirational, life-changing force.

It is our hope that in this anthology you will find "that something" that will give you the guidance and strength that you may need to live a happier, more effective life.

Dr. Norman Vincent Peale
Editor-in-chief

How to use this book

I SUGGEST YOU PLACE this book at a strategic place—perhaps on your night table if you like to read before going to sleep, or on the stand by your reading chair in the living room, or on the desk in your office.

Open at random, consult the Contents for an article to suit your mood. If troubled by a problem, select a story that seems to apply and read it through slowly. At the end close your eyes and say silently, "God is here with me now. He is filling my mind with faith and love and health. With His guidance and strength I cannot fail."

Mark certain articles to read to your family, friends, associates or to a Sunday school class. Remember the stories you want to use as conversational subjects or for speech illustrations. Concentrate on the truths that you can apply to your own problems and daily life situations.

If you will use this volume once a day, it will indeed serve as your guideposts to happier, more effective, more productive living.

NORMAN VINCENT PEALE

Contents

ꙮꙮꙮꙮꙮꙮꙮꙮꙮꙮꙮꙮꙮꙮꙮꙮ

HOW TO FIND AND USE
SPIRITUAL TECHNIQUES THAT WORK

THEY KNOW HOW PRAYER IS ANSWERED

HOW YOUR FAITH CAN BE
A DAY-BY-DAY GUIDE

HOW TO STRENGTHEN
YOUR PERSONAL FAITH

HEALING TECHNIQUES FOR SORROW,
FEAR AND WORRY

HOW TO HELP YOURSELF—
BY HELPING OTHERS

Five Famous Comebacks

—and How They Happened

Disaster Was No Calamity for Jane

by JANE FROMAN

*Stripped of material possessions, seriously crippled
and heavily in debt from a plane crash, singer Jane
Froman searched for hidden assets. One of Christ's
parables was of special help. An unforgetable story
of recovery and faith.*

I HAVE OFTEN HEARD the familiar remark, "When you reach the
end of your rope, tie a knot and hang on." Who, I used to wonder, gives us the power to hold on to the knot?

I found out during the years following that fateful March
day in 1943. The Clipper carrying our USO camp shows entertainment troupe, bound for service camps in Europe and Africa,
crashed in the Tagus River off the coast of Portugal. Of thirty-
nine aboard, only fifteen of us survived.

Conscious, but unable to help myself due to injuries, I was
kept afloat by Captain John C. Burn, co-pilot of the plane, who
held on to me in spite of his own head and back injuries. After
a rescue launch pulled us out of the icy water, they found both
my legs broken, one almost completely off; my right arm was
fractured and several of my ribs had been cracked.

Much publicity, sympathy and encouragement, far more than
I deserve, has followed my battle for recovery. But part of the
story has never been told—only now, do I know how to share it.

In a Lisbon hospital, awaiting emergency treatment, my mind
tried to take stock of the situation. All the personal possessions
I carried had been lost. The new clothes I had been wearing had
been cut from me with scissors.

As I lay naked under a sheet on a hospital stretcher I felt like

3

a new-born baby, entering this world for the first time. I felt I had nothing left from my years of living, nothing—except what was in my heart and mind: a set of memories of people who had been kind to me, and a lifelong dependence on Divine Power.

The doctors didn't tell me how hopeless they considered my case. In a way I sensed their unspoken verdict. "At best she will be a helpless cripple." All, except God and myself, thought I was finished.

I knew then that recovery would depend only in part on medicine and surgery; my greatest help would come from the storehouse within me. What had I been able to put away? Upon what spiritual capital could I draw?

Through the years I had built habits—among which was prayer. Like all good habits, it started early in life at Sunday and Wednesday Night Prayer Meetings, which were a regular thing in our family. When a situation was beyond me, I learned early to turn it over to God. I was also taught that prayers of thanks are as important as prayer requests. Gradually I had found myself saying, "Thank you, Lord," as I moved about accomplishing the everyday tasks. I discovered the habit gave an added glow to results.

I also owed a lot to my mother; and my pioneer grandmother who, years ago, had journeyed to Missouri in a covered wagon. Her only link with the life she had known before starting that great adventure, was a rambler rosebush carefully dug, packed and stowed under the wagon seat. Does one inherit courage and patience? If so, I was well fortified.

Like a storekeeper taking inventory I tallied them up: I was alive, wasn't I? I could think, hear, see. I could talk—and on a sudden impulse, I turned my head back and tried my voice.

The tones that echoed through the hospital startled everyone.

I could still sing! I tried the scales—a snatch of song—and my heart fairly thrilled.

With suppressed excitement I began planning a life again. How to use the important talents which had been spared me? Then I remembered the Bible parable of the talents.* Why couldn't I follow the example of the servant who increased his talents by putting them to work through other people? I would take what I had, without worrying about what I had not, and work for something constructive and good. I hoped in the doing that I could make people happy.

The process of recovery during the weeks that followed was like a slow climb up a tremendous ladder. Each rung was a step toward the horizon of a normal life.

Eight months after the crash I was in a wheel chair, singing in the Broadway musical, "Artists and Models."

They had to carry me everywhere. I was carted onto stages, lifted in and out of taxis. At the outset my pride suffered greatly, as it does with all handicapped people. I have noticed this also with soldiers in hospitals; they resisted, at times almost fought off, any help or assistance. It became nearly an obsession with me, too, and threatened to wreck the progress I was making.

While struggling with this I related it again to the Bible parable of the talents. Then I came upon a great truth: since I couldn't handle it alone God was using other people to render me assistance.

I began to see how trouble and privation fit into His Plan for man's development. To make personal progress in character building, human beings must give of themselves by helping others; therefore, my own need became a necessary part of somebody else's development.

Once arrived at this understanding, I could easily accept people's generosity and desire to help. Clearly visible to me was His Hand guiding and helping, not only me but hundreds of others, through my difficulties.

* *Matthew 25: 14-29*

In the years which followed, in and out of hospitals, with operations and re-operations interrupting my work, I had little time to feel sorry for myself. Huge doctor and hospital bills accumulated—I had to earn money. The only way I knew was with my voice.

My total expenses for doctors and hospitals during those years amounted to over $350,000. There were times when I thought I would never again be out of debt. But several years ago, when I paid the last bill, I received a statement from my bank showing that I had a balance of $37.62. That was the most thrilling bank statement of my life. And $37.62 to do with as I pleased!

Many months after my accident, I saw for the first time since leaving Lisbon hospital the man who saved me from drowning that night, Captain John Burn, the Pan American pilot. It is hard to describe my happiness when we were married in 1948— or the thrill when, a short time later, I threw away my crutches for good.

My husband and I recently purchased our own home in New York City. In the backyard of this house there is small area just big enough for a garden—something I have always wanted.

Several months after we were settled, my mother sent me cuttings from the very same rambler rosebush which my grandmother had carried West in a covered wagon, and which was later planted by the front door of our family home in Missouri. Its fragrant blossoms were an important part of my childhood memory. Since planting the rambler rose, I have watched it with particular eagerness. Now, transplanted again in Eastern soil, this rose and I have something in common. We are both beginning life all over again.

Whether it's plants or people, starting from scratch is an old custom in America. I thank God constantly for a country where the "nobody" can become "somebody," the handicapped rises above any obstacle, and the impossible is, through God's help, accomplished with regularity.

Technique for Victory

by JOHN SHERRILL

Shy, unpopular Ben Hogan was "through" as a golf champ back in 1949, his body smashed in a car accident. John Sherrill, Guideposts' Associate Editor, tells how it was, only a year later, that Hogan was able to rebound amazingly—on to new championships and to a popularity he would have never thought possible before.

BEN HOGAN once said: "Since I was knee-high to a stymie, I've had to fight for everything I got." His introduction to the game that made him famous illustrates this.

Born in Texas—the son of a blacksmith—Hogan was selling papers in Fort Worth's Union Station at the age of 12 when he discovered that caddies at a nearby club made 65¢ a round. He went after the job, not even knowing what "golf" was.

The boss caddy sized Hogan up, picked out another runt who wanted to work, and told them to scrap. The winner would get the job. Ben won.

A year later he decided to try the game himself. Hogan didn't have a natural swing. But he understood work, and the importance of detail. Commented one of his own caddies, "He will even memorize the grain of the grass if it will help his game." Hogan, the golfing machine, was born.

It was a plodding, mechanical, intellectual approach to the game that brought Hogan to tournament play, years later. "He swings with the business-like authority of a machine stamping out bottle tops," one reporter said. And Hogan himself, describing his swing, uses the tip-off phrase, "muscle memory."

To memorize a stroke muscle by muscle takes hours of solitary practice. Although these silent hours began to pay off in Ben's

7

game, they also took their toll on his personality. Hogan became dour, taciturn. On the links he did not know how to handle the distraction of the gallery . . . their hero worship, jibes, requests for autographs. The only apparent solution was to shut himself off from the crowd.

These are not qualities to make a popular man, although they did make a champion. After a slow start, Ben, in 1945, began winning title after title. Outwardly the galleries did not like him. But there was something about the very shyness and metallic discipline of Hogan's personality that doubtless made many in his silent gallery say, "You know, I am probably the only one who does, but I like that guy, Hogan."

Then on the morning of February 2, 1949, as Hogan was driving to his home in Fort Worth, Texas, he was critically hurt in an automobile accident. The golf champion had a crushed pelvis, a fractured left leg, a crushed shoulder, a broken ankle, and was close to death from shock. Doctors hoped he would live, but doubted if he would ever walk again. Hardly anyone considered the idea that Ben might ever resume his golf career.

It wasn't much more than a year later that short, 130 pound Ben Hogan amazed the world by entering the Los Angeles Open —one of the top tournaments in the country. Although suffering from leg cramps, Ben limped to the first tee as the crowd cheered. Instead of the tense, fixed expression usually reserved for the galleries, Hogan's face broke into a warm smile.

Ben played his usual concentrated game, careful not to waste his energy during the 72 hole match. His courage and determination brought him a tie for the championship. He lost the playoff, but everyone was speaking of "Hogan's victory."

The performance was remarkable in itself but the change in the "Texas Iceberg" was talked about even more. Sports writers all over the country were asking: What happened to Ben Hogan during those months of rehabilitation?

When I met Hogan at the Hershey Country Club recently, I asked the golf champ this question, and found that the Hogans had received thousands of letters during this period of recovery, letters from all kinds of people—housewives, salesmen, office clerks, students, the man on the street—each with basically the same message: "You can win out, Ben. We'll be praying for you."

Hogan revealed that several things helped him during his recovery. His theory of muscle memory on the golf course had been simply this: if he practiced one shot long enough and with enough concentration, his muscles would memorize the shot so that it would become almost automatic. On his hospital bed, Hogan applied the same theory. If he concentrated hard enough on getting well—believed enough—and practiced this belief hour after hour—day after day—just as he mastered golf, so could he overcome physical illness.

"Before the accident I took things for granted, even such things as trees and grass—except when they got in my way for a golf swing," he admitted.

"But all the time I lay in my hospital bed, I didn't even take breathing for granted. Then the letters started to pour in, people writing me that they were praying for my recovery. This was something that had never happened to me before. I had always tried to shut myself off from spectators during a match so that I could concentrate on my game. Before these letters came, I told myself that I never cared much whether people were for me or against me.

"The prayers of these people—and those of my wife, Valerie— had a lot to do with my recovery. Their belief in me helped me believe in myself. I *had* to repay faith with faith."

Ben Hogan, my wife and I talked for over two leisurely hours. There was nothing cold or ungiving in his personality. He spoke eloquently of the people who had helped him, his wife's tireless patience, and his many new friends among the gallery, the sports writers and his competitors.

For a man considered "through" three years ago, one of sports' greatest comeback heroes has surely achieved amazing honors. In 1950 he won the U. S. Open. In 1951, he won the Master's, the "World's Championship" at Tam O'Shanter, and repeated his U. S. Open victory, spectacularly coming from behind to do it. The Philadelphia Sports Writers Association voted him the most courageous athlete of 1951; both the Professional Golfers of America and the Associated Press voted him 1951 "Golfer of the Year."

Hogan's technique of victory can be applied anywhere, by anyone, as Ben did both to golf and to personal problems.

My Lucky Star

by FRAN ALLISON

A lovely young girl, injured and disfigured in an auto accident, knew she was dying. But a sudden great urge to live overwhelmed Fran Allison. Those who admire her beauty today on television little realize the extent of her personal victory.

THE BIG CRISIS in my life occurred when I was just starting my career.

A girl friend, Jessie, and I were driving to Des Moines for the weekend. An accident happened; so quickly I barely recall it. There was Jessie's mad wrestle to control the car; then I was pitched into glass, metal, noise and pain.

In a state of semi-consciousness I remember voices, a hospital and Jessie, unhurt, telling someone to call my mother back in Laporte City, Iowa, but not to frighten her. Then a priest came to say the last rites over me, just as I slipped into unconsciousness.

Later I remember more voices:

"She wouldn't be able to get here in time" (meaning my mother) . . . "It's useless to operate" . . . "Too late to do much of anything."

Weak as I was, somehow all this made me protest. They hadn't even tried. Nobody was doing a thing. My doctor at home would have tried.

With a great effort I made a feeble sound and called the name of my home town doctor.

My voice startled them. Jessie then tried to tell me that she had talked to my mother, "Nan," and that Nan was praying for me. (I learned later that my mother walked up and down the kitchen for 10 hours straight praying for my recovery. Anyone who came near her was asked to join.)

The fact that I was able to moan for a doctor, while seemingly on the verge of death, brought on some quick action.

It was 4 in the morning but the nurses immediately pulled out a doctors' registry. They assumed that the doctor I called for was located in Des Moines. Call it coincidence, but they located a doctor of the same name and got him on the phone: "Hello, Doctor . . . one of your patients is down here at the hospital . . . She's in a bad way. Could you come out immediately?"

Fogged with sleep, the doctor couldn't remember any patient by the name of Allison, yet he dressed and hurried down to the hospital. Of course he didn't recognize me, but it was enough that I had called for him. Gathering together his assistants, he went to work on my smashed face. He felt my condition was this side of hopeless. But he patched me together.

I believe to this day that if God hadn't given me enough strength to cry out that name, I would have been left unattended to die.

When I quit the hospital, whatever beauty I had was a memory. Behind my face was recurrent pain and dread onslaughts of headaches.

Yet there was much to be grateful for. My sight had been spared. My throat was all right . . . I could still sing. I could walk, hear. And I could laugh. Perhaps it was my brush with death and my awareness of my mother's prayers and my own—I had the feeling that God had bolstered my spirit when others had given me up.

In this period of recuperation, of constant headache and pain, "Nan's" (as everyone called mother) remarkable spirit and sense of humor were powerful therapies. My mother taught me by example how much power there was in prayer, and her own victory over tuberculosis made me realize how necessary it is to fight hard for life.

Despite a deep, self-conscious feeling about my scarred face, I decided to go on with my career. And since nobody *saw* you in radio, I felt secure in this field. Even before the accident, I was on the air in Chicago at the wonderful (to me) salary of $50 a week. I went back.

One day a man came in to demonstrate some new songs. We looked at each other, then he took out a song and sang: "You Are My Desire." A friendship grew, ripened, developed into love. Archie Levington and I are of different faiths, yet love, respect and understanding are the blended ingredients in our happy marriage.

My career developed and soon fan mail began to multiply. I didn't like to meet fans because I still felt self-conscious about my face and was very shy. One man wrote many times and finally came into the radio office, so I couldn't avoid the meeting.

We talked for a while, and he asked about the accident and insisted that I go to a famous doctor in Memphis. He made arrangements.

I went as soon as my radio season was over. After a thorough examination, the doctor sat down with me, an astounded look on his face. He told me that I had had osteomyelitis—that the bone of my nose and right eye showed its ravages—yet now there was no trace of the disease!

"Remarkable!" he cried. "There is no cure, yet you have been cured. Under what lucky star do you live?"

"The Star of Bethlehem, I guess," I told him.

I knew it was true too!

He performed what was a series of operations—done each year (except one) on my vacation time, until not only do I look almost like my old self again but I was rid of the pressure headaches that tormented me.

The year that didn't find me "vacationing" in Memphis was to have been the happiest year of our marriage—the coming of the blessing my husband and I wanted above everything. But our child was stillborn.

And once more I had to cling to faith—or lose it. My husband sought out the priest who had married us. And he and my mother prayed me through—and roused me again to faith.

If I had thought the battle after my accident was tough, this second blow had left me feeling numb and cold and forsaken. Only prayer and Archie's love helped me pull out of it.

During these past years, my work with the creative world of Burr Tillstrom has meant much to me. I had known Burr (and Kukla and Ollie) during the war years when we had done bond-selling shows. But since we have been together on "Kukla, Fran and Ollie," I came to know each of the Kuklapolitans and from each of them I have received a very definite something which I treasure.

Seriously—it's a good and blessed life with work of special dearness. Success, yes—beyond what we can quite believe. But when people wonder if my share of it will turn my head, when people tell me how pretty I am on television, I can't very well do anything but marvel, and give thanks to God and to my mother's prayers.

The Best Investment

by CONRAD HILTON

> *Buying the Waldorf Astoria Hotel had to wait at one point while Conrad Hilton did something more important. The warm personal story of a great hotel man who lost everything during the depression except the most important quality he needed to make a comeback.*

ON THAT SUMMER day in 1947 when my mother was seized with a heart attack, I was in the midst of some of the most ambitious negotiations of my life. Mother knew I kept a picture of an enormous hotel on my desk. Across it I had scrawled: "The Greatest of Them All." That day I had hoped to be able to tell her that at last I had bought the Waldorf-Astoria.

Once at her bedside, I knew she was dying. "It may be hours," the doctor said, "Or she may linger . . ."

Eighty-five years of vigorous, alert living finally running out! I sat down to wait and watch. My vigil was to last five weeks. They tell me that associates kept phoning that my presence at the office was vital. I can't recall any messages.

I was living again my years with this stricken lady, whose faith was my guiding star. Mother was the most religious person I ever knew; my father was the least. Gus Hilton made and lost fortunes; staking, claiming, working and buying land. A terror as a trader, he was a man's man, born for campfires, song, story, laughter, food and drink; totally without fear.

When Gus married Mary, he took his bride to New Mexico. It was a land of storms, where snakes, wild animals, Apache Indians, a horse under you and Spanish in your mouth, were all matter of course. There a man built with his own hands an adobe house, and a woman made it home.

Here, my mother raised eight children. I was the first son, born on Christmas. Mother rode me 11 miles, a body guard riding beside us, to have me baptized. She could do without most things in life, but never without her church. As a young mother, she and her kids rode every Sunday those 11 miles from San Antonio to Socorro, always with an armed escort because Indians had once nearly killed Gus.

I have heard many people say, "I just can't get to church," but I never heard mother say that.

Her program for us children was religion, food and learning and in that order, while father was becoming coal king of the countryside. We were sent away to schools. I planned going to Dartmouth and felt the world was mine. Came the 1907 panic and I couldn't go.

"Who says Dartmouth's best for you?" Mother demanded. "Maybe the Lord knows what's for the best."

It didn't seem for the best. Because after two years at the New Mexico School of Mines I had to quit. Dad's money was gone. We all came back home. Our house was ten rooms over a general store. Mother stowed all ten of us in five rooms, so that the others could be rented. She cooked for all.

That experience started me in the hotel business! I went to bed before sunset, got up at midnight to meet the southbound train at 1:00 A.M., and then waited for the northbound train arriving at 3:00. I toted the bags of travelling salesmen, hustled up eggs and coffee, pumped the strangers for news of the outside world, and bedded them down. Then I would catch a few hours' sleep before getting up again at 8:00 and running the store.

Gus was off, starting life afresh. Father was not a man to stay down long. Within two years he had organized a new bank in Hot Springs. Soon he built a home in Socorro and moved the family there where mother had her church. I was left behind to run the old San Antonio general store and "hotel" in full partnership, and I organized the first bank in San Antonio.

How often during those hectic years, mother would say to me:

"Don't talk to me about the important people you have to see, Connie. You get along over to church first and see God. Prayer is the best investment you'll ever make. Don't you forget it."

When I left for World War I, Mother threw her arms around me at the station and said: "I can't do all the praying for this family, Connie. Keep close to the sacraments."

My father was killed in an auto crash while I was at Army Headquarters in Paris in 1919. I got my discharge to become head of Pop's family with three of us still in school. His estate had shrunk and even with the remains of my bank (sold while I was in the service) my share was only $5,000. Since my one idea was to extend my operations, I bought my first hotel in Cisco. I put in my whole $5,000. Mother put in hers.

For a time things flowered and prospered. I bought more hotels on credit; I married a girl who had been visiting Dallas relatives; I tasted the thrill, too, of building a hotel, and incorporating.

Then, the stock market exploded and kept on going down. No salesmen were on the road, nobody taking vacations, everyone eating at home. By this time, I had 1,800 rooms. Desperately, I cut off floors to save heat; I even took out room phones to save 15 cents on each! But elevators had to be run, lights must be turned on, furnaces fed. First, no profits. Then I couldn't meet interest on notes. Next, I couldn't pay taxes—finally, current bills.

Imagine trying to pay a $100,000 furniture bill at $10 a week! Men were jumping out of hotel windows—*my* hotel windows! Mother said:

"Some men jump out of windows; some go to church."

An insurance company, the mortgagee on my hotels, foreclosed. There went my collateral. I prayed then . . . like a lost child.

It seemed everything blew up all at once. My brother Gus, Jr. had died suddenly that Spring. I owed over a half a million in debts. On sufferance I slept in a room of a hotel I once had owned. All my belonging were in a suitcase. If I wanted to make a phone call I had to talk publicly at the lobby pay phone.

When I got back from church that day a bellboy named Eddie Fowler called me aside and put his $300 savings in my hand.

"Just eating money, Mr. Hilton," is all he said. I couldn't answer.

There was a message for me from the insurance company president, asking if I would operate their hotels *and* my own. I went to Galveston and signed a contract which stipulated that if ever my contract was broken, I'd get one hotel back for every two that they took.

I went to work. But I was harassed by a boss who signed every check and watched my slightest move. When I found I had to explain buying 12 towels instead of 8, I decided to keep away from him. At that he entered suit to cancel our contract.

"What if he doesn't trust you," Mother said, "as long as God trusts you? You march yourself to church."

I marched to church every morning at 5:00 through that desperate time. Often Mother was in the pew beside me. One morning I marched out of church inexplicably full of courage. I filed a counter suit against my boss. Upon that, he decided court fights would do nobody any good. So he tore up my contract and gave me back my hotels except the best two.

I went back to the hotel—*mine* again now!—only to find a sheriff with a judgment from a creditor.

"Lay off," I begged. "I never skipped a debt yet."

"If you don't pay," he shrugged, "I'll tack this up in the lobby."

"Go ahead," I snapped. As I turned away I saw my mother standing, eyes closed, lips moving in prayer.

"This wall is marble," the constable called, "and I can't tack." We all burst out laughing.

"This chump can take his bill and stand in line," the sheriff decided and stalked off.

These and other memories filled me as I sat beside the woman who meant more in my life than any other person. Each morning, when conscious, she received Communion, while I knelt beside her. When she grew too weak to speak, she was still praying, her rosary clasped tightly in her hands.

I buried Mother in New Mexico, laying her beside Gus. The stores closed in her honor, and almost the whole town turned out, saluting one of the last of the frontier women.

Beside me stood my boyhood chum, J. B. Herndon, who has always been, until his recent death, one of my top hotel associates. I turned with him and left the past.

Not for another two years could I buy the Waldorf-Astoria.

When I first took up residence there, some columnists noted my daily church visits. Strangely enough I had to hit New York and its village interest in a Somebody's doing, for this habit to rate comment. But as I walk from the Waldorf each day over to the Cathedral, I feel like saying to everybody I see: "Come in with me, and visit the Lord. It's the best investment you'll ever make."

Out of Prison Darkness

by STARR DAILY

*While his father prayed for him, the boy was plan-
ning his next crime. Jailed, considered a hopeless
criminal and thrown into solitary confinement, Starr
Daily had a dramatic religious experience. He tells
of it here.*

PICTURE, IF YOU CAN, a man who lives exclusively for the execu-
tion and planning of crime. Picture a man whose health was
broken by the incessant hammer-blows of dissipation and prison
rebellion ... a man completely incapable of cooperating with
any save fellow criminals, and then only out of selfish motives.

This man was myself over 20 years ago.

I'll never forget the words of the judge who sentenced me to
prison for the third and final time.

"I know you are sick," he said to me. "And I know that more
punishment is not the remedy. I don't know what else to do. Our
helplessness is your hopelessness."

My earliest childhood memory is that of fear: fear of death,
fear of sin and a fear of being locked in. Yet I did have beautiful
spiritual dreams about Jesus Christ.

My mother, a lovely and sensitive woman, died shortly after
my birth. My hardworking father could not cope with my boyhood conflicts. I developed a sense of self-pity and false pride, and
started to run away from difficult situations.

I began to dislike boys of my own age and seek the society of
older boys, whose fellowship I won by copying their vices: chiefly
gambling, pool-playing, and drinking. At 12 came my first
drink. Then came stealing.

I began fraternizing with thieves and fugitives whose deeds
were black as Stygian Hell. With eagerness I looked forward to

the day when my record, too, would be long and black; when the police would refer to me with a shudder.

The picture of my patient father will always remain. His was a splendid indulgent love, a love that stood the severest possible test, since he saw me through my complete degradation.

For years he spent time, energy and money trying to keep me out of jail. Because of me he lost his reputation for being a man of sound judgment; he forfeited friends; he became an object of pity. It didn't seem to make a great deal of difference.

Yet how frustrated he must have been because his persistence in helping always seemed to be rewarded by the increase of my weakness.

Once, having arranged for the premature end of my sentence, he came all the way to the prison to meet me and share the joy of my freedom. As we rode away together, he spoke quietly of his faith in me. There was no preachment in his tones.

"You see, son, I want you to make good," he said. "Not for my sake, but to realize your mother's faith in you."

While he talked I was meditating upon my next crime. It seems almost a sacrilege, but I went to the little town of my birth to commit this act. In this village I was caught burglarizing a store.

The next morning my father heard the news. It broke his heart, but not his faith. He came immediately to the jail, put his hand through the bars and held mine. He suffered in silence. When the jailer told him his time was up, he spoke briefly:

"It's all right, son. Somehow, in some way it will all be made right." With that he left. Soon after I was sentenced to prison. I never saw my father again.

Strange how prisons, penal farms, chain gangs, the third degree of the police world—the whole futile program of punishment had tried to straighten out my twisted character and failed. How, also, good men, reaching to me with selfless hands, had tried to help to no avail. All for the simple reason that I didn't want to be corrected. Only God can help the man who has no desire to help himself.

I reentered prison for the third time with sinister ideas. Three times I tried to fight my way to freedom. The first two times were of the "lone wolf" variety; the third involved group action, destruction and physical violence. Our plan was to cause a mob riot and during its height to seize the deputy warden as a shield and hostage, then under threats of death force him to give the order that would open the gates.

The plot was discovered and I was sentenced to the dungeon.

The average time for a strong man in "the hole" is 15 days, at the end of which time the doctor ends the sentence. This time came and went. Finally, I collapsed. I seemed to be sustained by hate alone as I lay mired in the lowest hell earth had to offer.

Yet as I lay near death on the icy floor of the cell, a strange new thought came to me. I realized that I had been a dynamo of energy in everything I had done. I began to wonder what would have happened if I had used my powers for something other than destruction. It was a completely revolutionary thought!

What then followed is difficult to describe. I first began to dream disconnected dreams; then they took on meaning. These dreams were the same I had as a child—beautiful dreams of Jesus Christ, the Man I had tried to avoid for many years. He paused near my side and looked down deep into my eyes as though He were trying to penetrate my soul. In all my life I had never seen or felt such love.

Then I seemed to see all the people I had injured directly or indirectly, or who had injured me. I poured out love to them which seemed to heal their hurts. Then we were in a great auditorium and I spoke to all the people concerning love. I seemed to be assuring myself at the same time that I was awake and that I would never forget these words flowing over my lips.

When I consciously returned to my dungeon environment, the state of my mind had completely changed. The cell was illuminated with a new kind of light—the light of my own redeemed eye. Before that experience I was a calloused criminal; after it I was completely healed of my criminal tendencies! As a result, the prison doors swung open five years in advance of the time set for my release.

Often I've thought of my father and his faith in me. He had died before it was justified. Or perhaps it was my father's and mother's faith in me, which, with God's help, brought my transformation in that cold, foul prison cell.

I'd like to think so.

~~~~~~~~

Starr Daily walked away from his prison experience convinced that criminals can be healed through religious power. Despite no literary background, he decided first to write his story.

Mrs. Daily, whom he married shortly after his prison experience, tells how time after time he would receive his rejected manuscripts back in the mail, then patiently sit down and begin anew the laborious job of revision.

Finally, came an acceptance . . . his first book!

From author ("Release," "Love Can Open Prison Doors," and others) Starr Daily branched into the lecture field. Everywhere he tells his story frankly, hoping that it would spark prison reform, promote better methods for handling discharged convicts, and even touch the lives of criminals or men with criminal tendencies.

Starr Daily's thrilling personal story has given new hope and courage to thousands of defeated people.

THE EDITORS

What Can I Do?—
Stories of Personal Action

I've Charted My Course

by EDDIE RICKENBACKER

> *"Each of us needs a personal plan to help us, as a nation, rearm spiritually," says Captain Eddie. The famous automobile racer and aviator—now President of Eastern Air Lines—offers his own plan of action.*

IN RECENT YEARS the flames of freedom have been growing dimmer rather than brighter because, at a time when we wanted to win the peoples of the world more than ever before, our leadership was often weak and uncertain. Certainly, it has been misunderstood.

Why have we been failing?

Because too many of our generation worship the false idols of material possessions, from which they gain comfort but no enduring strength.

We are losing the spiritual bond of wisdom which, in 1776, sparked the creation of the Declaration of Independence. All dictators fear this document and fear what it stands for more than they do mechanized armies.

We Americans are part of the greatest experiment in the history of mankind; it has stirred and excited freedom-loving peoples the world over. The unique part of this experiment is that our country was founded on a religious foundation.

If this experiment ever fails, it would be because we, the people, failed.

Our leaders can't carry the whole responsibility. Each of us—businessman, housewife, doctor, factory worker, scientist, student—needs some personal plan to help us rearm spiritually. I present mine in the hope it may be helpful to others.

1. *Prayer has been the greatest source of power in my life.* I learned to pray at my mother's knee, and still never retire at night

27

without uttering those same simple prayers. I pray about my business problems, my friends, family, country. Prayer has saved my life on more occasions than I can remember.

2. *Believe in the principles of your faith,* in people, in your country—in life. Know clearly and fully what those principles are. Positive thinking is adhering to the fundamental teachings of the Bible. Think victory, and life becomes rich in achievement; think disaster and you will get it.

Once when in the hospital, I could almost taste the sweetness of death. It would have been easy to give in. Then through the radio beside my bed, I heard the announcement that Eddie Rickenbacker was dying. A tremendous urge to live actually gave strength to my muscles. It stimulated me so that I was determined to live.

In a few months, I was back at work.

I'll always fight like a wildcat for my life until they nail the lid on my casket. The fight should be not just to live, however, but to live to do something worth-while.

3. *Honesty.* There are no degrees of honesty. If you are honest with yourself, then you will be forced to be honest with your fellowmen. Honesty can be a hard master, but without moral discipline we are slaves to temptation.

4. *Work.* At our jobs, the positive word is opportunity. My parents migrated from Switzerland to America because of the possibilities they knew were in America. They taught me how to work; they taught me and six other children never to expect something for nothing.

At 12, when my father died, I worked as a glass blower to help support the family. I have worked in a foundry, carved tombstones (including my father's), was a railroad roustabout, and then fell in love with the automobile. To me, the right work is the most glorious experience in life. In Communist countries today a man is not allowed to work where and at what he pleases. That, to me, is degradation.

5. *Benevolence.* If God has given to us abundantly, we have a responsibility to share our abundance with those less fortunate.

6. *Thrift has always been one of America's greatest virtues.* Today it is mocked and labeled as selfish hoarding. I do not care how much or how little we make, none of us has the moral right—and this includes the government—to spend all we earn. The way to start to save is to think in terms of pennies, rather than dollars. Even in a vast organization like the Eastern Airlines, we think of economy in terms of pennies.

7. *Vote.* We cannot rearm ourselves morally, and not practice the privilege of voting. This is an essential part of any program to keep ourselves free.

8. *Country.* I say humbly and sincerely that there is nothing in the world—not even life itself—that I love more than I do this land of ours. No worldly goods can take the place of my country. And loving my country means loving my fellow countryman wherever he hails from originally, and however he worships.

No personal program for spiritual rearmament can be effective without day-by-day rededication, done with humility. Let's admit we don't know it all, individually or as groups; that we make mistakes, can fail and learn from others.

One of the greatest privileges we have in this country is the privilege to fail. Failure, adversity and suffering are the exhilarators of expanding mentality.

The first speech I made was a total flop and a great humiliation to me. This failure, however, made me go out and learn to speak. If our failures in the recent worldwide political crisis made us determined to devise a strong, positive program then these failures will have been useful.

No one group, or individual, can do the job that is needed today, but many of us, with the help and guidance of God can start our own spiritual program. I've made mine. Your own may be different—and better. I urge you only to make one earnestly and live it daily.

No Tips Today, Please

by MILTON BRONSTEIN

> *If you are going to church, or are on your way to vote, here is a cab driver who will give you a free ride. Milton Bronstein, and other drivers of the American-United Cab Association in Chicago, Illinois, are more interested in being good Americans than making money.*

TWO YEARS AGO, just before election time, I heard a guy say to his buddy, "Who you gonna vote for, Jim?"

"Don't know," said his friend. "Probably no one. I got a rough day Tuesday."

"Me too," said the other. "What's one vote anyway?"

I thought to myself: "Who do these guys think they are? They live in a free country; they get a chance to vote for anyone they like and they haven't got time."

I guess they're free not to vote, just as they're free to vote, but I still don't like it. I'm not trying to wave the flag about, but I'm certainly not too proud to say that I love my country. I drive my own cab, have a wonderful wife and two great kids. Our cab association is made up of guys who fought in the last war. In a way we're still fighting for the things we believe in.

Anyway, all this gives me an idea. The day before election I get out paint and brush and go to work on the side of my cab. The next day I pull up by our administration office—the American-United Cab Association—proud of my art. On the side of the cab is this sign:

"Be American. Ride American. No matter how you vote ... Vote today. Your ride free to the polls."

I showed the sign to other cabbies. "What do you guys say? Want to join me?"

Fifteen did.

See what I mean about our company!

Now I've no axe to grind about politics. I just believe in taking advantage of the rights we got in this country. We handled a lot of business free, that day. As for the lost fares, so what!

We got our cab association going the hard way after World War II. There's nothing tougher than breaking into a big city like Chicago with a new cab outfit. We stuck together, pooled our money and ideas and made a go of it. Some of our veterans were full colonels, one an air base commander in the war. We own our cabs. Come an emergency and we're mobilized, ready to go as members of the Civil Defense Corps.

I got a formula that I've followed ever since I started driving: For every dollar in my pocket, 50 cents belongs to anyone in need. I'm no fall guy; I just like helping people. A lot of my buddies feel the same way.

Don't put us down for no halos. The guys are rough-and-ready; several have trapped thugs and brought 'em in. Sometimes we scrap a little among ourselves, but let anyone else try to muscle in and see what happens.

On certain days we give free rides to anyone who will give blood to the Red Cross. Some of the guys have given so much blood, their arms are full of needle holes. I don't see how they walk around.

One day about 15 of our cabs jammed up the traffic in front of the blood center. A cop came running up, waving his arms and shouting, "Get these cabs outa here." But he quieted down quickly, and later went in and gave some blood himself.

On Saturdays and Sundays I have put this sign on my cab: "Believe in God and pray for peace—ride free to your place of worship." On Sundays I make 10 to 12 free rides to churches. Several riders called my home number as early as 6:30 Sunday morning.

Some days we put a sign inside our cabs, asking riders who intend to tip, to put it in the can for March of Dimes. We do the same thing, too, for the Cancer Fund, Crippled Children and so forth. We raised $4,800 for the Cancer Fund alone.

One of my favorite jobs is to drive up to the Navy Base and pick up vets back from Korea and give 'em a free ride to town and back.

But the rides I like best are with my own family. A number of years ago my wife and I started giving our kids a special geography lesson every year during our vacation. I asked the family what state they'd like to visit. They said Wisconsin. We studied every inch of the map; we knew every important spot, and then the four of us—Margaret, my wife; Sandy (16); Sharon (11) and I—all hopped into my cab and we started off.

We really covered that state. In three weeks we stopped at tourist cabins, visited historical spots, the capital, the parks, traveling up and down and crosswise. Did we love it!

The next year it was Michigan—then Colorado, Illinois, Indiana, Minnesota, and Pennsylvania. Lots more to go and plenty of time to do them.

There's too much living to do to waste any of it being unhappy because we haven't the money we'd like or don't belong to the best clubs.

Sometimes I've been hurt by cracks made about my religion. Happened several times in the Army. One answer always stopped 'em.

"That's okay with me if you feel that way, fellas," I'd say after some dig. "But if any of you men get hit by a bullet, I'll be glad to give you my blood. Then you'll have Jewish blood in you too."

After all, does it make any difference what your race or religion is if you try to keep God in your heart?

With a Song in Her Soul

by TEX MC CRARY

A lovely young singer, Ann Moray de Ceballos, had a chance for a glamorous musical career; instead, she chose dangerous work in a desolate corner of the world. Tex McCrary of the famous radio team, Tex and Jinx, relates a moving story of the Scottish girl with the haunting voice.

THE AUSSIE RAISED his forehead from the stone windowsill and looked out at the city of Caracas, Venezuela. He cocked his grizzled head to listed to the strains of a Scottish tune a red-haired girl was singing to him, in a delicate, haunting voice.

By yon bonnie banks and by yon bonnie braes . . .

"Before I die, Scotty," the Aussie said, "I want you to get me something. A bright red silk dressing gown!"

The girl, Ann Moray ("Scotty") de Ceballos, promised she would get him one. This man was different from most of the hopeless, despairing men and women of the colony; he was an Australian who had come to mine for gold in Guayana, and although his fortune-hunting had been cut short by leprosy, he faced his certain death with a cheerful resignation. The dressing gown was his last wish.

Scotty went to her husband, the leper colony's doctor, and to her father, the British Minister in Caracas, and together they combed the city for the brightest, loudest dressing gown in Venezuela. They finally found one—red and silk, with magnificent tassels. She presented it to the Aussie.

"I'm afraid we couldn't find any slippers to match," she said.

"Oh, I won't need slippers, Scotty. When my time comes, I'm going to float slowly and leisurely high over Sydney Harbour in my red silk dressing gown, and my feet'll never touch the ground."

The lepers will never forget Scotty, just as thousands of American and British soldiers of World War II will never forget the mystic quality in her voice, her soothing songs bringing comfort and hope to wounded men in hospitals all over the world.

Scotty's mission first started just before the war, when the late Mayor LaGuardia was presiding at a rally in Madison Square Garden. Since the singer of the Star Spangled Banner was late, LaGuardia appealed to the audience:

"Is there anybody in the house who can sing the anthem?"

A pretty redheaded girl, who reminded you a little of Greer Garson, came down the aisle. She walked on the platform and in a very British voice announced that she would be very happy to oblige.

The house became hushed when it heard her soft, ethereal soprano voice begin our anthem. She sang the first verse and the last, and many Americans really listened to their anthem for the first time.

A U. S. Army General was in the audience; he sent for her, and asked if she would sing for our troops. She became one of the most dedicated members of the USO, first in America, then in the outposts of the Caribbean and Italy. In army hospitals, doctors found her amazingly effective in psychiatric wards, with the sullen, almost hopeless cases.

In Italy, she stopped at the bedside of a boy they nicknamed "Soapy," who had cracked under the strain of walking in a field of land mines, and who lived in fear of trenchfoot. His hands were strapped to the bed to prevent him from scrubbing his feet until the skin rubbed off.

She asked him to name a song.

"Sing something about feet," he ordered.

Scotty was almost stumped. Then she remembered an old hymn: "How Beautiful Are the Feet of Them That Tread in the Gospel of Peace." When she had finished, Soapy said:

"Now sing something about water."

The only song she knew about water was another obscure one: "I Heard a Streamlet Gushing From Out Its Rocky Bay."

"Now sing them again, one after another," Soapy said.

She did. There were rings under Soapy's eyes from lack of sleep; he had been doped up so often he was immune to sedatives, but as Scotty finished singing, the strapped-down boy's eyes were closed. She sang Brahms Lullaby and tip-toed away.

Soapy slept for 16 hours straight. When he woke, he mused to the psychiatrist in the ward: "You know—feet and peace are the same thing. I should be washing the feet of others."

The doctor telephoned Scotty. "I don't know what you did for him," he said, "but it's the beginning of a cure. Soapy'll be all right."

Toward the war's end, she came to the bedside of a soldier whose eyes were bandaged. He was permanently blinded, but the doctors had not broken the news to him.

"I was hoping you'd get around to me, Scotty," he said. "Do you know 'Smilin' Through'?"

"Sure, soldier." Halfway through the song, she realized what the last two lines were:

When two eyes of blue
Come smilin' through at me.

She sang them. The soldier said, "Scotty—would you say my eyes *are* blue—or my eyes *were* blue?"

She didn't hesitate. "They *were* blue."

"I don't mind," he said. "I'll be a minister someday ... you don't need eyes to see God."

After the war, Scotty came back to New York and was about to start a radio program called "Lullaby for Grownups," songs to be sung at midnight, for troubled, sleepless adults. But she went to Caracas to spend Christmas with her uncle. There she met Juan de Ceballos, a young Venezuelan doctor who worked in the leper colony. She married him; and to Scotty, that meant working with him to help others.

Today, they live in a high mountain village near the colony, and also near an Old Women's Home, which Scotty often visits.

The favorite song of those old women is the same song that is asked for most by the lepers. Oddly, the Lord's Prayer has a special memory for Scotty, too. Whenever she sang for a front-line radio station, she closed every broadcast with it.

One night, an American corporal in a foxhole on an Italian hillside was listening to Scotty on a portable radio. German artillery bombarded that hillside for two thunderous hours. When the shelling ceased, the corporal was alive—but had lost his memory.

Two months later, a guard admitted Scotty to a locked psychiatric ward. She closed the door behind her, turned out the lights, and started singing the men to sleep. After a while, the movement and groaning changed to regular, heavy breathing. She finished with the Lord's Prayer . . .

Our Father, which art in Heaven
Hallowed be Thy name . . .

Singing in the darkness, she could hear a soldier climb out of his bed and crawl down the aisle toward her. The black shape came to within two feet of her and stopped. She broke off her song . . .

"You're Scotty Moray!" he choked. "I remember! You were singing the night of the barrage."

After a moment, Scotty finished . . .

For thine is the Kingdom
The power, the glory—Forever—"

Slowly the corporal nodded his head. "Amen," he said.

Once in a while, when Jinx and I see performers get blinded by their own glory, we smile at each other. We're thinking of the girl who chose to be prima donna for her young doctor-husband, an old woman's home, and a colony of lepers.

Scotty might have been a bright new star on Broadway—and yet maybe her name is up in lights already—in God's heaven.

King of the Highway

by JOSEPH J. ELLICOTT

> *What are these "spiritual stoplights" springing up throughout the country? Joseph Ellicott, the man behind this unusual project, is Assistant Superintendent of the Water Department in Chicago, Illinois.*

A CAR WAS SPEEDING down Chicago's Lake Shore Drive late one night recently, weaving slightly in a familiar, terrifying pattern.

"Please, Sam, slow down," the frightened girl in the front seat cried.

Sam, befuddled by too many drinks, laughed at his date cockily. "It's our world tonight, honey. Don't worry about a thing."

The wild ride continued a few minutes more, when the girl, staring ahead helplessly, suddenly leaned forward.

"See that light ahead by the side of the road? I want to stop there for a moment. Please, Sam, right there . . . now."

The car slowed, pulled to a stop. Reluctantly, Sam allowed himself to be coaxed out of the car. They walked a few feet toward the light, paused in front of a statue.

The glow in the night that caught the young couple's attention was the spotlighted figure of a Man with outstretched arms. In front of the statue was the inscription "Shrine of the Sacred Heart." The quiet, gentle look on the face of the Man held their attention . . . it pleaded for love of God and fellow man and for peace.

The young couple returned to their car without words. Sam, his head cleared, drove the rest of the way home slowly, carefully . . .

I heard of this true experience from a friend. It meant a great deal to me, because the project of placing these wayside shrines along the highways and byways has consumed much of my time during the past years.

It started back in 1946. Gladys, my wife, and I had lived very happily together for 30 years. My job during most of this time was in the City Water Department of Chicago, where I am now Assistant Superintendent. After Gladys died, life ceased to have much point or meaning for me. When I lost 50 pounds, my doctor feared for my life.

I do not try to account for the dreams that came to me then. In my weakened condition, I may have been delirious. Often Gladys' face would appear. Then the figure of Christ became mixed with the face of my wife. What was she trying to tell me?

These dreams tormented me. Finally, I confided in my pastor.

"Joe," he said, "you've been through a terrible heartache. The most important thing you must do is recover your health."

These dreams must not throw me, I agreed. But I did try to reason them out. Gladys, I knew, had always been devoted to the Sacred Heart*. Was she trying to tell me to construct a memorial to Him?

When I told my four sisters, all of whom are nuns, of this growing idea, they, too, at first tried to discourage me. Finally, convinced by my determination, one of them said, "Joe, if you feel this so deeply, who are we to say that God hasn't given you your marching orders?"

She wrote to Father Mateo, who in turn sent the letter to Father Larkin, National Director of the Enthronement of the Sacred Heart, in Washington, D. C. He called me by phone. "Do I understand that you want to build a wayside shrine out of your own funds?" he asked.

---

* *The devotion to the Sacred Heart originated centuries ago when Christ appeared in a vision, His Heart exposed in flames which, He explained, burned for love of sinners. Those who follow the devotion pray to God to inflame their hearts with love of Him.*

I told him that was my plan.

"We have the spot! Can you come to Washington?" An appointment was set.

Over the years I had saved a few thousand which could be invested in such a shrine. Could this idea grow into something big? "If God wants it to be done, nothing can stop it," I repeated to myself.

Upon arriving in Washington that December day back in 1946, I was met and driven out to the southern outskirts of the city. Just off the end of South Dakota Avenue we left the pavement and bumped along on a dirt road. At the top of a muddy hill Father Larkin pointed to a spot covered with scrubby brush.

I was terribly let down. Father Larkin sensed my disappointment.

"This area is to be developed greatly," he explained. "In a short time it will be heavily traveled."

"We'll build here," I agreed.

On June 8, 1947, the first road shrine was dedicated. The muddy, scraggly hill had been converted into a carpet of green grass. Today the road is paved, traffic is heavy, and attractive homes dot the surrounding area. The figure of Christ, with outstretched arms, captures both travelers and nearby dwellers.

Each night a certain truck driver on the way home is seen on his knees for a brief prayer by the statue. Children come regularly to place flowers at the feet of their Lord.

The response to this first shrine crystallized my dream of constructing such "spiritual stoplights" throughout the country. The next was built in New York City on upper Broadway, while the altar mentioned at the start of this story was erected here in Chicago on Lake Shore Drive at Devon Avenue. Another has been constructed at Menominee Drive and Burleigh Avenue in Milwaukee. Others helped in financing these projects. More are planned for Denver, Salt Lake City, Philadelphia and other cities.

In order that the shrines, on a smaller scale, could be made available for private homes, we established certain patent controls to prevent anyone from ever commercializing on them. Replicas, a foot high, are now available. I keep one here on my office desk.

The other day an irate woman approached my desk in the Water Department with fire in her eyes. She had a complaint, and her wrath exploded all over me. I hadn't been able to say a word when suddenly the storm subsided.

"What is that?" she asked, pointing to the small statue.

I told her what it was and, briefly, what it meant to me.

"Where can I get one?"

I wrote out the address for her. Suddenly, the complaint didn't seem to be important to her at all. We straightened it out quickly.

No longer am I uncertain about my vision of the shrine. I make myself available to go any place in the world, at my own expense, to help expand this project.

Meanwhile, the dream of making Christ King of the highway is coming closer to reality every day.

What a Nickel Can Do

by RAYMOND THORNBURG

A boy and a nickel started one of the largest cotton mills in America. The founder's grandson today maintains the family tradition of individual initiative. Raymond Thornburg, Guideposts' Publisher, tells the story of a famous family—the Callaways of LaGrange, Georgia—and the unique philosophy behind their successful business.

HE WAS JUST a ten-year-old boy, with a determined chin and short, dark hair. One day he started walking barefoot from the plantation where he and sixteen brothers and sisters lived. Destination—the small country town of LaGrange, Georgia, a few miles away.

In his hand he clutched a nickel. When he reached the general store in LaGrange, he paused, tempted, at the candy showcase.

"How about some licorice?" the proprietor asked helpfully. The boy shook his head. "Six spools of thread, please."

His merchandise carefully pocketed, the lad returned home. Then, with a keen sense of business thrift, he went from neighbor to neighbor, selling his thread, three spools for a nickel. Soon he was back in the general store, with two nickels clutched in his hand. This time, along with the spools, he bought some needles.

Several days later he set up a small store of his own in his father's dairy barn. His business grew on the strength of persistence and sturdy leg-work.

At the age of 13, the boy hired a mule and rented a piece of land from the small profits of his business. The resulting crop was sold at a profit of $36.45.

He was 18 when he borrowed five hundred dollars to begin a new business venture which he named "Callaway's Mammoth

41

Five and Ten Cent Store." With shrewd calculation he stationed boys along the busiest streets, each armed with a tin pan and an iron rod. They banged away and led the gathering crowd to the store, then went out for a new crowd.

The first year he made $1600 on his five and ten cent store, turning over his stock twelve times. Then he decided the store was profitable enough to cut off the word "Mammoth."

His next venture was a department store. At the age of 29 he, with a group of associates, organized the Unity Cotton Mills in LaGrange, the first of a group of manufacturing corporations he was to head.

This boy, who back in 1880 looked for business opportunities in a South where business was in the doldrums, was Fuller Earle Callaway.

Fuller never claimed that he had a great vision about the industrial enterprise he created. He was just a hard worker, often toiling 16 hours a day. For direction he relied on prayers; God was his beacon.

"Life is like a ball of yarn," he would say. "You begin winding, and at first it runs all askew and crooked. But if you keep on winding, you find eventually you have something that begins to look like a ball. Then it gets bigger and bigger, and you roll it faster and faster, and soon it doesn't take near as much trouble as it did at first. Then it gets so big you hardly know you're winding—and you've got the ball."

Mr. Callaway not only built up industries, he also constructed schools, churches, hospitals, greenhouses, gardens and homes for his workers. He never let the problems of such a large enterprise blind him to its future possibilities.

Before his death in 1928, he was asked, "What are you going to do when the children of the mill operators grow up? Under the leadership they have, they are going to want better homes, better wages, and constantly higher standards of living. How are you going to handle that?"

"Of course they are going to improve and change," Callaway said promptly. "We'll keep up with them. Remember, the mills started with nothing but a few spools of thread. Anyone would have said all of this was impossible then. But here they are. The best foundation for a business enterprise is just to set down in your mind one phrase: 'Everything happens that couldn't.' When you learn that, you'll believe. I found it out as I went along."

He taught his children the importance of such qualities as self-reliance, capacity for hard work, thrift, integrity, friendliness, civic pride, and above all, faith in God. The fruits weren't theirs just because of blood relationship with him. They were expected to work their way up the hard way, as he and his forebears did.

There have been Callaways in the South since 1665 when Thomas Callaway came over from England. In the family cemetery plot in LaGrange lie six generations of the family, all of whom lived on land which has never been sold, and all of whom worshipped in Sardis Baptist Church. The family has turned out 25 preachers, including Fuller Callaway's own father. Such history counteracts the idea that all big families are going to seed, with each generation getting weaker. Perhaps some do, without a solid foundation of faith.

Two sons, Cason and Fuller, Jr., followed Fuller Callaway's pattern in training and development. Cason, first, then Fuller, Jr., directed the destinies of the Callaway interest, each retiring before reaching the age of 45, so that new leadership could be developed and used.

His grandson, Fuller Earle Callaway III, carries the name of the man who started business with a nickel. His first job was in the testing laboratory of the mill.

In his search for opportunities Fuller III worked one summer as a laborer in the Texas oil fields, another in the mills, another summer found him in Finland, toiling with a timber cutting crew.

Then he conceived the idea of operating a "rolling store" right in LaGrange during his summer vacation from Georgia Tech. He wanted to see what would happen, today, when a lone figure applied the principles of initiative his grandfather had used over 60 years ago.

He bought a second-hand school bus for $500; $400 more went into repairs. Another $200 provided such merchandise items as groceries, ice cream, cold drinks, household items. He called his enterprise "Callaway's Square Deal Traveling Store."

When he started out, he covered substantially the same routes his grandfather had taken. During his first days, some of the merchandise fell off racks. The water from the ice box overflowed and spoiled three bags of flour. His brakes locked. Children left the ice box open and the dry ice evaporated. A talkative woman bought a quart of ice cream, then held him up with conversation so long it melted in her hands. He had to replace it.

Three generations haven't changed the working habits and incentives of the Callaways much. Like his grandfather, Fuller III also looks about for opportunities, not an easy set-up. Also following the path of his grandfather, he is learning first-hand how to start a business, operate it, pay taxes, and be of service to others. Fortunately, our country has ample room for those who will work hard, sacrifice and believe in what they are doing.

Today the Callaway enterprises include 11 plants, a complete research division, and more than 8,500 employees. They make dozens of textile products. Yet the founder always had the dream that the Callaway organization would be known more for its community and human development than merely for business success.

If he could be here today, he would be pleased with the neat, well-kept homes, with yards, gardens and trees (most Callaway employees now own their homes). He would certainly take pride in the 23 churches in the communities because he always felt that American life should be built around the family and the church.

"Religion is the dynamic factor motivating the energies of people," he once said. He started the policy of a monthly pledge to each church and paying one-half of the cost of maintenance and improvements. This policy is still being carried out.

Mr. Callaway loved to watch children at play. Therefore, the Callaway Educational Association with its community centers, swimming pools, playgrounds, health clinics, and greenhouses is the culmination of his dreams.

The world has changed a lot since his era, but the fundamental principles of life never change. Character is the same in any age— also qualities of the spirit, love, integrity and courage. Fuller Callaway often said: "We make American citizens first, and run the cotton mills to pay expenses."

This still goes.

The Foreman and the Proofreader

by GRACE LUMPKIN

What can one woman, a proofreader in a printing plant, do to counteract Communistic propaganda? Grace Lumpkin, a former Communist herself, faced this situation and did something about it.

I STARTED TO WORK in this printing plant several years ago. There were six of us; the plant foreman, the pressman, two linotypers, a "bank boy" and I was the proofreader. All of us brought our lunches and ate together in one corner of the huge plant that was big enough to house several airplanes. Lunch was the time we talked.

Pete, the foreman, dominated the conversation. He was an excellent worker, but somewhere along the way he had got off the track in his thinking. He spoke bitterly about the rich and pointed out all the faults of our country. While not a Communist, he talked their line.

Luncheons were not very pleasant because not only did Pete try to tear down all the values which I had learned were important, but the others sided with him. The talk was rough. The plant, with its huge machines, the dirt, the low level of conversation and prison-like supervision, was an ugly place.

It had become a practice of mine to pray about certain people and problems, so each morning before work I stopped in a church and concentrated on the situation in the shop. This became a daily habit. I knew that it was up to me to be one of God's workers there in the plant.

One day at lunch Pete was in a particularly propagandizing mood. "Human beings are nothing but a higher form of animal," he said. "There's no right or wrong. Everything is relative. It's the churches that stir up the trouble."

"Not the churches, Pete," I spoke out suddenly, "but you and I, because we have denied God."

"What do *you* know about it?"

"I know because I was with the Communist Party for ten years," I answered.

The others stared at me in amazement, perhaps wondering how a mild looking woman like myself could ever have become so involved.

"I used to preach all those things you have been saying," I went on. "I sneered at God and the Church . . . I told lies, cheated and approved of stealing and murder because I believed the end justified the means. In spirit I was a traitor to my country. We talked a lot about the equal rights of man, but it was only when I accidentally read our own Declaration of Independence, which says: *. . . all men are created equal and are endowed by their Creator with certain inalienable rights . . .* that I understood we have no rights and no equality except as we believe in God."

The foreman was speechless at my outburst.

"My wife and I were married in a church," contributed one of the other men lamely.

Pete didn't say another word then, but I knew he was angry. Later he called me into the shop, where I found him holding a sheaf of proofs in his hand. In a rasping voice, aimed to be heard by all, he pointed out every minor mistake I had made in the last week. I didn't attempt to justify them because I knew the work was basically all right, that his rage had nothing to do with proofs.

Yet it was a humiliating experience. I walked to my desk fighting back tears of anger. Furious, I wanted to triumph over him, to humiliate him as he had humiliated me. Then I remembered my recent vow to pray over upsets at the *very moment they occurred*.

"Thy will be done in this place and in my heart," I whispered fervently. At first I couldn't possibly mean it. I had to say it over and over again until peace came in me—peace and confidence and love.

From then on there were fireworks almost daily during our lunches. I was determined to answer all false statements with the truth as I knew it, and I was armed with the facts about Communism. But only through prayer was I able to do this without personal animosity.

Pete and the others, like so many who had been disappointed in life, were the obvious, easy marks for the Communist line. Several times I stressed the fact that Communism's emphasis on materialism as a way of life made its followers virtual slaves to their leaders. It had done so to me until I transferred my loyalty to another kind of leader—Christ—Who never broke a promise, Who never let anyone down, and Who makes men free.

For months they tried to shake my stand. I would sit there eating my lunch or knitting—and as I did so I prayed for each one in turn, as well as for myself, that I could be honest, sincere and understanding.

One noon Pete said: "Why do you say Communists are against religion? They let the churches alone in Russia."

"While still with the Party," I answered, "I was told by first hand observers how religion was fought there. Really religious people get no benefits. They are last when it comes to ration cards, last to get essentials, first to be oppressed. Just as it was in Nazi Germany. These are facts. Communist children are expected to tell the secret police if their parents worship God."

"Well, what makes you think America is so wonderful?" Pete came back. "That book we are printing points out that all newspapers in this country are controlled by the rich—that 75 per cent of the news is lies. Russian papers tell the truth."

"You are misquoting that book."

He insisted that he was not.

After lunch I found the galleys and brought them down to Pete. "Read this galley," I said.

Reluctantly he did. The galley stated that some 75 per cent of Americans are misinformed on foreign affairs through poor newspaper reporting, not that 75 per cent of the newspapers print lies.

When Pete finished reading his face was livid. "Go back to your desk," he yelled. He picked up a wrench and flung it clear across the room against the wall.

I left, trembling. An urge to try and rouse the others to mutiny welled up. I knew they too, resented Pete's behavior. And then I sickened at what I had been thinking. I was not there to have a personal fight with Pete. It must be God's will and God's victory —not mine.

Suddenly it struck me that I must go and say something to Pete *at that moment.*

Pete was at one of the linotype machines with his back to me. I hadn't adequate words, so I walked up to him and touched him lightly on the shoulder. When he turned around dourly, I smiled, at the same time praying hard. The tense muscles around his face relaxed and he smiled back. He stuck out his hand. I shook it, then went to my desk.

More months passed and I began to notice a definite change in the plant and in Pete. Nothing startling. We still argued at lunch, but without the bitterness.

One morning I said: "You know, Pete, you and I both have had a lot of disappointments in our lives."

His nod was friendly. Then he told me how he had married young and had never been able to complete his education. He had never owned his own home. I told him how often I give my disappointments to God.

Shortly afterward Pete said with an air he tried to make casual, "Amazing coincidence, but I went to church with my family last Sunday and the minister preached about giving your disappointments to God. How do you figure that?"

Although he had gone to church, I could see that Pete was

ashamed to have the other men know. Even to say the word "church" during lunch had always produced a dead silence or ridicule. How could he acknowledge that he had gone back on all those things he had said?

One morning during my prayers, I asked God to show me how to get Pete to do this without losing "face." That day at lunch Pete began to tell us about a Sunday excursion he had taken with his wife and kids. "Was that after church?" I slipped in.

"That's right," Pete said without blinking and finished his story.

After that religion came naturally into the conversation. One man who had been most profane in his swearing and had backed Pete most emphatically, spoke one day of church in a very familiar manner. A younger man said: "What do you know about it, Bill? You never go to church."

"What the hell!" Bill retorted. "What do you mean I don't go to church! I was in church last Sunday." We all laughed.

The biggest thrill came shortly after. Pete's kids were baptized —and so was Pete! He became an active member of his church, vividly punctuating the Bible phrase "with God all things are possible."

One day Pete said: "Will you pray for me today? I am going to meet some lawyers to talk over buying a house."

Would I! I didn't tell him that for weeks I had been praying that God would make this possible. I think I was as happy as Pete when he came back and said it was all arranged.

Today our shop is a different place, but it won't stay that way if we let up. People are always changing one way or the other. If it isn't a steady change for the better . . . it will be for the worse.

I have learned this—Keep God as Foreman and "all things work together for good." It takes courage to demonstrate that law. But God gives us courage. If you try, you'll see.

They Can Always Spare More

by STARR WEST JONES

> *Ten hungry Italian children used paper bags for clothing until their parents' letters to Francisco Marinosci, a barber in New York, started flowing a most unusual relief supply. Starr West Jones, a Guideposts editor, reports on how one man is loving his neighbors.*

IT DOESN'T LOOK LIKE MUCH," Frank said when I stopped in to look over his barber shop. "But it's fed me and my wife, enabled us to raise three children and now has made me known throughout my native Italy."

The small establishment was shabby; odds and ends of clothing and boxes cluttered the place.

"I came to America from Italy 40 years ago, when I was 17. I was going to make my fortune, just like the stories I'd heard."

But there was no trace of bitterness in Frank's voice as he said it. Rather, he was chuckling as he lathered the face of a man in the barber chair.

Later, Francisco Marinosci, or Frank, took me to the rear of his shop where there were stacks of letters, heaps of clothes and packages being prepared for shipment.

"Look at some of those letters," Francisco waved toward a stack of envelopes piled in a box. "These people are all in such bad shape. They need food, clothes, medicines. It makes you realize how lucky we are—here in America—makes you glad of the chance to help."

Francisco Marinosci has been doing that for many years now. He has sent over 2,000 packages of food and clothes to needy strangers in his native country.

"It began in 1945," said Frank. "I got a letter from Francavilla

Fontana, my old home town in the province of Brindisi. Neither my wife nor I knew these people, or how they got my address here. But the family had ten children. They were very poor, they had to use paper bags for clothing. If you've got a heart, you've got to do something. . . ."

Francisco sent them four packages of clothing and twenty dollars. Soon, other letters from the needy, of all kinds, up and down the boot of Italy, found their way to Frank's Barber Shop, 629 Westchester Avenue, the Bronx, New York.

He and his wife, Maria, were soon spending most of their spare time preparing boxes. They scoured the neighborhood for old clothes, bought uncalled-for items from the nearby dry cleaners, patronized the Hadassah rummage and the Salvation Army sales.

Sometimes money orders were added to the gifts where the need seemed greatest. Postage on each package ran to about a dollar and a half. I asked him how he could afford to help so many.

"Sometimes my shop only clears fifteen dollars a week," he said. "But my wife has a job too, so—we can always spare a little more."

Requests came from families, churches, schools, and organizations of every type. About a thousand have been helped—an old woman's home, a girl in Palermo suffering from tuberculosis, a church that needed a statue.

An orphanage in Francavilla was sent seventeen packages, enough to outfit all of the 23 children; four hundred dollars also went for rubber sheets, bedding and the beginnings of a much needed annex. Nine other orphanages have been aided.

I asked him how he could be sure all those he helped were worthy. His silence was eloquent. He believes in his fellowmen. Did the "Good Samaritan" inquire into the status of the stranger before caring for his wounds?

"Others are offering to help me now," said Frank. "So I send them some of the needy letters. Many have sent money, and I have kept careful account of it all in a little book, with notes on who and where it is sent to.

"I just got a letter from the little girl in Palermo who has tuberculosis. She wanted to give thanks for three packages and ten thousand lira sent to her by a lady in Illinois who wanted to help.

"A man who works for the Department of Welfare has volunteered to work three to four hours a night answering letters for me. A man in Alaska, and another in the West Indies, wrote asking to buy the stamps that come on the letters. That money will help more families. . . ."

I examined several carefully labeled packages sewed up in cheesecloth to prevent pilfering. "In Italy they probably think I'm a pretty rich man," said Frank with a twinkle in his eye.

He wasn't rich, but Frank's happiness was obvious. He admitted he and his wife had been unable to save anything, but many a millionaire should have their sense of security!

How To Find and Use
Spiritual Techniques
That Work

The True Road to Greatness

by CHASE WALKER

> *Buying opera scores with his meal allowance, young Arturo Toscanini decided at an early age to trade comfortable obscurity for the possibilities of musical greatness. It called for some hard choices.*

IT WAS BEDLAM. Thunderous boos and angry hisses from the Brazilian audience swept toward the Italian conductor, a last minute substitute, as he took his place in the pit. After a futile attempt to start the music, panic grabbed the musicians and they fled behind the curtain.

The audience was enraged because the substitute conductor had replaced one of their own countrymen. It all started several days before when the opera company received a bad press in Rio papers after their first performance. In a public statement the Brazilian conductor blamed the singers, then quit. Loyal friends decided to hiss the rest of the touring Italian company right out of town.

It looked as if they had succeeded as a frantic conference was held behind the curtain. Directors turned toward their cellist, a 19-year-old youth by the name of Arturo Toscanini. Just out of school, he had impressed them with his ability and knowledge of scores. He was their last hope.

Once again the musicians took their places. Then a slim, adolescent figure shot from behind the curtain and into the pit. He picked up the baton and, without even glancing at the score, started them off from memory.

Surprised spectators didn't have time to level their boos before the lively music had grabbed their attention. At the end, young Toscanini received a tremendous ovation. Since that wild night back in 1886, "Maestro" Toscanini has had 65 years of unparal-

57

leled greatness as a conductor right up until his retirement last spring.

How has he achieved it?

Young Toscanini did not come from a musical background. His father, as a village tailor, barely earned enough to feed his family; his mother was a seamstress. Arturo, at the age of nine, entered the Royal School of Music in Parma, Italy, on a scholarship.

There, he regularly sold his meat portions to fellow students so that he could buy more scores. He studied these in his spare time, committing hundreds to memory by the time he graduated. Thus, he was ready for opportunity when it came.

There was the incident of an important graduation piece he had laboriously practiced on his cello. Two days before the examination, he told his teacher he would not play it.

"Why not?" the stunned teacher asked. "You can play the notes well enough to pass the examination with a good grade."

"I do not understand the music, so I will not play it even if I do fail the course," Arturo said.

The teacher, in despair, let young Toscanini switch to a concerto—a piece he hadn't practiced in months. Arturo, in a few hours of tremendous concentration, worked the concerto into good enough shape to pass the examination with a flourish.

Toscanini has always been uncompromising in his moral convictions. He has cancelled concerts at the last moment because he felt the orchestra was not prepared. No pleas or financial threats ever made him waver if it was a question of the integrity of the composer's work.

Under the same convictions he is constantly outraged by man's inhumanity to man.

When in South America a number of years ago, he was beaten by young Fascists for refusing to play the Fascist anthem. His reaction: "Truth we must have at any price, and freedom of speech.

I have said to Fascists time and time again, 'You can kill me if you wish, but as long as I am living, I shall say what I think.'"

When Mussolini's brand of dictatorship took over in Italy, Toscanini publicly denounced him. Il Duce never dared take official action against him, even though the Maestro repeated his convictions often.

He has never conducted in Russia, although invited; he refused to play in Germany under Hitler. Because of Hitler's treatment of Jewish musicians before the war, Toscanini (a Catholic) went to Palestine at his own expense and helped organize the Palestine Symphony Orchestra. The Maestro has always tried to reveal publicly his support of any persecuted group.

The Maestro works on the development of his orchestra's spiritual expression to bring about artistic completeness; he believes that without the spirit of God, man is incomplete.

Once after a very emotional performance, he told a musician: "God tells me how the music should sound." Again, in the heat of a rehearsal, he knelt and intreated: "Come with me to heaven . . . come on wings."

On still another occasion, during a rehearsal of Beethoven's Ninth Symphony, he abruptly stopped the orchestra and leveled his intense eyes at the soloist.

"Do you know what you are singing about?"

The man hesitated.

"You are singing of brotherhood, but in your face you look like you hate everyone. That will show in your music."

This spiritual leadership of his orchestra is founded in discipline; to him discipline is respect. He never expects of others what he is not himself. Musicians can sit while they play, singers come on and off the stage, but the Maestro tirelessly stands, coaxing, urging, imploring them to do better and better.

His quest for perfection often brings on emotional outbursts on the podium which make him most penitent. After one rehearsal, he sidled up to a musician and said with downcast eyes: "I have a bad character."

"No Maestro, just a bad temper, sometimes."

It is in his humility that the Maestro's greatness lies.

The great scholars who wrote the Bible described him: *Likewise, ye younger, submit yourselves unto the elder. Yea all of you be subject one to another . . . and be clothed with humility; for God resisteth the proud, and giveth grace to the humble.* (I Peter 5:5)

He shuns publicity with a modesty as retiring as his conducting is aggressive. On the rare occasion when he did sign an autograph, it was for a small eleven-year-old boy. Beside his signature he wrote: "Don't try to be a superman. Just to be a man is sufficient in this world."

At the conclusion of an unforgettable performance of a Beethoven symphony several years ago, which everyone thought was certainly perfection, Toscanini thanked the musicians and said simply: "We shall try to do better next time."

The Best Living Insurance

by CLINTON DAVIDSON

> *As a boy, Clinton Davidson was shy and awkward.*
> *Yet between 1930 and 1938 Mr. Davidson sold more*
> *life insurance than any other man in the world. He*
> *tells here how he did it.*

"DAVIDSON, you're not the type to be a life insurance salesman," a co-worker told me many years ago. "Why did you ever pick this field?"

I wondered about that too. My qualifications couldn't have been less impressive when I arrived in Indianapolis from Kentucky to start this work. Shy, self-conscious, awkward, raised in poverty, I lacked social graces, proper clothes or funds.

Each day I would make about fifteen blind calls on prospective policy buyers. Out of this pavement pacing, I was fortunate to get one good interview a week. My monthly income was around $35—hardly enough to support my wife and youngster.

Two sources of comfort in this period of discouragement were the love of my wife and the inspiration I got from the Bible. Mother had read The Book to me often as a boy, and I had been stirred by the dramatic stories of David, Daniel, Paul, and Jesus.

One night I began thinking about Paul, who certainly was one of the greatest salesmen of all time. What a job he faced in trying to sell to pagans the idea, first, that there was only one God instead of many gods, and secondly, that a simple carpenter was the Son of this one God!

How many salesmen today would go out on such a job—with no expense account—to "sell" a product unwanted by the people and opposed by the government! On top of all this, he faced stonings and beatings for his trouble!

With rising excitement, I read in Acts 17 about Paul's technique in reaching these unsympathetic people. In Athens, for example, he discovered the inscription "To An Unknown God" on many plaques about the city.

So Paul stood up before the people and began, *Men of Athens, I perceive in every way that you are very religious . . . what therefore you worship as unknown, this I proclaim to you.* (Acts 17:22.)

Paul thus began his talk with a subject in which his listeners were interested—their unknown god—and proceeded to tie it to the subject in which he wanted to interest them—Christ, Son of God.

Arrests, whippings, taunts never stopped him. He persuaded, persisted and eventually evangelized much of the world.

Just as Paul believed completely in what he was preaching, so did I believe, too, that my business was benefiting others. And Paul's selling techniques could be just as effective today, I thought to myself. I tried Paul's principle with an auto tire dealer, who greeted me gruffly, bent over the hood of a car.

"May I talk to you, Mr. Smith, about a non-blowout, puncture-proof life insurance policy?" I asked.

He straightened up, surprised. "What in the world is that?"

I explained that because of rising expenses and the extravagance of some heirs, the principal from insurance policies might be dissipated in a year. The remedy was, of course, a special policy guaranteeing an income for life. This got his interest.

Later I called on a man named Anderson who had on his door just one word, "Paper." That gave me another idea.

"Mr. Anderson," I began, "I would like to talk to you a few moments about a fortune on paper."

"What is that?" he asked, his imagination stimulated.

"In about 85% of the cases," I continued, "the only fortune an average man is able to accumulate for his later years, or for his dependants, comes from the few words printed on the paper that makes up his life insurance policy."

A full time interview was granted me. By selecting prospects from the classified telephone directory, and preparing an opening sentence for each along the above lines, I turned 80% of my calls into interviews. Thanks to Paul I learned how to get my foot in the door, and my income quickly jumped to around $300 a month.

During these early years, I met all kinds of disappointments and made every mistake that could be made. "Is $300 a month going to be my limit in this line?" I kept asking myself.

While indulging in a slight case of self pity at home one Saturday afternoon, I picked up the Bible and read: *Arise ye, and depart; for this is not your resting place.** Somewhat startled, I began to pace the room. Perhaps I was lazy. Was my thinking too small?

Seldom did anyone stay in the office on Saturday afternoons. Why couldn't I spend two hours every Saturday afternoon there, alone, planning, thinking and developing creative ideas?

Out of one such Saturday afternoon session came an idea. It happened during National Thrift Week which, according to the Thrift Society, was to emphasize savings, buying homes and life insurance. I went to the main office of a local railroad employing 2,000 people and was given permission to address one department on Thrift Week.

The session, during which I showed charts on life insurance, was so successful that I was able to sell the idea to other departments. The result was helpful information to employees and a number of sales for myself. Later the National Association of Life Underwriters began promoting one day in National Thrift Week. Their activities increased so much each year that now it is called Life Insurance Week.

It wasn't long before I felt ready for a try at New York City. When I heard that my company had a vacancy in the Manhattan Office, I called on the Vice President.

* *Micah 2:10*

I had prayed hard for this change, but the Vice President turned down my request. Again the Bible buoyed me up in a period of discouragement. Moses, at forty, thought he was ready to lead the Israelites out of bondage, but the Lord knew better and made him wait forty years. God is always right in his timing.

Three years later I did get my transfer to New York City.

I always seemed to be waging a battle with my inferiority complex; no one ever loses it entirely. Thanks to the practical inspiration I drew from my study of the Bible, I was able to chip off most of my inferior feeling, one by one. The example of Jesus—His faith in Himself, in His proposition, in His God—never failed to inspire me.

Men who have only self-confidence develop into insufferable egotists. Study of the Bible, however, builds confidence while at the same time helps eliminate egotism. Paul said: *I can do all things through Christ which strengtheneth me.**

But this one thought returned again and again, "How can an ordinary person like myself achieve, with God's help, extraordinary results?" I thought about those whose accomplishments had lived down through history—Moses, Abraham, Jesus, Paul.

In Matthew I read, *The light of the body is the eye; if therefore thine eye be single, thy whole body shall be full of light.*† There was the answer. Let thy eye be single. One-eyed men—all with bodies filled with light—had been the greatest accomplishers.

I wanted to be like that in my own profession. Would it not be better to concentrate on one good prospect than fifty small ones (out of which I might still be able to serve but one or two)? Since my company followed the policy of hiring a large number of mediocre agents whose success depended on the number of small policies they could sell, I decided to resign and stake my future on the "one-eye" policy.

*Phil. 4:13
†Matthew 6:22

It was a big risk. The office rent, stenographer's salary, family expenses and expenses for one assistant who insisted on taking the plunge with me, amounted to a thousand dollars each month. At the time I had less than $300.

I carefully selected one good prospect, who kept no regular hours and traveled widely. Days were spent sitting fruitlessly in his office. Several times I caught him on the run for short interviews. The other salesmen soliciting him dropped in off and on, but could not wait as they had too many other prospects.

When I finally sold him the policy, he made this revealing statement: "You didn't get this business because your company is any better than the others, but because you got your message before me often enough." Commissions on this one sale were over $2,000.

"If thine eye be single . . ."

To those who say, "I haven't the capital to be a one-eyed man," I advise them to be one anyway. Pick the best prospect, no matter how difficult it looks, and concentrate on it. You will be surprised at the results.

The more I matured and developed my business, the more I realized that there was wisdom inside the Bible to meet every situation.

One of the most powerful passages of all is from Romans: *All things work together for good to them that love God . . .* * To those bruised by many disappointments, it is hard to believe this promise. Yet I have found it to work over and over again.

I believe that God expects and wants His children to use these marvelous Biblical promises in achieving more effective living. But certainly these principles will not work for those who have selfish motives. Along with one's efforts to live by the Bible must go constant prayers for God's will and a basic commitment to

Romans 8:28

His ways. The benefits realized then, belong to Him—let's not forget it.

God has been very generous to me, and I expect to spend the rest of my life trying to make return payments. My wife and I were recently able to purchase some property in Mendham, New Jersey, including a small chapel. Today the chapel is open to the public and filled to capacity as a church on a non-denominational basis. We hold Bible classes in the basement of the chapel for the teaching of Jesus' principles, which will always be the best living insurance.

His Talent Is a Trust

by LOUIS P. LOCHNER

*"One very essential quality is needed to accomplish
great things," says Fritz Kreisler. Here is a close-up
of one of the world's greatest violinists written by
Louis P. Lochner, Pulitzer Prize winning foreign
correspondent.*

"I WAS BORN with music in my system. I knew musical scores in-
tuitively before I knew my A-B-C. It was a gift of Providence. I
did not acquire it.

"It is to the cause of true art, and to the marshalling of its forces
as the sublime God-inspired pacifier—and to the priesthood of
artists all over the world as the human bridge to understanding
between nations . . . that the major part of my earnings has been
and shall be devoted as long as I shall be permitted to exercise my
profession."

This famous statement by Fritz Kreisler, one of the greatest
violinists the world has ever known, is the basic philosophy of
his life.

All through his unexampled career of 61 years, he has regarded
himself merely as a guardian of a talent which the Almighty laid
in his heart and brain. He has felt that this obligates him to devote
most of the income earned through his artistic effort to the allevi-
ation of human suffering.

As a result, no artist, living or dead, has allotted a greater percentage of the proceeds from his concerts, compositions and re-
cordings to humanitarian endeavor.

Not that he considered it obligatory as God's steward to live as
an ascetic and deny himself those pleasures in which the life of a
successful artist normally abounds. The work, self-discipline and
concentration which are required to develop his talent, he feels,
gives a man the right to full support.

When in July 1945 it was my painful mission as War Correspondent entering Berlin with the first American occupation troops to relay by mail that his exquisite home was a ghastly heap of rubble, not a word of complaint or self-pity came from his lips. Instead, he expressed only his joy that his employees on the place were unhurt, so I'm told.

His celebrated library was sold at auction in January 1949, every cent of the $120,372.50 proceeds going to the Golden Rule Foundation and Lenox Hill Hospital of New York.

Most of his violins were sold for charity in 1946, including the celebrated 235-year-old "Earl of Plymouth" Stradivarius.

"I think, Louis," he once said to me, "I never was so carefree as when I had to worry about the next month's rent ... I worried in a wholesome sort of way until I could come home with a contract in my pocket and be able to tell my wife that our next month's housing problem was settled!"

Fritz Kreisler is imbued with the feeling that he can approach God more directly through the medium of music than in any other way.

"The nearest approach to the Infinite God available to any of us is through some form of music," he often says. "I am what might be called a mystic ... How can one be a real musician and not a mystic?"

As a man of broad and deep culture, to whom the various philosophies, the applied and pure sciences are as familiar as musical scores, he sees no conflict between science and religion. He seemed like a happy boy to me when, in 1948, he read du Nouy's "Human Destiny" and saw that this noted French scientist asserted as a central theme of his book: "Science was used to sap the base of religion. Science must be used to consolidate it."

During the hysteria of World War I, Fritz Kreisler devoted the major part of his income to the upkeep of a home—founded by himself—for Allied musicians stranded in Vienna, his native city.

Yet Allied musicians were technically his enemies! Despite his emphasis upon the "priesthood of artists," however, his charities are all-embracing, never limited to profession, class, race or religion.

For almost 48 years Fritz and Harriet Kreisler have known a truly happy marriage in spite of vicissitudes of wars, spotlight and fame, and its attendant lack of privacy.

Once Mrs. Kreisler's love and faith were put to a severe test a few weeks after the outbreak of World War I: her husband, serving as a lieutenant in the Austrian Army at the Russian front, was reported dead, killed in action.

Harriet Kreisler would not believe it. To everyone's consternation, she refused to accept the report or to act accordingly.

"I have prayed and I know he is not dead," she said. And people regarded her announcement with pity for her disbelief in the face of the facts.

What really happened was told me by Fritz Kreisler in these words: "The report of my death originated through a mistake of the surgeon. Next to me in the hospital was lying a man who was dying. After the surgeon had looked at him, an officer in the hospital said, 'Did you know that was Kreisler, the violinist?'

"The surgeon thought he referred to my neighbor, and when he unfortunately died, reported my death."

When, shortly after his arrival at the hospital, Harriet received a wire from her husband correcting the erroneous telegram, she dropped to her knees and gave thanks.

Both Kreislers are deeply religious. "No man can accomplish great things unless he has a heart full of love." Kreisler states this often, and he and his wife live these words.

Friends and well-wishers who attended the celebration a few years ago of Kreisler's 75th birthday noted that he was deeply engrossed in a conversation with Msgr. Fulton Sheen. I asked him what it was all about. He replied:

"We were discussing the paramount duty today of all believers in God to join in a common fight against atheistic communism. I believe that in this struggle all who worship the Almighty and acknowledge His existence and omnipotence, must stand together. The world's crisis today is between good and evil, between God and anti-God. It is as simple and as important as that."

Not By Bread Alone

by MARGARET RUDKIN

> *While their young son struggled for breath, Mr. and Mrs. Rudkin practiced all kinds of medical advice. Finally, a high protein diet for the boy was suggested, and Margaret Rudkin tried her hand at baking bread. The result changed the lives of a whole family.*

THERE'S AN OLD Irish saying: "God broadens the back to bear the burden." Grandmother used to quote this proverb each time we launched some new project. "You children have talent," she would say. "Don't be afraid to step out. You won't be alone."

I never had to learn exactly what Grandmother meant until the day my husband, Henry, and I first heard low, gurgling sounds come from our son's chest. The child had asthma: We were on the threshold of needing broader backs than we had ever imagined necessary.

For seven years Henry and I went through torture, listening to this little boy struggle for breath during the attacks. We spent half our time following doctors' instructions, but there seemed to be nothing we could do except pray.

Finally, we made rules for ourselves: no more doctors, no more "cures." But, of course, that didn't work. When your child can't breathe, you grasp at anything. Then, one afternoon, a friend came to our Connecticut farm and told us of a famous doctor who had gotten results in allergy cases with a high protein diet.

"Why don't you drop in and see him?" she said. "Tell him I sent you. It can't do any harm."

This doctor's theory was that man is harmed by his own blundering treatment of natural foods. Our bodies are often starved for lack of right food values, such as is found in stone-ground

71

whole-wheat flour. I went home and boldly announced that I was going to buy some real whole-wheat, and bake my son a loaf of bread.

Now I'd never made bread in my life, but in the kitchen I struggled to reproduce an old-fashioned home-made loaf. All the old cookbook recipes had a long list of ingredients: whole-wheat flour (stone ground); pure honey; fresh, whole dairy milk; pure butter; and so forth. "Nobody makes bread with these anymore," I said to myself. But I decided to use them all.

The noise of clanging utensils that followed must have sounded like a battery of bakers at work. Not knowing what I was doing, I made a dough, and stuck it in the oven. An hour later I took out my first loaf of bread.

It was awful.

On the outside it was crooked; it sunk low in the middle, and was about as solid as a brick. When I put it on the table, I could see my family choke. It took weeks of repeated trial and error—still not knowing what I was doing—before at last I produced a loaf that caused Henry to sit back, his eyes bright, and say: "Now that's *bread*."

Slowly, with his new diet, my son's wheezing and coughing lessened, and the child grew stronger. I certainly do not want to say it was my home-baked bread that cured my son of asthma. There was another factor working: strange "coincidences" that I seemed to have no control over. The development of this first successful loaf into Pepperidge Farm bread was to come about through a chain of such unusual coincidences that I hesitate to use the word. Some people would call them "accidents." I like to think that God and prayer work through people in remarkable ways.

For instance, many friends, tasting my bread, began to suggest that I put it on the market. Hopefully, a few days later, I made eight loaves of bread, then took them down to a local grocer.

"I would like you to taste a piece of bread," I said, and happened upon a very successful sales technique. The grocer's face brightened. Three hours later he telephoned me excitedly that the bread was already sold out and asked for a regular supply.

Although I knew nothing of manufacturing, of marketing, of pricing, or of making bread in quantities, with that phone call Pepperidge Farm bread was born.

One evening Henry casually mentioned that he was helping a fund-raising campaign for the Visiting Nurses. He told me the story of Lillian Wald, the wealthy Jewess, who was devoting her life to service for others, through her nursing program.

"I'd love to meet this woman," I remarked, but knowing how busy her life was, I never dreamed it would be possible. About a year later I was out for a drive when my car broke down, "accidentally." From a large house nearby a chauffeur appeared and personally did the repair work. He would accept nothing for his trouble.

"Surely there's some way I can thank you," I said.

"It was my employer sent me down, Ma'am. Miss Wald."

Taking the opportunity, I walked up to the house, rang the bell, and met Lillian Wald. We became close friends. It was she who inspired me to think of my bread-making as both an enterprise and a form of service to others.

Perhaps it is through such "coincidences" (our son's illness, inventing our bread recipe, friends suggesting making bread en masse, and now the meeting with Miss Wald), perhaps through these accidents, God broadens our backs to do work we never dream lies within our capabilities.

Certainly, the problems that arose seemed beyond my capabilities. First, as the demand for our bread increased, we had to get stone-ground flour in large quantities. Almost all the stone grinding mills disappeared decades ago. We even considered setting up our own mill, but that would have required thousands of dollars and I was determined to let all new equipment come from profits. Yet there could be no profits without flour.

One day, by *chance,* we heard from an acquaintance this completely casual remark: "You know, there's a man up in Connecticut who has an interesting hobby. Has an old-fashioned stone mill. Grinds his own flour."

My husband and I rushed up to meet him and discovered a mill that had ground flour since Revolutionary days. I explained my project.

"You realize, of course, that my mill is just a hobby," the gentleman said. That was the trouble. None of us knew anything about milling; the art of the stone mill had been almost lost. We went ahead, though, using his flour, knowing we were doing many things wrong for lack of technical knowledge.

Somehow we expanded, moving our pots and pans from the kitchen to the stables. Then, one day a woman reporter was sent out to the farm to do a story on us. Later she called me at my office in the stable.

"Mrs. Rudkin, I'm down at an old second-hand book store. I just *happened* to run across a book you might be interested in."

It was an old, technical volume on stone milling. It turned out to be the bible of the trade—and had all the answers we needed to operate the old stone mill.

This last event drew my husband into the business. Henry had always taken my commercial bread-making somewhat as a joke. Now, through the technical side of the business, he became greatly interested.

"You know, our stones aren't far enough apart," he would say. "We've got to do something about that. It says here you can burn your wheat if the stones aren't properly set." Out came his calipers and measuring tapes.

Henry today is one of the outstanding milling experts in America. Bit by bit he began turning his full time away from Wall Street towards making bread.

Henry at first laughed at the way I kept books. He would walk into the stable, and see me scribbling on little scraps of paper. This was my bookkeeping: so much in, so much out; the rest was profit.

Now his attitude changed. "Anyone who puts out a thousand loaves of bread a day is in business, Peg. Let's set up a regular bookkeeping system so you'll know where you stand."

A thousand loaves of bread a day. Then 4,000 . . . 10,000. We moved from the stables to an abandoned gas station. Then we had to build a new plant, specially designed for hand-kneaded bread.

As we increased production, we were, of course, faced with difficulties keeping the home-made quality. Yet we've done it. When I was invited to give a lecture before a group of manufacturers, I said, "We succeeded at Pepperidge Farm by breaking all the rules of manufacturing." We have kept each of the theories of bread-making we started with in the kitchen of our farmhouse.

This means extra help, no rigid standardizations, and family relationship with every employee.

Today, we are producing thousands of loaves a day: whole-wheat and white. We have three bakeries, four mills, over one hundred employees. Our bread has been eaten, literally, half the world over.

If, as I worked over that first soggy loaf, I had seen the modern bakery, I would have said, "That's impossible. It belongs to someone else." I didn't realize that you walk a mile by taking one step at a time.

Grandmother's first words to us, "Don't be afraid to step out," have come to a fuller meaning. We know, now, not to be afraid to get started on some new venture just because the end of the mile seems so far away. We don't worry about the *end* of the mile —we just take the first step. God will broaden the back to bear the burden.

Of Faith We Sing

by FRED WARING

Thirty-two times sponsors replied "No" to Fred Waring's idea of adding a Glee Club to his orchestra. But something surprising Fred's mother had once said kept him at it. What was it that all sponsors had overlooked until at last one took a chance?

I WONDERED what mother's reaction would be that day when four of us came home from high school and organized our first band.

There was no point in being secretive about it, so my brother, Tom, Freddie Buck, Poley McClintock and I—all "self-taught" musicians—decided to hold our rehearsal in the parlor of our home there in Tyrone, Penna.

When the chandelier began to swing and the furniture to shake, mother appeared in the doorway—not to bawl us out, but to give us cinnamon rolls and cocoa. She not only encouraged us, but what was much better, she listened to us. Because of her understanding and sense of humor, our house became headquarters for the gang.

Her advice: "Whatever you do, son, make sure it's worth the doing. Then do it with all your heart."

Mother's ambition for me, however, was singing. How well I remember the Sunday mornings when the Waring family would hustle off to the Methodist Church in Tyrone, where we all sang in the Sunday School or Church choir. At that age my idea of Heaven was millions of angels rendering beautiful songs.

On Sunday evenings after church, Tyrone musicians would drop in for a musicale and a long session of hymn singing. My mother was captivated by choral music. "You can't give them too much sacred music, Fred," she told me often with rapture in her eyes.

Devout as she was, she never preached religion at us. She and father lived it together. Their faith was rich and warm with love and human goodness. The memory of the wholesomeness of our lives in Tyrone has never left us.

When I entered Penn State College, my ambition was to make the glee club. Music had been such an important part of my youth that I felt quite confident during try-outs. When the final roster was posted, my name wasn't there!

Surely, there must have been a mistake, I thought. But a check-up revealed the conclusive fact that I had not been chosen.

Looking back now, I can chuckle about it. Then it was a major blow, and I was petulant. Yet it was one of those divinely-guided experiences that direct a person out of one situation into a better one. God helps us when He provides a setback, but we seldom see the wisdom of it at the time.

My hurt was eased somewhat by the popularity of our banjo orchestra, which defrayed my college expenses. The Pennsylvanians were born soon after. Of course we always sang as a band, and it wasn't until years later that we added a glee club to the orchestra. It was a slow process convincing radio sponsors that the blending of choral singing and dance orchestra was music at its soul-stirring best.

The first offer of a commercial radio show was a milestone. Then came the hitch. The sponsor wanted only the orchestra. "Choir singing," he declared, "is good only for Sunday morning. It will flop as an evening show."

I used every kind of persuasion without success. It was a hard decision and an important one. I felt a sense of mission about our choral group, thanks to mother; without the glee club the Pennsylvanians were just another band.

The offer was refused regretfully. Thirty-two times in all we gave auditions for prospective radio employers. Each time the answer was "No." Then in 1933, our faith was rewarded when a sponsor appeared who took a chance on our entire show.

In the years of radio work that followed, the Pennsylvanians have always reached the peak of their performance in sacred music. I have felt the swelling response in our audience, in our own singers and musicians, and very much in myself.

Some of the Pennsylvanians have been with us for thirty years; a few are grandfathers. Disappointments as well as successes, friendships and a sense of teamwork have helped weld us together into a family-like group.

Mother's slogan: "What you do, do with all your heart" has been our unconscious motto. A sense of loyalty and common purpose built this kind of atmosphere, but I think something else has been added too. I think the spirit of the Lord has guided us.

At times I am amazed by the spiritual sensitivity of the Pennsylvanians. We need no research department to answer questions about any of the religions. If one arises during rehearsal on a point of interpretation involving the Protestant, Catholic or Jewish faiths, I'll ask the group. Someone always has the answer.

Let me put it this way. No atheist could stick with our orchestra very long. And we have learned that just creating music isn't the most important thing; our special opportunity lies in rendering sacred music so that it can help stir the hearts of people to love of God and each other.

The springtime of the year is always a high point for me. First, on March 14th comes mother's birthday. Our program on this date has always been dedicated to her, for she certainly deserved all the attention we could give her. She liked so many numbers that selecting her favorites has been easy: "Holy, Holy, Holy," "The Battle Hymn of the Republic," "The Rosary," "Onward Christian Soldiers," and "The Lord's Prayer," were just a few.

Easter for us is a spiritual climax of hard work and prayer. Our television program that evening is a holy service of music, stories and Bible passages. From the response of listeners in past years, we feel they receive the same spiritual uplift as do we who take part.

Finally, comes Mother's Day on the second Sunday of May. She who had been unselfish, encouraging and a source of inspiration to me all my life, passed away several years ago. Yet her memory grows stronger every week. It is in tribute to her and to mothers everywhere that I have shared these personal experiences and convictions.

Young Hearts—Big Dreams

by RALPH EDWARDS

> *As a boy on a Colorado farm, Ralph Edwards played a game of forfeits with his brothers. It was the rare quality of love and warm humor in Ralph's family life that helped inspire two famous radio and television shows: "Truth and Consequences" and "This Is Your Life."*

OFTEN I HAVE BEEN ASKED, "Ralph, you must have driven your mother crazy as a kid; where do you get so many ideas for pranks?"

It began many years ago . . .

When we lived on a farm in Merino, Colorado, I went to school till mid-afternoon, then milked the cows, had supper, and did my homework. There was still an hour before bedtime for a little merriment.

So, Mom was caught up with an entertainment problem for three animal-spirited youngsters. While Dad would usually be out looking after the horses, Mom dug into her creative reservoir and out came a game of forfeits.

Paul asks Carl, "What's the capital of Arkansas?" Carl can't answer, so he does the dishes. Carl asks me, "What's the biggest state in the country?" I say, "California." That's wrong, so I empty the trash.

All the time the kitchen is a radio station, Mom is the coast-to-coast audience and we are giving each other the works. We are also getting the chores done.

My folks were of old pioneer stock. Dad's been gone now for years, but Mom just goes on forever. I can remember as a kid watching her gee-haw and reign-in a runaway team of wagon horses, her feet braced against the foreboards and me hanging on for dear life around her middle.

If she heard noises at night, while Dad was off in Omaha shipping cattle, she would say, "Paul, you make sure Carl and Ralph finish their lessons." Then she would pick up a potato masher and hunt out a prowler in the chicken yard.

Like other American pioneers, my parents built their lives around the church and family Bible. During devotions we were often reminded: "This is a free country where opportunities come to those who work the hardest. God made these opportunities possible. Don't forget it, boys."

When we moved to Oakland, California, after some sub-zero weather killed our livestock, I handled a paper route, later jerked sodas. The first play I wrote was put on in our local church, where my brothers and I were janitors, and where Mom always made coffee for church suppers.

I had an experience with stage fright, too, during an Easter service. Just as I was to recite, the Sunday School teacher handed me an Easter lily to hold. I was so mortified I could only sputter. Any fluffs I make on radio or television today remind me of that Easter lily.

While working my way through the University of California, I did my first announcing on a local radio station. After graduation, my burning ambition was to go to New York and try for a spot as a network announcer. Mom didn't say much when I left. Just one final sentence, "Go to church, son."

Upon my arrival in New York, I rented a room for $9 a week. This, plus my fare East, left me with $90. Then I began my trek from studio to studio, including every radio listing in the telephone book. Week after week passed with no results.

I moved out of my hotel room to a twenty-five cent cot provided by the Methodist Church. There was a Bernarr Macfadden health food shop on Third Avenue which doled out meals for two, three and four cents a clip (remember, this was back in 1936).

The lowest point came one night when I was down to my last

15¢. During my weeks in New York, I had followed Mother's advice, and this night I again slipped into the Actor's Chapel off Broadway. Yet I had never really sunk into what you might call an empty pit, primarily because of my belief, and faith, that opportunities could come to a fellow no matter how rural his background. The knowledge that Mom, my brothers and friends were praying for me bolstered me.

When I came out of church, there was a friendly moon above, even a scent of fragrance in the air. A neon-lighted cafeteria looked inviting. I blew my last 15¢ on a salmon sandwich and coffee.

Next day, before giving up entirely, I decided to make a final round of the studios. At CBS, the receptionist announced, "Auditions at 11 A.M. for a staff announcer." Sixty-nine of us were to try out!

Immediately, I forgot about my growling stomach and the hole in my coat sleeve as I went in for the audition. Later I was summoned back a second time. Still later they called me in and told me I was hired.

What followed was a blurred period of excitement: "Meet Ted Husing! This is David Ross! Here is Andre Baruch! Meet Paul Douglas! . . ." My heart was doing half-gainers, while I held my hand over the worn spot in my elbow.

For the next few years I worked joyously as much as 15 hours a day, announcing soap operas by day and variety, dramatic and musical shows at night. Meanwhile, I began to dream of having my own show. And another "dream" came into my life: the girl I married—Barbara Sheldon. Barbara and I were exploring ideas for a new program when I said suddenly, "Say—as kids on the farm we used to play a game called 'forfeits.'"

Truth or Consequences! Everybody, including a sponsor, jumped for the idea at once.

I would have bubbly feelings all week when we had a particularly crazy stunt planned for the next program. Like the time we had our first water tank on stage. One fellow walked the plank, fell in, and when I reached in to pull him out, I fell in too—tuxedo and all. On another occasion, I'll never forget the stunned expression on a housewife-contestant's face when we told her that the following week we would broadcast our entire show from her home—seals, elephants and all!

But it was more than just clean fun. The show had a strong body, now we wanted to give it a heart. And there are many opportunities on both radio and television to bring hope, faith and courage to others.

Thanks to a chain of wonderful people, Lawrence Trantor, a paraplegic in a veteran's hospital, who hadn't much will to live, and whose only interest was watch-making, was sent to the Bulova School. Upon graduation, Trantor returned home, married his sweetheart, and our coast-to-coast audience listened as he received keys to a jewelry shop completely equipped for him; plus $1,000 to start his bank account.

The story of Lawrence Trantor on Truth or Consequences led me to develop the "This Is Your Life" program. I would never be interested in doing a program that, in addition to providing fun and laughter, didn't contribute in some way to good works, church attendance, prayer or religious understanding.

Several years ago Mom, Barbara, and our three youngsters were given a "homecoming" at Merino, Colorado. All 259 residents of Merino were there, plus thousands of other wonderful well wishers. A part of the festivities was a bumpy wagon ride through town, with all the Edwards holding on for dear life.

This ride was sort of a gag to get back at me for all those we had kidded and made do crazy stunts on "Truth or Consequences." Yet the friendship of our old friends was no gag, nor our joy in coming back and reliving old memories.

The ride ended at the Community Church where all assembled

for a church supper. I realized, suddenly, how many important things in life change but little, year in and out—the sweet odors of flowers, trees and grass; the love of friends and family, the vitality of the church.

As I looked around, I saw myself in every boy with torn coat sleeves. There will always be, please God, thousands of young people with growling stomachs and patches in their clothes, who will never stop dreaming, then finally realizing the opportunities that await them in this wonderful country.

They Know How
Prayer Is Answered

On His Own Two Feet

by GRACE PERKINS OURSLER

> *The eyes of parents and son met and held. In a moment of crisis they made a decision beyond common sense.*

THE BOY HAD FALLEN, running home after school, and skinned his left knee. It was no more than a scratch—there wasn't even a rent in his trousers—but by night the knee started to ache. Nothing much, he thought, being 13 and the sturdy son of a frontiersman. Ignoring the pain, he knelt in his nightgown and said his prayers, then climbed into bed in the room where he and his five brothers slept.

His leg was painful the next morning, but he still did not tell anyone. The farm kept the whole family relentlessly busy; always he had to be up at six to do his chores before school. And he must be thorough about them or he would be sent back to do them over again, no matter what else he had to miss, including meals. In their household, discipline was fair but stern.

Two mornings later the leg ached too badly for him to drag himself to the barn. That was a Sunday and he could remain behind, while the rest of the family drove into town. School homework finished, he sat in the parlor rocker, examining and comparing the three family Bibles; one in German that held the records of all their births and deaths; another in Greek that was his father's proud possession and finally the King James version shared by mother and all the sons.

One night this week it would be the boy's turn to lead the family devotions. He could select his own passages from the Old and New Testaments and read them aloud and try to get a discussion going; sometimes they became exciting. But now the pain

With credit to Soldier of Democracy *by Kenneth S. Davis (Doubleday). Copyright also by Reader's Digest Association.*

blurred his attention; he put aside the Scriptures and dozed until his brothers returned from Sunday school.

Mom and Dad did not come home with them because Sunday was parents' day off; the boys did the housework and cooked the big meal of the week, while father and mother stayed on for church service.

But by the time dinner was ready the boy had climbed into bed. The shoe had to be cut off his swollen and discolored leg. Why on earth hadn't he told somebody? Go quick and fetch the doctor!

Mother bathed knee and foot and thigh, applied poultices and wiped the boy's sweating forehead with a moist, cool cloth. She was an intense and vital woman. Confronted with this angry infection, her manner remained serene. Mom had nursed her brood through accidents and ailments from toothaches to scarlet fever; one son she had lost, but that only made her calmer and more determined when she had to fight for the others.

Old Dr. Conklin examined the leg and pursed his lips. "It's not likely we can save it!"

The invalid sat up stiffly. "What's that mean?" he asked huskily.

"It means," explained the doctor gently, "if things get worse we'll have to amputate."

"Not me!" stormed the boy. "I won't have it! I'd rather die!"

"The longer we wait, the more we will have to take off," urged the doctor.

"You won't take any off!" The boy's voice broke with an adolescent crack, as his mother turned away, shaken. But there was no adolescence in the eyes that defied the doctor's reproachful gaze.

Dr. Conklin stalked out, nodding to the mother to follow him. As he stood in the hallway explaining to both parents about what could and probably would happen, they could hear the boy calling for his brother: "Ed! *Ed!* Come up here, will you?"

The brother stamped in and then they heard the sick lad's

voice, high pitched with pain: "If I go out of my head, Ed, don't let them cut off my leg. Promise me, Ed—*promise!*"

In a moment Ed came out and ran to the kitchen. When he returned his mother said, "Ed, what's your brother asking for?"

"Fork! To bite on; keep from screaming."

Then Edgar stood outside the bedroom door, his arms folded. Quite clearly he was standing on guard.

Ed looked straight at old Dr. Conklin. "Nobody's going to saw off that leg!" he announced.

"But, Ed—you'll be sorry," gasped the doctor.

"Maybe so, Doc. But I gave him my word."

And nothing changed that.

If Ed had not stood his ground, father and mother might have yielded. They were not yet convinced that amputation was necessary; they were doubtful. The adamant attitude first of the sick boy and then of his brother was incredible, for defiance of parental authority was unknown in this household. Yet there was Ed, standing before the sickroom door.

"Guess we'll wait and see how he looks by tonight, eh, Doc?" said the father.

For two days and nights Ed stood guard, sleeping at the threshold, not leaving even to eat. The fever mounted, and the suffering boy babbled in torment, but the older brother showed no weakening of resolve, even though the discoloration of the swollen leg was creeping toward the pelvis, just as the doctor had predicted. Ed remained firm because he had given his promise, and also because he shared the frontiersmen's horror of being less than physically perfect.

The parents knew that their son would never forgive an amputation, and Ed's attitude continued to be decisive, time after time, when the doctor returned. Once, in helpless rage, Dr. Conklin shouted, "It's murder!" and slammed the front door. Nothing but a miracle could save the boy now!

Mother, father and watchful brother Ed shared the same thought, as their anxious eyes turned from the doorway. Had they forgotten their faith in the turmoil of their fears? Why, this sick boy's grandfather, that vigorous and inspiring old farmer-minister who had been leader of the River Brethren Colony in Pennsylvania, had always believed in healings wrought by faith. Now, in this desperate hour, the three went to their knees at the bedside.

They prayed, taking turns in leading one another. Father, mother—and at last Edgar—would rise and go about the farm work and rejoin the continual prayer. During the second night the other four brothers would kneel from time to time and join in the prayers.

The next morning, when the faithful old doctor stopped by again, his experienced eye saw a sign. The swelling was going down! Dr. Conklin closed his eyes and made a rusty prayer of his own—a prayer of thanksgiving. Even after the boy dropped into a normal sleep, one member of the family after another kept the prayer vigil.

It was nightfall again and the lamps were lighted when the boy opened his eyes. The swelling was away down now, and the discoloration had almost faded. In three weeks—pale and weak, but with eyes clear and voice strong—the boy could stand up.

And Ike Eisenhower was ready to face life.

So Long Son

by ARTHUR GODFREY

> *This famous radio and television star once had an
> amazing dream. The warm story of a father-son re-
> lationship, the memory of which Arthur Godfrey
> still carries with him.*

SOMEWHERE IN THIS UNIVERSE is a timeless, undeniable force. It's
stronger than granite, steel, majestic mountains towering into the
sky—or nuclear fission.

Sooner or later—in strange and different manifestations—that
force touches every human. Sure, some pass it off as a phenom-
enon that somehow cannot be reduced to exact scientific formula.
To others it is the hand of the Almighty—a reminder that regardless of the grandeur of man and his accomplishments—God is
still "running the show" here on earth.

Now, I want to tell you of such an experience. I have remembered it across the years and it will ring in my memory for as long
as I live.

It's about my dad—God bless him!

Let me explain a little about my dad. He was one of the most
brilliant and warm persons I have ever known. A lecturer, newspaper man, magazine writer and raconteur—he was at home in
any society. He was the well-rounded man I always wanted to be.

Of course, he had his failings, too. One was a disinclination
towards business and finance. As a result, he went through several small fortunes and sometimes things were tough at home.
That's why I went on my own at 15. But, I never blamed dad.

All this is prelude to the point I want to make. But, if in telling
it—one human, faltering on the precipice of lost faith or shaken
belief—takes heart—my telling the story will have been worthwhile.

For out of it, I learned first-hand about that timeless force in this world. Now, whenever the adulation of the crowd dins in my ears . . . whenever temporary wealth and fame assault my senses and balance—it helps me remember that force—transcendent above the world itself.

It makes me remember how the hand of God is at work constantly and I am humble in His presence.

It was in 1923. I was stationed on board a Navy destroyer—in charge of radio communications. I had knocked around a lot since I left home. The years and life had not been too kind but the Navy had been a sanctuary, the only security I had known for a long time. One day, tired, I fell asleep in my bunk and I dreamed.

My dad—I had not seen him for years—suddenly walked into the room. He offered his hand, saying, "So long, son." I answered, "So long, dad." I said some kind of prayer. It wasn't eloquent but it came from the heart.

I never saw him again. When I woke up, my buddies told me that at the exact time while I was asleep, the wires from shore hummed the news of my dad's death.

Don't tell me about science and its exact explanation of everything. Some things are bigger. God is the difference. He gets around.

Prayer Was My Racquet

by ALICE MARBLE

*When Alice Marble, famous tennis champion,
awoke on what had promised to be the most exciting
Saturday of her life, she couldn't move. Yet there is
a superhuman power within everyone which can be
tapped in an emergency, as this outstanding athlete
discovered.*

IN THE OFFICE of our Ambassador, Joseph Kennedy, I heard these
words, some years ago, "England will be at war with Germany
in two months."

Selfishly I thought, "What if war comes before Wimbledon is
played!"

Wimbledon, to a tennis player, compares with the Metropolitan for the opera singer. When one wins Wimbledon he is considered champion of the world. I had previously made two unsuccessful trips and knew that if I were going to win I would have
to do it that year. I just had to win!

I managed to get to the finals in all three events. Here promised to be the most exciting Saturday of my life. I wasn't even
the slightest concerned about having to play the three finals in
one day.

The big Saturday dawned or rather, it crashed with a bang,
for I couldn't get out of bed. I screamed at my teacher, Eleanor
"Teach" Tennant: "I'm hurt."

She thought my paralysis stemmed from sheer excitement. But
as she tried to help me out of bed she, too, realized that I couldn't
navigate. Always efficient in an emergency Teach called our
friend, Dr. Dunning, who came running.

I had torn a stomach muscle and he advised me not to play, saying that I would undoubtedly do some permanent harm. When I

93

insisted that I would play he said he would take no responsibility for my foolishness.

Dr. Dunning then bound my middle with heavy adhesive and was about to leave when I said rather brusquely, "Please take it off."

The doctor thought I had taken leave of my senses, but acquiesced. I explained my reasons to him—that perhaps the excitement of playing on the center court would make me forget the injury; that I didn't want to be reminded by the pull of the adhesive.

After the doctor left I couldn't look at the disappointment on Teach's face. I asked her to help me dress as I wanted to go down to the lobby of the hotel. She finally agreed, probably because she, too, wanted to be alone. It meant as much to her, my trainer, as to me. My success meant much to many who had invested years of faith in me.

All the way down in the elevator I thought, "I must at least make an appearance on the court." I was to be in three of the four finals. Twenty thousand English fans would be there: 5 thousand had camped on the grounds overnight for the privilege of standing all afternoon to watch the tennis.

In the lobby of the hotel, our genial manager, Mr. Burdet, rushed over, all smiles until he saw my face. I told him what had happened and asked if I might use his suite for an hour or more as I wanted to be alone. He personally escorted me upstairs and silently left the room.

I found myself thinking of my mother who had died the year before. I remembered the hundreds of times we had heard her say, "Trust in the Lord." In my despair I had forgotten all about Him. Then I did a strange thing; strange because I had never done it before. Mother had always allowed us to say our prayers any way we liked. We didn't kneel formally.

But now, injury and all, I got down on my knees and prayed to God not to let me make a fool of myself on the court that afternoon. I never asked Him to let me win. I asked Him that I would not let my supporters down.

Somehow I felt better and stronger, and able to face Teach and to tell her that everything would be all right. I rose feeling calm and sure in spite of pain.

Neither of us could eat the lunch sent to our rooms nor did we speak a single word in the car as we drove out to Wimbledon. When we reached the grounds, Teach impatiently brushed aside the autograph seekers on our way to the dressing room.

Ordinarily I warmed up for half an hour before an important match but of course the warm-up was forsaken that day. As I sat in the little cubicle Teach laced my shoes as it was impossible for me to reach up or down. At the given moment the official escort, Teddy Tinling, escorted my opponent, that grand gal, Kay Stammers, and me to the center court.

On that sunny afternoon the stands were packed with 20,000 enthusiastic people. When the welcoming applause died down Kay and I curtsied to Queen Mary; or at least I made a slight bow, hoping that nobody would notice.

Queen Mary smiled and nodded to us.

I let Kay toss her racket to decide the service. She won and elected to receive. The idea of having to reach up to serve was frightening.

How can I explain two selves? My bodily self was agonized and in terror. My inner self was secure and above body: All that I knew or felt was Trust in the Lord.

After the short warm-up period of two minutes allotted by the umpire, we began. I shall never forget as long as I live that first game. Each swing of the service made me want to scream. The score went to deuce four times before I won the game. Then, from the moment we changed courts on that odd game, I did not, for an instant, remember the torn muscle. Twenty-five minutes later I had won the championship of the world.

Then came the biggest thrill of all. Kay and I were presented to Queen Mary, considered Wimbledon's patron saint. I was proud and happy and grateful.

Yet I wanted to be alone. Success was very sweet and very sobering when the first breathtaking excitement was over. During the next few days that I spent in bed I had plenty of time to reflect upon my victory and to realize that despite my years of work and preparation, I was merely the medium of a Greater Power. He looks after us if we only give Him half a chance.

His Own Magic Wasn't Enough

by GLENN D. KITTLER

"This is one trick I can't muff," said Carl Ballantine after hearing the doctor's verdict. The story of how this magician-comedian then found the all-important prop is told by Reporter Glenn D. Kittler.

THE TALL, strapping young man standing in the wings of a famous theatre heard the master of ceremonies introduce him:

" . . . and now—The Amazing Mr. Ballantine, the World's Greatest Magician!"

The orchestra blared a raucous tune. Carl Ballantine gathered his props, straightened his broad shoulders, and began the bravado strut that was one of his trademarks. Suddenly, a wave of nausea swept over him, and Ballantine collapsed to the floor.

Within 24 hours, he lay in the Will Rogers Memorial Hospital, a sanitarium for actors at Saranac Lake, New York.

"You've got tuberculosis, Mr. Ballantine. And you've got it bad," the doctor told him. "I'm afraid there isn't much we can do for you. You've got six months to live, at the most."

Six months. Not much time. Dazed, he turned his face to the wall, his heart refusing to accept this deadline.

"This is one trick I can't muff," he told himself soberly. "This one *has* to come off."

He remembered the first time he had muffed a trick, a mistake that changed his life and turned him into one of the country's leading comedians. Until that horrifying moment on-stage in Atlanta, Georgia, he was a straight magician, competing to win popularity against the best magicians in the world. Then it happened.

He was doing the old trick of ripping a sheet of newspaper into a string of paper dolls. Actually, the dolls, cut earlier in his dressing room, were supposed to be up his sleeve. When he reached for the hidden dolls, they weren't there.

Horror exploded on his face. Stunned, he looked out at the expectant audience. Then he threw up his arms in resignation and said, "Oh, well, you've all seen that trick anyway. Let's go on to the next one."

Laughter started at the back of the house and rolled down on him like a tidal wave. It was the first big laugh the act ever got, and it was the turning point of his career. Ballantine twisted his entire performance to frustrated, fumbling tricks that never worked, and for an added note of satire, he billed himself as the world's greatest magician.

Success was immediate. Higher and higher he rose in the entertainment world until his collapse in the wings.

Now he had only empty hours of staring at a blank ceiling, only the torment of fighting the fact that he had probably given his last performance.

The days petalled off, and Ballantine counted each one. One evening during his third month in the sanitorium, his eyes fell on the Bible on his night table. It had been placed there earlier by the hospital chaplain, and for the first time Ballantine reached for it. Propping it on his chest, he flipped the pages. The phrase that caught his attention was in Matthew, Chapter 7 . . .

Ask, and it shall be given you.

To Ballantine, this was news. He read it again, his brown eyes filled with doubt and surprise.

Ask, and it shall be given you. "This sounds like *real* magic," he said, half-aloud.

Ballantine, like many vaudevillians, had never had much time for church. Up late for the Saturday midnight show, then back at the theater for an early afternoon performance precluded the true meaning of Sunday for him.

But now this. Ballantine had an innate belief in God, but he rarely gave it any serious thought. It never occurred to him that the Creator of the universe would listen to the requests of ordinary people.

Yet, there it was in print before his eyes. Later, after the orderly clicked off his light, Ballantine looked out the window at the stars.

"All right, God," he whispered, "I'm going to try this. The doctors gave me six months, but I think You've got more to say about that. God, I'm asking You to stretch that out—indefinitely. Please."

For weeks, there was no perceptible change in Carl Ballantine's condition. Half-afraid that his prayer had not been heard, he repeated it again and again, each night. The morning of the sixth month, he sat up in bed to welcome the doctor on his morning rounds.

"Well, Doc," he said, beaming, "I've passed the deadline. Now that it looks as if I'm going to be around for a while, I want you to know that the food in this place is terrible."

A strange thing began to happen. As the encouraged doctors started to plan treatments for Ballantine, they found that his unexplainable but definitely gradual recovery made them unnecessary. Months passed, and Ballantine became stronger. Eventually, the bewildered staff arranged to discharge as cured a man who had come to them with a time-limit on his life.

Three years after an ambulance had hurried him out of New York, Carl Ballantine returned to Times Square. Standing at 47th Street, he feasted himself on the millions of lights glittering along Broadway.

"Well, we made it," he said to himself and to God. "How am I supposed to say thanks? Everytime I breathe, I'll know it's because You're letting me do it. And how's this: wherever I travel, I'll do benefit shows for TB patients so that they can see what You've done for me, and what You can do for them. But that means You'll have to put me back to work, doesn't it?"

There were no doubts now, no surprise: merely the confidence of faith. Ballantine's agent, however, had different ideas.

"Sure, everybody's glad to see you," the agent said. "But you've been gone three years. A new audience has grown up. They never heard of you. No big producer will take a chance on you."

"Forget the big producers, then," Carl said. "I tell you I'll be headlined at the Paramount in six months."

The agent laughed. "What do you think you are, a real magician?"

For weeks, there was nothing. At last Ballantine was offered a weekend appearance at a resort hotel and this was followed by a tour of infrequent one-night stands in the Midwest. Adhering to his pledge, he performed in TB hospitals wherever he went. After each show, he would stroll through the wards.

"Been reading this?" he'd ask, picking up a Bible. "It's the best medicine in the world. I know."

Then, the telegram from his agent reached Ballantine in Ohio.

Hurry back to New York, you prophet. You open at the Paramount Thursday.

On the train, he thought about the sudden call to New York. Had word of his out-of-town performance seeped back to Broadway? Or had there been a stronger influence . . . the Strongest Influence in the world?

That happened several years ago. Carl Ballantine is now back in the big time, back in the nation's best theaters, and he is one of television's brightest personalities. Many still wonder how he did it.

Was it just plain luck? Or was it—as Carl Ballantine believes it was—evidence of the unseen hand of God, moving in answer to prayers of simple faith?

Prayer in Shorthand

by MINNIE WAITE BROWN

*What was the message the distraught teacher jotted
down—that helped change a life twenty years later?*

BILL WAS A handsome boy of 14, full of animal spirits and deviltry.

More often than not, he managed to keep Mary's whole classroom in a titter and Mary on the verge of tears, for it was hard to
get even the minimum amount of work out of her pupils with his
distracting influence.

One morning Mary told God about Bill. Then she wrote a
prayer in shorthand and slipped it into her Bible.

At that moment Bill himself appeared in the door, and, like a
friendly dog mischievously wagging his tail, he stopped in front
of her desk.

"What are you writing, Miss Mary?"

"Something I want God to do for me," she replied calmly.

"You think God can read shorthand?"

"I think God can do anything—even answer that prayer!"
Mary said vehemently.

Bill's curiosity was challenged. He could not stop thinking
about that note written to God in shorthand. After class he
slipped back into the room, took the bit of paper from the Bible,
and went around the corner of the schoolhouse to look at it.

All he could read was his own name. But he kept the note and
put it in the back of his Typing Book.

The years went by and Bill grew into manhood. Eventually he
entered a successful law practice, married, and became the father
of two children. He still pursued his irresponsible, egocentric
ways, just keeping on the safe side of disaster through luck and
charm.

Then, after several years, luck appeared to be on the wane. For the first time in his life, his home seemed to be on the verge of break-up. People were getting wise to Bill.

In the midst of this personal turmoil, Bill's father died. Bill left immediately for the West Coast to be with his mother, where he remained until the family house had been disposed of. She was coming to live with him—another responsibility heaped onto those he could hardly cope with now.

As he went through old trunks and papers in his mother's attic, he came across something familiar, his old Typing Book.

As he thumbed through the yellowed pages, the memory of Miss Mary, tormented by his own provoking antics, came back to him. A slip of paper fell to the floor. With a start he recognized the prayer Miss Mary had written in shorthand.

What had she written about him? He seemed to hear, just as clearly as he had heard it that day in his boyhood, her sharp answer that God could do anything!

He took the worn bit of paper to his secretary and asked her to decipher it. As she read an embarrassed expression came over her face, and he noticed that she blushed.

"It's a very personal message," she said. "I'd prefer to write it out and leave it on your desk."

He found it there when she had left for the day. The words stared up at him: "Dear God, don't let me fail this job. I cannot handle this class with Bill upsetting it. Touch his heart and make him a good boy. He's a boy who can be very great or very wicked."

The words struck hard. "Very great—or very wicked." For a long time Bill sat at his desk, thinking of his headlong years; trying to see himself as his harassed teacher, his distraught wife, his children and his business associates must see him. It was dark when he left the office.

For days the message was like a living thing. It would not leave him. He kept it in his pocket and at intervals he took it out, reading it and rereading it.

Finally, in desperation, he decided to consult a minister.

"Do you believe that a prayer can be answered after 20 years?" he heard himself asking.

The minister smiled. "Sometimes God waits until the heart of a person is ready to receive it. And—the recipient of the blessing must do something to merit the answer," he replied.

Something of merit that he had done? He tried to think.

He had taken his mother to live with him, at a time when his marriage was going on the rocks, when he wanted to evade the issue. Yet, after all, that was a small thing to do, all things considered. But—certainly it was one of the few unselfish things he had done during his whole life ...

His thoughts began to clear just slightly. It was as if a door opened and a ray of light tried desperately to come through. He considered. Thoughtfully, slowly but very surely, he made his decision: he would go back and make that marriage a success.

They talked for a long time, Bill and the minister, and Bill went away with an inner peace that he had not known before. From that day, his whole life changed. Today, Bill is on the way to becoming "very great."

Months later he sent a letter to his old teacher, who is my sister. As she read it, a light came into her eyes.

"Yes," she said. "I do believe that God answers every prayer."

Each in His Own Way

by DON MCNEILL

> *Would radio listeners think prayer out of place on an entertainment show? The famous Breakfast Club toastmaster tells what happened when "prayer time" was introduced and the lives it has since affected.*

I'LL NEVER FORGET the morning during World War II when I first asked Breakfast Clubbers:

"All over the nation ... each in his own words, each in his own way, for a world united in Peace—bow your heads, let us pray!"

The studio audience of 500 followed the example set by the cast and the orchestra seated with me around the breakfast table, and for twenty seconds silently blended their thoughts with ours. For a fleeting moment I wondered about the reactions of the unseen audience, accustomed to our early morning foolishness. Part of my personal prayer was that everyone would participate.

I had reason to believe the result would be favorable. Breakfast Club had been founded on inspiration, good music, audience interviews, clean family fun and nostalgic memories, at the time of day when a person's outlook would influence his daily efforts. Furthermore, I believed that prayer—the greatest single force in the world—was urgently needed at this moment while we were at war.

Our Breakfast Club mothers, fathers and sweethearts, I reasoned, needed a vehicle through which they could spiritually unite with their boys and friends overseas as the last supreme efforts were being made to bring order out of chaos.

Family prayer, I believed, was the vehicle. For 12 years the Breakfast Club family had laughed, sung, marched and reminisced together. Why not pray together?

Reactions were mixed. Some thought prayer out of place on an entertainment program; others applauded it. Several told me it was a courageous thing to try. The manner in which people expressed hope that I would continue "Prayer Time" made me feel they didn't think it could last.

Frankly, I hadn't visualized "Prayer Time" as a permanent peace-time fixture of our show. I regarded it as a call to action on the home front. With the war ended, our prayer for peace might be superfluous, I figured.

But ninety percent of the 100,000 Breakfast Clubbers who wrote us insisted that prayer *belonged* on the Breakfast Club program.

The first piece of evidence I received on the power of our prayer time came early in 1945 from a Pennsylvania woman.

"My mother in England," she wrote, "had a stroke during the first bombing of London and has been helpless ever since."

I suggested she say a prayer at exactly 2:25 P.M. London time each day which is 9:25 A.M. E.S.T. "This is the time," I wrote her, "when I, with the rest of your Breakfast Clubbers here in Chicago, will be praying with you."

"Believe me, Don," she answered later, "today I received a letter from my Dad saying that mother had given him such a surprise. He was cooking their dinner when she peeked around the kitchen door. She had managed to get up and walk downstairs! I am sure your minute of silent prayer has helped her. May God bless you!"

On May 7 of the same year, six minutes after we had said our usual prayer for "a world united in peace," an excited newsman interrupted our program with the announcement that the Germans had surrendered unconditionally.

Nancy Martin, our vocalist at the time, was singing "Oh, What a Beautiful Morning." It truly was a beautiful morning!

As a unit, the studio audience arose and gave a mighty roar. An

Air Force Lieutenant in the front row hugged his wife who had tears in her eyes. An elderly man sent his hat sailing into the air. An Army Private began dancing with an officer. Persons who had been total strangers a moment before shook hands and hugged each other.

While we were not the only people praying for peace, it meant only one thing to a multitude of Breakfast Clubbers. A prayer— their prayer—had been answered!

Because there was still a war and a peace to win in the Pacific, our moment of silent prayer remained unchanged until late in 1945. Then listeners offered several variations. My mother, for example, asked that Breakfast Clubbers offer thanksgiving on one day for all the blessings received during the week.

Another variation is found in our prayer "for better family understanding." A woman with five children wrote that she had decided to give her husband the divorce he wanted so badly—until she heard me offer the moment of silent prayer for broken families.

"That sounded like it was meant for us," the letter read, "and I prayed so hard. The following evening my husband returned home. Thank you, Don, that was the guiding hand we needed."

A St. Paul columnist told about a pretty girl he sat next to at a dinner one night. She confided that she had not completely subjugated her desire for drink.

"I wonder each morning," she said, "if I'll get by the day without falling off the wagon. One thing that has helped me stay on keel is Don McNeill's Breakfast Club program. During his moment of silent prayer I always ask God to help me. In two years, He has never failed."

The other letter came from a mother: "I have a son who is a member of A.A. and they use your daily moment of silent prayer as a starter-offer for the day."

Frequently, we are asked to offer a public prayer for a private individual. These requests are divided among the members of our cast who "in their own way" remember the pleas in their silent prayers.

Prayer time means much to people of all faiths, races and position. But none is more appreciative of family prayers than the McNeills.

My wife, Kay, and I had occasion to pray as only desperate people can pray back in September 1947 when our eldest son was stricken with polio. For seven straight days we prayed at the bedside of Tommy, then 12 years old. On the seventh day, the doctor reported that he could move his leg, and we knew that Tommy would be all right.

The next morning I told our Breakfast Clubbers about the crisis we had been through and asked that they join me in thanking God. Not only did they join us in prayer, but they literally showered Tommy and his friends with 15,000 letters, cards and gifts.

How Your Faith Can Be A Day-By-Day Guide

Too Busy to Live

by FAITH BALDWIN

A beautiful morning gave this famous author the tip-off for peaceful living in a hurrying world. A charming little story that makes you glad to be alive.

FOR A LONG TIME I had been troubled because there had not been enough hours in a day to do all that I felt I must do. Interruptions, emergencies and irritations came in such numbers that when I did have a quiet hour and sat down to work, I could not, with the best will in the world.

Then came one especially beautiful morning. A warm day; a cloudless sky, without flaw; and a clarity of atmosphere like crystal. It came to me that all who had eyes to see this beautiful world must, of necessity, rejoice and be thankful.

Then it seemed to me, that all my life I have not been sufficiently grateful for these things which appear commonplace and are in reality little miracles.

I began to count them; and found I could not.

The birds, flying free, and the flowers springing from the earth; the gentleness and understanding of friends; the sky at night, alive with stars; the warming cup of tea, the letter with good news . . .

I like to think that if I had my life to live over again, I would remember to thank God for every delight, however small, or brief. But I've been too busy to notice.

Why do we manage to remember with rebellion what we have *not*. We do not stop to consider what we *have* now.

I have spent so much time begging and beseeching God; and so little in being grateful to Him. Gratitude is not a common attribute. Each of us remembers the wrong far longer than the kindness.

I think back over my long way of work and achievement, dream and fulfillment, a way beset with obstacles and personal grief, which brought me to this study, this desk and chair and window. And I am grateful.

For no matter what turn the path has taken, no matter how veiled the road beyond the turn, I can find it in my heart to say, with thankfulness, as the Psalm has said "Thou hast set my feet in a large room." *

A room with many windows. Not just this room, which is not really large, but the room of my life . . . There was never a time when I could not look from the windows and see my blessings. But I was always in such a hurry that I did not look.

I was too busy to live. I shan't miss that joy any more.

*Psalms 31: 8

Better Than a New Fork Ball

by FRANK HILLER

Here is a Major League Baseball pitcher, with a bouyant personality, who has applied spiritual principles on the ball field with remarkable results.

IT ALL STARTED one afternoon in Yankee Stadium.

The New York Yankees, for whom I pitched back in 1948, were several runs ahead in the eighth inning of a hard-fought game. As a relief pitcher, I was warming up in case the Detroit Tigers rallied.

Then a couple of solid base hits, a walk and a double tied the score. I was called in to put out the fire.

Yankee Stadium is a tremendous place, seating around 75,000 people. There were perhaps 40,000 fans there as I walked out to face the Detroit batters, and some of the fans let go with the usual treatment.

"Why bring in Hiller?" one cried. "There goes the ole ball game."

"All he's got is a fast ball," came the cry from the Detroit bench.

This last cry really hit home. My right arm had been operated on not too many months before, and I had great trouble throwing a curve. Word of this weakness of mine had gotten around to the other ball clubs.

My first few pitches were wide of the plate. I was nervous and very anxious to make good—so much so that my shoulder began to tighten. The next pitch was down the middle.

"Smaack." The ball soared over the right fielder's head, into the stands for a home run. Three runs crossed the plate.

"Take the bum out!" someone yelped. "Ship him back to Kansas City," groaned another.

A few minutes later, the Yankee manager sadly waved me out

113

and another relief pitcher in. I walked to the club house, sore at the manager for not using me more, sore at the fans, but mostly sore at myself. And we lost the game.

In my own mind I wondered if I could pitch at all. Mentally, I was in a bad state.

A major league pitcher needs a lot of equipment: fast ball, curve, control and the right mental attitude—call it a winning attitude. Sometimes he can get by with just three of these qualifications. If he has only two, brother, he's in bad shape.

I lacked a curve ball, which was bad enough. But even worse, I had no confidence in myself; I had a defeatist complex.

The brightest spot in my life, at this point, was my wife, Helen. Married but a short time, already my life, away from the baseball field, was taking on more purpose and meaning. Although my wonderful Dad and Mom saw to it that my two brothers and I, as kids, attended Sunday school and church, I hadn't learned to apply religion fully to my everyday living.

Helen convinced me that we should join a church in Irvington, New Jersey, and attend regularly. Recently blessed with a son, we wanted to start him off right.

Our minister, The Reverend Albert Charles Freeman, took an interest in us. Perhaps he sensed that I was groping through a fog of spiritual confusion and in need of strength.

We talked about God and Christ's love—and how love conquers all. "Hatred makes people tense up so that they never do their best," he told me. "You probably find that true, even on the ball field, don't you?" he queried.

Now that was a new thought! I hadn't any particular hatreds against players, umpires, manager or fans, but I did have feelings of resentment which contain the same kind of poison. It never occurred to me that there could be any possible connection between religion and my performance as a pitcher.

I had to chuckle at the idea of facing slugger Ted Williams of the Red Sox, for example, and trying to love him out of a base hit. Yet a new line of thinking began to open up to me. I did some experimentation.

We started reading the Bible aloud, as a family, every morning after breakfast. At night we began to pray together. It wasn't easy at first, but I found that the relationship between Helen and myself was greatly strengthened.

I found that rising earlier in the morning, to spend time with my New Testament, helped me plan my day's work and made my mind more receptive to creative thoughts.

All these changes came slowly, one at a time. Life became happier. This feeling of joy was helped if I stopped several times a day just to thank the Lord for all my blessings—health, wife, sons, my mother and father, my country.

Meanwhile, on the basis of my poor showings, the New York Yankees released me to the Minor Leagues. This is a tremendous disappointment for any player. Yet, in the Minors I began to pitch regularly and regained my confidence. Self-pity and resentment were thrown off. At times, however, I'd pitch games under a hot sun and lose from 8 to 14 pounds. When I felt a pain in my arm or shoulder I'd begin to worry about it.

One day it occurred to me that I should practice my religion right there during a game. I don't mean by praying for a victory, but by letting some of the strong passages from the Bible run through my mind to help relax and coordinate me in a tight situation.

It was 109 degrees on the ball field a few days later; by the fourth inning my uniform was soaked; I was tired. I repeated to myself: *They that wait upon the Lord shall renew their strength; they shall mount up with wings as eagles; they shall run, and not be weary; and they shall walk and not faint.**

Some skeptics may laugh, but I repeated that phrase over and

Isaiah 40: 31.

over and it did help me a lot. I stopped worrying, felt more confident, less tense. I even seemed to feel cooler and went on to win the game.

As my winning percentage increased, it wasn't long before I was back in the Major Leagues again—this time with the Chicago Cubs. Meanwhile, I had developed a new type of pitch for me, a fork ball, to help out my fast ball and curve. Even better than this pitch were the spiritual techniques I had learned.

Many times during the ball season I'd walk out on the field for practice two hours before a game and say aloud: "Hello Lord. Thanks for this beautiful day, the sunshine, the green grass, the fresh air and my team-mates." Sure, I'd even include the umpires and the opposing team.

Some ball players perform best if they get mad at the opposition. Anger just tightens me up. I found it most effective to glance good-naturedly at the batter facing me, then dare him to hit the ball. Result: I'd be loose and free and have more on the ball.

I still took my lumps, but not as often. All ball players brood after a defeat, especially pitchers who lose a tough game or are batted out. I've found that if I burst into a song when I'm alone after a defeat, I can take it much easier.

One game in 1951 against the St. Louis Cardinals at Sportsman Park in St. Louis will always stick out in my mind. The Cardinals have one of the greatest hitters in baseball in Stan Musial and are an aggressive team. Stan has always been rough against me, as he has against all other pitchers.

It was a beautiful evening; having practiced all my positive techniques, I brimmed over with confidence. The ball was doing just what I wanted it to; I walked one man and a double play erased him. Enos Slaughter hit a single off me, and he too was rubbed out on a double play.

Then in the fifth inning I twisted my back, fielding a slow roller along third. My confidence was shaken; it was very humid and I suddenly felt tired. Stepping off the pitcher's mound, I paused a minute to rest my back and started repeating the quotation: *They that wait upon the Lord shall renew their strength . . .* I said it over and over again.

If hard-boiled players and fans had known what I was doing, they would probably have thought me slightly cracked. But the important thing is that I felt new strength; my confidence returned.

Twice during the rest of the game I struck out Stan Musial with fork balls. Not another man reached base; only 27 men faced me, the minimum amount, during a regulation, nine inning ball game. We won 8–0. I hope the Lord will excuse a little boasting over this game—He should, since He made it all possible.

I know only too well that my years as a player are numbered. Once you get in your thirties, as I am, the pace begins to tell. I love the game, but knowing that an injury or advancing years can end your career at any point, I have my own insurance business in Kansas City.

Spiritual principles, by the way, can work in selling insurance just as well as on the ball field.

In a way, through baseball, I found my place with God. Then, through God, I found a new place in baseball as well as in all of life.

Faces of Faith

by WILL OURSLER

> *In the subways, in the Automat, artist Guy Rowe
> found the faces he needed. Will Oursler, war cor-
> respondent and mystery story writer, tells the story
> Guy Rowe's models never knew.*

REGULAR CUSTOMERS at the Automat on New York's 59th Street,
knew him only as "The Old Man"—a white-haired old-timer
with sparkling eyes who dropped in daily to sip his cup of coffee.

They accepted the little man as their friend—with no questions
asked. None of them knew his name or suspected he was any one
important. Certainly none dreamed these daily sessions would result in a series of Biblical pictures which would be known across
the nation—with they themselves as the "models" for Old Testament figures.

They could not guess that each day he hurried back to his studio to put down, from memory, what he had seen, the faces of
faith he had found among the Automat's clientele. These were
the preliminary sketches for the famous book of Biblical selections, *In Our Image*—with magnificent full color illustrations by
artist Guy Rowe.

In 1946, when Rowe first entered upon the arduous assignment
of doing this book for the Oxford University Press, he was already an artist of established reputation, with a record of achievement in both fine and commercial art, including nearly a hundred portraits for Time Magazine.

These portraits he had done in a unique grease pencil technique he himself developed. They were careful, detailed studies,
seeking to capture not only likeness but innate character, the essential personality behind outer features.

That was why Houston Harte of Texas, who made the Biblical

118

selections, wanted Rowe to do the Old Testament illustrations—in vivid Twentieth Century style which would make the Biblical figures alive and vibrant to modern readers.

The assignment was a challenge. Although a man of deep human compassion, Rowe was agnostic in his views and had never before been drawn to religious subjects. Brought up in the Midwest, he had travelled widely and worked at assorted jobs before launching his art career in New York.

His diverse occupation brought him into close contact with every type of person—from the rough woodsmen in the logging camps of the Northwest to the tinseled comraderie of the vaudeville stage where he performed with an acrobatic team as "top man on the pile."

"Always wherever I went I drew and painted," Rowe declares. "I was interested in people and in form. I seemed to see beauty where others saw none. Yet often I myself didn't understand what that beauty was."

When he began the assignment, he planned to use strictly the Time cover technique. "We study the life of the subject and examine hundreds of photographs of the subject at different ages, in changing mood, from various angles."

The artist's eyes flashed as he recalled the beginnings of his three-year project. "But there were no photographs or angle shots of Noah, Joshua, Saul or any of the others. I had to find real, living people."

So Rowe set out to search for the people of the Bible in the streets, the subways, the restaurants, wherever he could find the character, the expression, the personality he envisioned.

After weeks of reading and re-reading the Scriptures he began to picture in his mind some of the characters—particularly the frightened, golden-haired Eve, and the towering massive strength of Abraham, the man of faith.

"One day, out walking," he remembered, "I saw a pert blonde

carrying a little suitcase. She reminded me of Eve, so I followed her. Then she vanished into a dancing studio. I didn't have the nerve to go inside."

Disappointed at losing Eve so suddenly, he dropped into the Automat for a cup of coffee. "It was almost as if I had been told to go inside. For there at the next table sat Abraham—in modern dress. A man about 80 years old—with a snow-white beard. He was engrossed at the moment in his scrambled eggs. But this was the Abraham I saw in my mind.

Rowe's extraordinary religious adventure had begun. He stayed that day long enough to study the face, to hurry back to his studio and sketch down a few details. "I couldn't ever tell him— or any of the others later—what I was doing. They would have become self-conscious and changed their whole expression."

Each day he came back to the Automat to study Abraham. Later he began to talk to others who came in regularly—the shifting parade of humanity in the Automat of all ages and types, from many walks of life.

These were his people—his models for Joshua, Ezekiel, Abraham and many others in the Old Testament. Sometimes he would use only a feature, a nose or ear or hand. The glint of Elijah's hands from one—the defiant glance of Jeremiah from another.

He did not, of course, confine his research solely to the Automat. Constantly—wherever he went—his eyes were searching. The questioning look of Amos, for instance, he found in the eyes of a soap box orator.

For Samson he studied the expressions of the sightless at an institute for the blind. Gideon was based on a photograph of an American General in action in the Pacific.

The only models who ever knew they were being drawn were Adam and Eve. That began one evening when Rowe and his artist wife and son were discussing the problem of finding Eve.

Rowe's son, Charles, declared, "I know a girl, Dad. Her name's Nikki. She's golden-haired and pretty. I wonder—"

He paused. The father smiled, "Bring Nikki home to dinner one night," Rowe said. "Only—don't tell her the real reason."

Charles told Nikki he wanted to take her home to "meet his mother." When she arrived and found Mr. Rowe at work over a drawing board, and Mrs. Rowe, in slacks, toiling over an oil painting, the golden-haired girl glanced around at the somewhat Bohemian scene with a mixture of pleasure and panic.

"When I saw that look," Rowe declares, "That excitement— the desire to stay mingling with her inner apprehension—I knew this was Eve."

The facial portrait of Eve was actually that of Nikki, and the Adam at here side was the artist's own son, Charles. To add a story book finish—Adam and Eve were later married and are now the proud parents of their first born

But none of the "models" at the Automat ever learned of the role they played—nor of the spiritual metamorphosis they helped to bring about in their friend.

"You think you've read the Bible," Rowe told me, "but you haven't. You have to go back, again and again, to read and reread. Each time you learn something new. For the Bible is a fertile field. Everything that is in life is there—to read, to know—and to paint."

In his three years of reading, learning and painting—Rowe came to look with new eyes on the faces he loved to draw. The agnosticism of three years before was gone. "I was searching for something special, not just for meanings; I searched for the face of the Divine, for the fire of religion and belief."

The Strongest People I've Known

by JACK SMITH

> *They call him "God's roughneck" or "the truck driver's Ronald Colman." Jack Smith, who has also been a stonecutter, cab driver and professional wrestler, is now an expert on physical culture as the General Manager of Postl's Health Club in Chicago, Illinois.*

WALTER HUSTON, the late stage and screen actor, was sitting at my desk several years ago, staring hard at a row of markings on my desk calendar.

"What do the letters 'A-P-R-P-B-W-P-R-A-A' stand for?" he asked.

"Affirmative prayers release powers by which positive results are accomplished," I replied quietly.

Huston's jaw dropped four inches. "Well, I'll be. A big roughneck like you thinking about religion."

"I write the first letters of a quotation on my pad in hope someone like you will ask what they mean," I told him. "It's my way of showing people I believe in God and am out plugging for Him."

Since Walter had come for a physical workout from a nearby Chicago theatre where he was appearing, I soon had him sweating hard on the handball court. As time went on we became good friends, and it was during a visit to his beautiful California home, a veritable mountain retreat, that I learned how deep his spiritual feelings were.

One Sunday, Mrs. Huston suggested a five-minute Bible reading for the three of us. Right there we made a vow to spend 30 days each year together at this mountain retreat, and we did so until his death.

Walter had lived a more Christlike life than any man I've ever known.

Many people whom I've met at work or at one of our Wednesday morning breakfast and Bible sessions, ask me how come my interest in religion. I'm led to tell the remarkable story of my mother and father.

My father, Peter C. Smith, ran away from his home in Aurora, Ill., when only 13. Seven years later he came back to find his family gone. He never did locate a trace of them!

Soon after Peter Smith wandered into a small restaurant in Melrose, Iowa. One of the customers was insulting the waitress, Anna Marie McGowan. Peter threw him out. Anna, he found, was also without any relatives, so the two young people were drawn together by a common bond of loneliness.

They were married and spent their honeymoon in a boxcar on the way to Chicago. As the family grew . . . four sisters, an older brother and myself . . . it was tough going. We kids peddled newspapers and my father worked at the stockyards. Mother took in washing, scrubbed floors, and did extra work.

My mother, although she had no schooling, did have a simple faith in God which helped her hold the family together through two panics and the Chicago fire. Her belief in Good, her kindness to all whom she met, her loyalty to her family, will remain in my heart always.

I grew up stubborn and needed the bumps and spills that came my way. I have been a professional wrestler, driven a truck, a taxicab and served five years as a stonecutter. It took 17 years and 17 broken bones to tone down my "wise guy" attitude.

Other things helped steer me toward religious thinking. One was an experience with a fellow stonecutter named Holland Oates, who had been saved from alcoholism by Evangelist Billy Sunday. Oates, whenever troubled, would get down on his knees, in the stables, out in the yard, in the office, any place, and pray about it, no matter how many people were about. I loved the guy and followed him around to outdoor prayer meetings.

One night on Skid Row a tough character began heckling

Oates, who himself was just a little fellow. Finally, the atheist got under Holland's skin. With a holy light in his eye, he threw off his coat and invited battle. When two more ruffians moved forward, I did too. After a brief struggle, the Lord raised our hand in victory and the worship service continued. It showed me muscle and religion didn't have to be strangers.

People occasionally ask what my church is.

"All of 'em," I tell them, "including Protestant, Catholic and Jewish."

Not that I think everybody should spread their religion around like this, but I find something I particularly like in every church.

Rabbi Louis Binstock of Chicago's Temple Sholem is one of the many clergymen who attends our keep-fit club.

One day the Rabbi came in, and I deliberately put him on the handball court with Sid Luckman, football star of the Chicago Bears. Although a rough-and-ready type, I have found in Sid a deep spiritual philosophy, and often wondered why he wasn't more active in his temple.

I confided to the Rabbi, "In my opinion, Sid Luckman has more God in him than most people who go to church regularly."

The Rabbi was interested and played harder than usual to give Luckman a good game. The football player's sense of fair play impressed the Rabbi and the clergyman's sense of humor appealed to Sid. It was my hope that Luckman's faith could somehow be put to work.

I used a lot of prayer in this situation. Then one day the Rabbi phoned me. "Drop over to the Temple tomorrow morning, Jack, and you will see something interesting."

There I found 750 kids sitting on the edge of their seats listening to a speaker whom they had previously admired only through the sports pages. It was Luckman all right. He was dishing out the best brand of good morals and spiritual faith you have ever heard—and carrying the ball better than at any time in his

13 years as a Chicago Bear quarterback. Later, Sid told me this was the most important score of his career.

I don't know much about the philosophy of religion, but I do know how faith has worked for me and for others in recent years. For example, one day while on vacation in Wabeno, Wisconsin, I accidentally stuck my fingers into the business end of a circular saw. The doctor looked at the chewed remains doubtfully. Working in a lumber camp, he was used to this sort of thing. "I'll have to amputate," he told me.

But I had a different plan. "Patch them up as best you can, Doc," I said, "I'm going to put my faith to work and pray about those fingers."

One of the fingers did heal perfectly. The other gives me a little trouble but it will come around all right.

I had to learn that my blunt manner at times rubs people the wrong way, but there is one approach that sure helps. In any kind of an argument, if my opponent looks like he'd enjoy changing the design of my face, and I myself am frying inside, I say a prayer, like, "God, you'd better get into this situation quick." Then I calmly suggest that we sit down and talk the matter over.

Looking the guy squarely in the eye without talking, I ask the Master to help us both feel God's power. Each time I can feel the anger melt away. If I think this, feel it, and want it with complete sincerity, the fight goes out of us and we wind up friends. This weapon of love sure has 'em all beat.

That's what I mean, see? When I honestly try to love someone, I forget my earthly troubles. Maybe it means I've got to smile a lot and pray plenty, and try and live out some real genuine prayers, but I do it. It makes me feel great, and when I look into any person's face with an eager desire to find good, it's there all right.

My Bus Has a Scottish Angel

by CLEMENT L. LOCKWOOD

Passengers aboard a New York to Baltimore Grey-hound bus may be surprised to hear their driver re-cite poetry. Clem Lockwood, who has driven 12 years for Greyhound, began writing poetry to put his own life in focus. He discovered that it can also be useful in helping others to do the same.

ONE DAY not long after World War II, while I was making my regular run from New York to Baltimore, I noticed a young man leave his seat and walk to the front of the bus. He seemed hesi-tant.

When he drew opposite me, he tried to say something, then changed his mind and sat down on the steps at the front of the bus.

There was something about the young man's attitude that prompted me to leave him alone. Out of the tail of my eye, I watched for 20 minutes as he pulled nervously at his khaki trou-sers. Then I decided it was time to act.

I began quoting poetry. In a voice loud enough for the whole bus to hear, I recited a war poem of mine published in the Army newspaper, Stars and Stripes. When I finished, there was a silent period of surprise, then a buzz of whispering. The young veteran turned and, at last, spoke . . .

"Where did you find that poem?" he asked. I told him, but I did not mention that I had written it. After a moment came the question I had been waiting for: "You been in the war, then?"

"Air Corps," I said. I didn't take my eyes off the road.

"I was in the Army. Engineers. . . ." Then, as my bus ate up the miles, he began a story that paralleled so many other stories I had heard.

During the war he cleared mine fields. He had seen so many of his friends blown up that his subconscious mind could not let the experience go. When he got back to civilian life, he would wake up in the middle of the night, haunted by the vivid memory of his Army life. Each new dream was the twin of the last: he, too, was blown up.

"Funny thing about that story," I said. "When we were flying B-17s over Germany, I knew a lot of men who were ashamed of being afraid." At that time I had written a poem which I now quoted to the young veteran. One stanza goes like this:

> *"Be not ashamed if your fear is great,*
> *For never a hero dear*
> *But fought his fight*
> *And won in spite*
> *Of the cold, old hand of fear."*

"Yes, I know that poem!" the young man said, and pulled out a much-wrinkled Stars and Stripes clipping. He looked at the name under the poem, then at the name-plate which hangs over my seat on the bus. We both smiled and that was the opening wedge I needed. For two hours as I drove along we talked about what it was to remember fear.

I remember the first time, three years ago, when I smashed my fear of sharing poetry with strangers.

I had thought of poetry as private—my way of putting life in focus. Then, one blistering July day I was loading my bus, getting ready to pull out of Baltimore. Everyone was sullen and tempers were short-fused.

Suddenly, as if a wisp of fresh air had entered the bus, we all sat up and smiled. An old, old lady arrived. She was short, wiry, and very Scottish.

She got in the bus humming and she sat down laughing. She joked with me about my driving and poked fun at herself for being Scottish. Passengers who had been grumbling a moment before, turned to each other to smile and then to chat. It was one of the pleasantest trips we've had.

Afterward I took this little Scottish angel aside and thanked her. "Dinna come to me with yer thanks, young mon," she said. "My laugh and song air not mine, really; they belong to other folk. 'Tis God ye should be thankin', for He gave them to ye through me." She walked off in a busy, gay shuffle.

The next trip was just as sweltering. Again passengers pushed and grumbled and I found myself remembering what a pleasant trip we had with my little Scottish angel.

I started the motor and pulled into traffic, still thinking about her and about what she said, "My laugh and song air not mine, really; they belong to other folk . . ." How hypocritical I was. I always pray for the safety of my passengers just before starting a trip; I pray and then sit back to drive. What if I asked for the happiness of my passengers? What if I did something about it as my Scottish angel had done?

It was then that I began to quote my poems. At first it was very difficult: I was embarrassed. It was part of my own self held up to the public, a part that was secret, even to me.

But I've been quoting poetry regularly since then. It makes trips brief for my passengers, and each day is new experience for me, helping people forget their humdrum lives and cares.

I've had an exciting life driving my bus for 12 years, spending three years in the Air Corps as an aerial gunner, working on a Camden daily newspaper, and before that, taking my first swing at life as the son of a farmer.

Most of this time I've noticed one thing about people and about myself: we are all too much tied down by the strings of everyday living.

That's why I wrote poetry in the first place. I found I could make molehills out of mountains through a poem. When I was in the Army in England, I wrote about the war and haphazardly stuffed stacks of verse into my foot-locker, until one day a buddy sneaked three of them to Stars and Stripes. They were accepted and published. I took four more in; they were printed. Eleven more were accepted.

The odd thing about this poetry was that hardened men enjoyed it. One of my training buddies was a husky, rough, fast-living 20-year-old. We ended up in the same squadron and I am positive that only I knew he had another secret side to him.

We were getting ready for a mission that promised to be rough, when this boy caught me alone and shoved a Stars and Stripes clipping into my hand. It was a poem I had written called "Fortress."

"This yours?" he asked.

I nodded, and he said, "Not bad."

For him, this was a wild expression of release. I was particularly glad he spoke out loud, because three hours later he bailed out over Frankfort, and I never saw him again.

People often ask what my passengers think about having a poet-driver. Once a lady in the back seat scolded me for keeping her awake. But as a rule people enjoy listening to poetry; it makes the trip seem shorter.

Yet, whenever anyone thanks me, I try to say, in my own way, the same thing my little Scottish angel said:

"Don't come to me with your thanks. Be a poet yourself, whether it's with a poem, or a song, or a laugh, or simply with a smile."

When One Reaches
A Crossroads In Life

It's Time for Decision

by JIMMY DOOLITTLE

> *During his adventurous life, Jimmy Doolittle has faced many emergencies and has been called on often to make split-second decisions. The famous Tokyo raider tells here how he has been fortified inside for those occasions when the chips were down.*

MY RELIGIOUS FAITH has always meant something very personal to me. So much so that until recently I have hesitated to talk about it lest I sound sanctimonious or like a "holy Joe."

Yet the world needs people to take a stand on their religious beliefs. Silence on the part of those who believe in God can actually aid the cause of atheism. Today one must be for something rather than just against an evil. I am for the building of a peaceful world based on the concept of the Fatherhood of God and the Brotherhood of man.

Since my travels take me to so many places throughout the world, I never think of my faith in relation to any one church. I have always felt that acceptance of God as the Controlling Power, and the advancement of religious understanding among all faiths, are far more important than the promotion of any one faith or religious group.

My experience along this line began in my early youth when mother and I went to Alaska to join my father who, although a carpenter by trade, was there to prospect for gold. In Nome three churches were located in our neighborhood—Methodist, Congregationalist and Catholic. I recall vividly my first Christmas. The Methodists had a Christmas tree for the kids, the Congregationalists gave away prizes, and the Catholics served ice cream. I went to all.

My buoyant youthful reaction to all this was more temporal

than spiritual, but the idea did sink in that there was much good in every faith and denomination. I haven't found anything since to make me feel differently.

Prayer has always been a vital, personal force in my life. Whether in cathedral, country church, or alone on some remote mission, I could always talk with God. And I do pray, daily.

Stories of those who have used prayer in time of crisis always stir me. With each person it seems to work differently. I pray before undertaking a critical mission, making a big decision, or doing anything that might call for that extra something. In such a prayer I ask for wisdom and strength—the rest, I figure, is up to me.

For when the chips are down, there's often too much to do during an emergency to send out a prayer for help or guidance.

I know that bringing God into the picture has made a big difference in many situations I've faced. Not that God should remove obstacles or grant special protection or favors, but He helps give one confidence and power to overcome the difficulty and fear.

During the North African campaign in the last war, we discovered that the Germans were supplying their forces in Italy mainly through an airlift of Ju 52s and huge six-engine Me 323s. Carefully, we planned an ambush so that we could knock them all out with one attack by our North African Air Force fighters.

A few days before this great plan was to materialize, we were out over the Mediterranean on a mission against enemy shipping with eight P-38s and six B-25s. Suddenly out of the northeast came a huge armada of these cargo-type planes, carrying valuable material to the German armies in North Africa.

The temptation was great. Here were hundreds of perfect targets, but with only a handful of planes we couldn't knock them all out. Still, this equipment was going to the African front to kill our soldiers. Yet if we attacked now, it might spoil our big plan to bag the whole airlift armada later.

It was a tough decision, and although I knew the boys were drooling, we turned away and went on with our search for shipping (in which we were, about 30 minutes later, successful).

A few days afterwards, however, through careful planning and skillful reconnaissance, we managed to get all our fighters in the air at just the right time to intercept another such airborne armada. The pilots did a masterful job of shooting down over 200 of the big planes. This broke the back of the German supply airlift and was instrumental in hastening the surrender of North African Axis armies a short time later.

The first vital decision not to attack was a split-second one. Did prayer determine it? Not in any dramatic way—no. But I always prayed for wisdom before every such mission.

Prayer doesn't need a dramatic answer to be effective. And there have been times when, without prayer to help guide me, I've done stupid and foolhardy things. This is enough proof for me.

Religion to me means recognizing the existence of God and living according to His precepts. It means applying the Golden Rule, and opposes the idea that the end justifies the means.

Such faith is exemplified through worship, in kindness, unselfishness, honesty, decency, morality and purity. This kind of religion needs to be brought to all mankind before we can have the better world we talk about.

The three R's no longer are sufficient to meet the complicated requirements of today's children. Tomorrow's citizens need the 4th "R," religion, as well as geography, the sciences, and human relations. The time has come now for all religious beliefs to band together against atheism. Certainly then, religious ideals shouldn't be kept out of schools just because of differences of opinions between various faiths.

There may be discord in a family, but when a stranger intrudes, the family "gets together." There may be honest differences of opinion between members of different political parties in a nation, but if the nation is attacked from the outside, all factions pull together against the enemy. So should all who believe in God, work together against the common enemy, atheistic communism.

As one of the ancient prophets said: "Trust in God with all thy heart, and lean not upon thine own understanding. In all thy ways acknowledge Him, and He will direct thy paths."

My Toughest Mission

by JULE SPACH

> *His B-24 out of control and plunging into the Medi-*
> *terranean on a mission back in 1944, Army Pilot Jule*
> *Spach bailed out. The miraculous experience that*
> *followed directed this young pilot into a field of*
> *work he would never have chosen otherwise.*

IT IS FEBRUARY 15, 1951, as I write this. Tomorrow my wife, two children, and I sail from New York to Brazil on the liner Mormacdale. We are to be Christian lay missionaries in the northern part of Brazil in a town called Garanhuns.

Many people have asked me, "Why, at only 27 years of age, do you want to be a missionary?" Now is a good time to trace back through the years for the answer.

As far back as I can remember, thanks to devout parents and grandparents, the teachings of the Bible and the word of God have been present in our home. But the older I grew, the more I drifted from my faith and the more I seemed to doubt the existence of God.

I joined the Air Corps at 18. By my 20th birthday, I was a pilot of a B-24 with the 460th Bomber Group stationed at Spinazzola in Italy. On August 1, 1944, we took off on our fifth mission, which was to bomb the Genoa dockyards.

The weather was perfect, enemy resistance negligible as our squadron of heavy planes winged over the Mediterranean to northern Italy. Suddenly an oil line broke. In a matter of minutes all four of our engines had "conked out."

After pulling out of formation, our entire crew of 10 bailed out about 3 miles off the coast of Italy. My parachute billowed past me as I struck the water, and I quickly slipped it off.

137

When my life vest wouldn't work, I was frantic. Being only an average swimmer, this stroke of bad luck seemed to seal my fate. In addition, it took me 20 minutes to get rid of my clothes and shoes. Then P-51 pursuit planes flew over the top of the water looking for us, and the whole Italian coast seemed to open up with a barrage of flack.

I never felt so completely lost, alone, and afraid.

Exhausted from my struggle with clothing, the only thing I could do was to start swimming toward shore which I saw dimly. Then, like so many others who ignore God and prayer until in a desperate situation I began praying that He would help me. I really talked to God, almost shouting the words, for fear He might not hear.

Then it seemed that in one moment all the planes went away, the shooting stopped, and everything was deathly still.

That was the assurance I needed to know that God was near. Convinced that I had nothing to worry about, I relaxed, talked to myself, whistled, and even sang as I swam. Little did I realize that this section of the Mediterranean was shark-infested, or that German patrol boats were about, or that bullets from one boat had already killed one of my crew members, or that five others of my crew had already drowned.

I swam for nearly six hours before reaching the shore. The amazing thing is that I do not recall being tired and never once doubted that I would make it. After this experience I was ashamed that I had ever doubted the existence of God.

The coast was under German control, so I hid for the rest of the day in a haystack. The next morning a group of Italian women discovered me, but instead of calling for help, one gave me her shawl to cover my nearly-naked body, and the others brought food. Unfortunately, several Italian men got wind of my arrival. One jammed a gun in my back and marched me to a nearby German military unit.

My nine-month period in German prison camps was fortunate in one way, because it brought me in contact with one of the greatest men I have ever known. In prison camp Stalag Luft 3, near Breslau, I met "Padre." He was a Scottish paratrooper chaplain.

A year before my arrival German officials had given him what they thought would be good news. "Padre," they said, "you can go back to England in exchange for a German prisoner."

But he shook his head. "I'm needed more here," he told them.

In the months that followed, he stood up under hardships which few other men of his age could have endured. He seemed to be everywhere at once, cheering us up, making us laugh when we most needed to. He talked about the Lord quite a bit, but in a warm, human way that made religion seem dynamic and full of vitality. The more I came to know, respect, and love the man, the more I began to realize that you could reach for higher goals, but that the way to reach these goals was through Christianity.

The end of the war brought my liberation and return to the United States. I soon enrolled at Georgia Tech to study chemical engineering, and like other returning service men, was uncertain about the future, indefinite about what I wanted to do, and somewhat let down.

I had quickly gotten over the idea that America owed me a living just because I had served my country a few years. Everyone had made sacrifices of one degree or another.

During Christmas of 1947, I returned home from college to my home town of Winston-Salem, N. C. One night I double-dated with an old friend, whose date was a girl named Nancy Clendenin. I was intrigued by hearing Nancy tell us that her ambition was to be a missionary.

Months later, back at college, I found myself walking restlessly down the street one day. "Jule," I said to myself, "you just don't know what you want to do. Here God practically pulls you out of the Mediterranean, guides you back home, and you're all mixed up."

The idea came: "Maybe I should be a missionary." I recalled the Padre in the German prison camp; his was certainly a consecrated and vital work. Then I laughed. "What a foolish thought for a guy like me."

Three weeks later this same thought returned. This time I really faced myself squarely. How in the world could I be a missionary? I didn't know how to teach people about the Bible or about Christ. All I knew was chemical engineering and how to fly a bomber. "Be yourself, Jule, you're just not the type for missionary work," I cautioned.

But the idea haunted me. I couldn't sleep, my studies suffered; I didn't know where to turn. Then, I remembered the girl in Winston-Salem.

I made a special trip home that weekend to talk with Nancy. While she talked about her own ambition to be a missionary (a dream she had cherished since she was 11), I noticed her soft, brown eyes, the warm sincerity in her voice, and the proud arch of her head. We talked for two days; then I returned to school.

For several months we wrote back and forth. Finally, through her guidance and a lot of prayer, I began to realize that it might be possible for me to do this work after all.

"If you really decide that you'd rather be a missionary than anything else in the world, Jule, it wouldn't matter how much training you had," she told me. "The most important thing is how much you love God and how important you feel it is to share this love."

Within a few months I had made two decisions: first, I did want to be a missionary; second, I wanted to marry Nancy.

Nancy liked both ideas, so we were married in September 1948.

We then wrote to the Board of Missions of the Presbyterian Church. The Candidate Secretary paid us a visit to tell of an opening in Brazil for a man who could teach science, chemistry, mathematics, and athletics, and who had, in addition, a sincere Christian fervor. Everything he told me was something that in some small way I felt I might be able to do. We accepted the offer.

Looking back, I can see how God helped me along step by step —from the adventure in the Mediterranean, to my experience with the "Padre," and finally my meeting and then marriage to Nancy, who has been such an inspiration.

Even though this mission will be the toughest one I've ever faced, I feel a happiness and sense of satisfaction I have never known before nor thought could be possible.

Pickaxe Vacation

by COLLEEN TOWNSEND EVANS

> *One moment a movie star in Hollywood, then a personal decision, and Colleen Townsend soon afterwards found herself in Italy digging ditches and eating spaghetti three times a day.*

IN THE SUMMER OF 1951 my husband, Louis, and I saw a unique formula in operation. With young people from 15 different countries and widely diversified beliefs and backgrounds, we built a road on top of an Italian Alp.

No easy picture had been painted for us of Work Camps prior to our going. If we volunteered under either the World Council of Churches or the Friends Service Committee, we agreed to help the people help themselves . . . *their way*. We were to eat what they ate, do the work they did, sleep wherever we could. Further, we Americans paid one dollar a day for such food and lodging, plus our fares.

Our home Church, the Hollywood Presbyterian, was sending and helping to finance a team of ten, and the director who talked to us put it pretty clearly. "In Europe anyone can volunteer for this work. You'll run into mixed thinking . . . agnostics, atheists, communists. Your job is to help them build, or lay bricks, or dig ditches.

"You're not going there to be a martyr but to share Christ in some way with everyone you meet. If you haven't actually found Him and the joy He brings, you have nothing to share. Don't volunteer."

Louis and I volunteered. We drew Agape, Italy, a Christian conference ground for young people being completed near the tiny town of Ghigo, thousands of feet up where the borders of Switzerland, France and Italy meet.

At our orientation in Paris we were told that in Greek, Agape meant Divine Love. "But don't let that deceive you," warned our young instructor from the World Council of Churches. "Agape is Agape . . . spaghetti three times a day . . . poor sanitary conditions. The only way up is by trolley, bus, and your own feet."

Then, as he looked sharply at us, trying to estimate how we would adapt to new situations, he added, "If you want to back out, do it now!"

Because of my background as a motion picture actress, I felt he was speaking directly to me. I already knew that the road to "Divine Love" wasn't easy . . . and I wasn't backing out.

A feeling of inadequacy had started me on this path years before while I was still in college. I was constantly prodded by an awareness that something was missing in my life—not the material things that so many of the world's people need. In my deep underlying sense of lack, I wanted a purpose and goal.

Upon leaving college for Hollywood, I carried my restlessness with me. While a motion picture career came fairly easily, the answer to my real search didn't.

Eventually, I was led to a group at the Hollywood Presbyterian Church, where 400 young people between 20 and 30 met two or three times a week. They came from every walk of life: young advertising executives, filling station attendants, secretaries, actors, students. But they had two things in common. They were in absolute earnest. And they knew God.

There was no doubting the joy they had found.

"But how?" I asked a good friend of mine.

"Through Christ," he said simply. I dimly knew what he meant. I wished he could be more explicit.

For six months these young people worked with me; they were confusing, groping months, but I saw amazing things happen. One boy with an exceptionally good singing opportunity was leaving night club work to join the Westminster Choir School. A successful young TV song and dance team was dissolving, the husband to study for the ministry while his wife danced for his tuition. They were doing it simply because they couldn't keep this joy for themselves. It overflowed.

All this changed my life. No visions, nothing supernatural, just a very natural spiritual rebirth. I found that I could walk with Him all day long. Then I too began to experience joy, and serenity, and adventure without fear that came with surrender to Christ.

In this bright new light my career became dimmed. My happiness lay in the work I did weekends at the Church, going to the Main Street Missions or the jail camps. Tours, locations, hours on the set only seemed to interfere.

Truthfully I didn't "give up" motion pictures. They simply got crowded out because I had found something so much better.

Next came studying for full time Christian work . . . a summer working in a French refugee camp . . . then a most wonderful thing happened. Louis Evans, a young Divinity student, who was the son of our minister at Hollywood Presbyterian Church, asked me to marry him. After the wedding, studies continued at the Theological Seminary in San Francisco, and then this last summer . . . Agape.

Our instructor in Paris told us it would be rugged . . . that was a good word. Our project was to build a road from the little Village to the four conference buildings a mile away.

The girls worked 8 hours daily, the men 10. We all slept on gunny sacks stuffed with straw, the girls in the Ghigo schoolroom, Louis and the boys in teepee tents. (Louis and I later did live together in a small room.)

Since my husband was elected a camp foreman, I reported to him every morning with my shovel and went where he sent me. He had no worries about my strength.

What our instructor said was true—as far as it went. But he did not know Wolfgang, nor the girl, Maria, nor the other campers. They were the real adventure.

Maria, a beautiful Italian girl, had been through much in a short life and was deeply unhappy. In the first four weeks of camp we failed to win her confidence. She watched us, came to our prayer meetings at night and just sat listening. Not once did she mention the deep problem we knew she was carrying.

One afternoon she asked Louis and me to come with her. We went to a little grassy knoll far from camp. Then Maria told us a wrenching tale of heartbreak and terror.

"I tried so hard to find God," she cried. "And I failed so completely."

We told her how we too had searched and searched ... and finally found our way to Him!

Then for over two hours we read promises that He has given us ... *I came that you might have joy ... peace I give unto you, not as the world gives ... I will instruct thee and teach thee in the way that thou shouldst go ...*

The sun had gone down and it was cold now on the mountain. But not one of us felt it as the three of us prayed *together* for the first time.

Since then we have received many letters from Maria, the essence of each one the same. "Now I know what you meant. It *is* thrilling. It *is* the big adventure."

At Agape we shared all the camp work. Language barriers, differences in creeds or education seemed to wash down the drain with the dirty dish water. It is hard to maintain superior feelings with your hands in dish water up to the elbows.

No one asked, "Are you a Methodist, Lutheran, Jew or Gentile? Are you an Italian, Armenian, American?"

Truthfully we didn't care. The bond of joy between those of us who had found faith set agnostics and atheists to wondering just what this treasure was.

It was this spirit, too, that refreshed Wolfgang.

Wolfgang was a 21-year-old theological student from Otter-burg, Germany, in the Russian occupied sector. His father had been sent to Siberia. His mother and 14-year-old brother were forced to work in a factory for 180 East German marks per month (about $12 in American money). Wolfgang had taken large chances bicycling across half of Europe to reach us.

Many of us at Agape wondered at Wolfgang's determination to stick to his Communist-dominated community in East Germany. There, divinity students, while given comparative freedom, are the subject of distrust by Communist authorities. Now he proposed to go back and face the added risk that someone might expose his trip to Agape.

"I take the chance because that is where I am needed," he said. "I was thirsty to share the joy you all have together in a free Christian life. I needed to make sure you still had it. Now I can go back refreshed . . . to give hope. To tell what I have seen."

Maria and Wolfgang are only two of the hundreds who have worked at Agape and gone away "refreshed." Each has given something, and each has taken something away.

Louis and I took to Agape an eagerness to share our spiritual convictions—plus a thoroughly American viewpoint. There hadn't been enough vitamins in the food to fuel bodies digging ditches. An American bulldozer could have done in six months the job these people had worked five long summers to complete with their hands. Yet we came away with much more than we brought.

We *had* built a road on three bowls of spaghetti a day . . . and stayed amazingly healthy. With a bulldozer Agape wouldn't have been Agape: the work of a thousand hands, a link in a chain of understanding of each other and of God—a new hope for the future, a positive proof that we can all work together in peace and have a wonderful time doing it.

You Have a Story to Tell

by JOHN RYDER

An advertising man took his wife to a prayer meeting because he thought she needed it. Instead John Ryder, President of the Norm Advertising Agency, was captured by a new challenge. One of the results was a Job Finding Forum, which has since helped over 25,000 men and women.

I RECALL A DAY in a long-dead past when I occasionally would sit in the pew of a church—if I hadn't had a bad night before, or too pressing a golf date! I can remember sitting there fuming and crabbing . . . the sermon was never right, the music could stand improving, other members of the flock didn't look too good. I got what I gave: nothing.

Frankly, I had no idea that I had any real need for God in my life. I was "doing all right" . . . making good money in advertising, had plenty of friends and a nice family. I vaguely believed in God, attended church now and then, paid my bills. What more could a man want?

The idea that God knew more about controlling and guiding my life than I did—or might bless me and my family more richly —never occurred to me.

My first real step toward God was totally unconscious on my part—a gathering of men and women at Calvary Church in New York to discuss faith on a practical basis. As husbands do, I agreed to go only to encourage my wife, figuring it might be a good idea if she were a little better Christian. I had no idea the shoe might fit me.

I was due for surprises. First, the quality of the people was much higher than I had anticipated. Instead of dull, "mousey" types or well-meaning but impractical people, they were an attractive, stimulating bunch—the kind you might meet any night at the Ad Club. Second, there was a genuine friendliness and sense of humor, and a spontaneous eagerness to share and help each other. Third, there was none of the fanaticism or kill-joy philosophy I had expected.

These people were really living—they spoke with a quiet conviction and enthusiasm I had to admire—with a sincerity I had to respect—and a humility that really reached me. For these people were just like me, with similar problems and interests. And similar failings and temptations.

It wasn't until I heard people of my own kind tell how prayer and God worked in their lives that I became convinced that religion is a practical thing—that it could work in my life—and was what I wanted and needed!

But it was not until I began to offer every area of my life to God —and to share my prayers and experiences of Him with others as these people shared with me—that my life began to change.

Three things stand out. As soon as I began to put myself completely in God's hands by forgetting myself and constantly praying only that I be guided to do *His will*—I was directed first to form a prayer group in my office. Second, as soon as I began sharing or "witnessing," new people, interests and opportunities began coming into my life. Third, fascinating new projects opened up to me for which I had no background or experience—*yet that did not seem to matter!*

When your life is God-centered, He sends you the right person or the right words at the right moment—tells you when to go ahead and when to stop because He knows we *need* His help to do His will.

The Job Finding Forum of the New York Advertising Club is a direct result of this kind of guidance and sharing for God.

When Charlie Green, the Club's Executive Secretary, and Herbert L. Stephen, Field Editor of Printers' Ink, first suggested such a project to me back during the days of heavy unemployment, I wasn't sure I was the one to tackle it. Or how. So I took the matter directly to my early morning office prayer group. At the end of our prayers and "quiet time" together, there seemed to be a unanimous feeling among the group that I should head up the project.

How could we help these men and women find jobs? Obviously you can't resort to a lot of pious prattle with deeply discouraged, unemployed men and blandly advise them to, "Go home and read the Scriptures for the answer."

The day came when I stood before 25 jobless men . . . with a prayer in my heart. And the prayers of my associates back in the office. Our prayers brought the right people—experts—contacts—data . . . everything we needed to meet the individual needs of these jobless men.

Based on Christian principles, the Job Finding Forum has since helped over 25,000 men and women, with every conceivable employment problem, from age to disability, land *not just jobs, but the right jobs for them individually.*

One of the most striking facts to come out of this endeavor is that the person who forgets himself and sincerely tries to help other fellows at the Forum is usually the first to land a job, and to profit the most.

In the eleven years of Forum operation, no charge has ever been made for services rendered except the Christian observance, "Freely ye have received, freely give." *For God means his love to be used* if we are to receive more.

You have a story to tell! And I have a story to tell. Because God expresses Himself through each of us differently, He needs and wants every one of us to share our experiences of Him. If you have ever had a healing—or other spiritual proof of God's help and power—share that experience and faith with someone now. Maybe you don't feel your experience counts. Or you don't know much about religion; or you haven't had any dramatic answer to prayer. Or you think, "I'm not the type."

Both your friendship and your experience are much more precious than you think.

Whom did Christ pick to found His church? Peter, a simple fisherman. Matthew, a tax collector. Luke, a physician. No background for the work, a modern-day efficiency expert would say. No college education. No experience, no important contacts. Yet Jesus chose these men to found the whole Christian church.

A lot of people have asked me how to bring the comfort and healing power of God into the lives of "intellectual" friends who neither feel the need for God nor recognize His existence. Perhaps you, yourself, have wrestled with certain doubts beyond your understanding.

Have you ever enjoyed the scent of a rose . . . or felt your heart soar at the evening stars? Have you ever loved anyone or anything more than yourself?

Certain experiences, certain truths come to us only through our hearts. We can't explain how we recognize them, scientifically. We only know that we do know them and experience them . . . *that they do exist.* Science, in spite of all its miracles, has never been able to produce a piece of protoplasm from which all life springs . . . which is life itself. Nor can science reproduce love, or explain either one completely.

Nor can the existence and power of religion be fully understood and explained on an intellectual battleground. Yet it is a sure fact that we *will* draw closer to Him, if we come humbly to Him on our knees, with the deep sincerity and eagerness of a little child to learn. And it is a sure fact that God *will* come into our lives and those of our friends if together we ask His guidance and love. Otherwise, Christendom would have caved in centuries ago.

Your Hour of Decision

by BILLY GRAHAM

as told to LEN LESOURD

> *"I have fifty million dollars and I am the most miserable man in this city," one businessman told Billy Graham. A racketeer once missed a date with death because, by chance, he stopped in to hear this famous evangelist. For the lonely, the unhappy, the wrongdoers and the skeptics—and perhaps for you—Billy Graham has an answer.*

PEOPLE COME up to me and say: "Why should I make a decision about God? I'm happy doing what I'm doing. You call it sin—I call it fun. Live and let live."

If they don't say it in these words, the thought's there unspoken, in their faces.

There's pleasure in sin—but only for a season. Deep down there is a gnawing, dull dissatisfaction.

I sat down with a 69-year-old business executive in a large Eastern city recently who told me, "I have fifty million dollars and everything I could ever want—and I am the most miserable man in this city."

One of the biggest names in Hollywood, a tall, strapping, swash-buckling type, revealed the same thing in different words. His life, he admitted, was lonely and empty.

These are two prominent people who have discovered that wealth and fame aren't enough in life. Millions more feel the same way. Telling lies and dodging the facts cannot shield them from the real truth—that because their consciences are black with acts against God, they can find no inner peace. To cleanse out this dirt, they need the injection of a driving spiritual force in their lives.

Jim Vaus came out of World War II a master of electronics.

Within a few years he was in the employ of big gamblers on the West Coast, drawing down huge fees for his craftsmanship at wire tapping and communications.

One night Jim dropped in on one of our meetings in Los Angeles to kill time before he was to take off by plane for a very important deal in St. Louis. Outwardly indifferent, he stood at the rear of the hall. When the call came for those in the audience to come forward and make a decision for Christ, a quiet man next to big Jim tapped him on the shoulder.

"Will you go forward with me?"

Jim whirled on him. "Lay off me or I'll knock your head off."

The other man didn't retreat. "You can do anything you like to me," he said gently, "but that won't right things between you and God."

Something clicked inside of Jim Vaus at that moment. His face twisted with emotion, he started walking to the front of the hall. Jim then made a decision to break clean with his old life and contacts. Today, he is one of the Lord's hardest workers.

Jim Vaus found out later that the plane he didn't catch that night of decision was met in St. Louis by gunmen *who had instructions to kill him.*

This is a spectacular example of what God can do with a person. Hundreds of men and women are reborn, less dramatically at every meeting.

"But, Billy," some people say, "What do you mean by being born again?"

To be born again means that the Divine Life has entered the human soul. God's objective then is to have that person start life anew, living in the image of His Son, Jesus Christ. The two conditions of this rebirth are repentance toward God and faith toward Christ.

At our meetings emphasizing the family and home, whole families have come forward to make their decision together.

Once a husband and wife, who had parted, came to the meeting separately. He started forward at the end. So did she. Startled, they met face to face, then joined hands with tears in their eyes.

We hold these meetings over periods of four to eight weeks in cities and towns, usually where we have received a joint invitation from the churches in the community. The effectiveness of our meetings, we have found, depends on working with local churches and ministers and giving them the responsibility of following up our efforts with a program of their own.

The results so far have been heartening—for which we give God the glory. Our continuing prayer in these days is that we can remain in a position of usefulness to God and play a part in calling the world back to Him before it is too late.

If you are a disbeliever, a skeptic or just indifferent, I know what you're going through. I've gone through it all myself. If you feel that you are just naturally weak, let me assure you that many persons who once were weak, today are the strongest workers for God. The Scripture says that strength comes from weakness.

When I wandered into my first revival meeting back in 1934 in Charlotte, North Carolina, I was a gangling kid of 16 with a consuming ambition to be a major league ball player. The last thing I wanted to be was a preacher. From our worldly crowd, two of us, Grady Wilson and I, went to the meeting to see what the shouting was about.

The first night I hid behind a stout lady's big hat. I recall vividly the smell of pine shavings in my nostrils ... also the strange stirrings that churned up inside me to know more about Christ. Although my family had reared me in a fine religious background, I had shrugged much of it off during my teens.

The second night I sat up closer and battled with the questions everyone asks. Was it sissified to embrace Christ? Could you be religious and still have fun? Who would be looking if I were to go forward at the end of the meeting? Why couldn't I make a decision without walking all the way to the front?

All these questions are rooted in man's pride and egotism. God didn't come through to me as a real Presence until I publicly made the decision to be a living, breathing worker for God. Not an evangelist, though, I said to myself.

Months later, after some of the most exhaustive prayer sessions I have ever had, I decided to make religion my career.

To earn enough money to pay my way through Bible school, I spent one summer selling brushes. This experience taught me that regardless of whether I offered brushes or faith in God, without convictions and enthusiasm I was wasting my time.

Being jilted at 18 made a terrific impact on me. The fact that the girl in question said she didn't think I would amount to anything helped light a fire under me. After a long session of self-analysis, I decided I did want to amount to something—not for myself but for God.

While attending the Florida Bible Institute, I began to practice preaching in a nearby woods. Almost daily I would slip into the swampland, lay my notes on a stump and offer my sermon to the birds, alligators, frogs and all who would listen.

Then came the question that nags many who start out doing God's work. "How do I know God wants me to do this?"

The only way I knew I could get an answer was through prayer. "God," I said, "if You want me to preach, help me locate a pulpit."

That same day a man came up to me, said he had heard me preaching and asked if I would give a sermon at a gospel meeting that night down the road. This—my first real answer to prayer—started my career for the Lord.

Today when a cynic asks me—"How does giving your life to God pay off?" or, "If I change, what will God do for me?"—I can answer by telling him what He has done for me.

He forgave my sins; He gave me peace of mind; He took away my fear of death. He stirred up creative powers within me that I never realized existed. But more important than what we receive from God are the efforts we are able to make for Him.

How Youth
Measures Up To The Challenge

Boys Will Be Big Shots

by JAMES F. FARLEY

Why do boys become criminals? Whose responsibility is it? A challenge to everyone by one of America's most distinguished political figures.

WHEN I LOOK on the older generation, *my* generation, struggling with terrifying world conditions, I realize the wonders we have achieved, the advances we have made, the marked improvements and progress. Yet I also see the errors we committed, the mistakes, the wrongs, the many, many stupidities, and my heart is heavy.

When I look upon the generation after us, which was so often called "The Lost Generation," I marvel at their magnificence in World War II. They were boys to make the blood sing and the heart exult with pride. Those were our G.I.'s who are now pulling the load with us.

But most important is the *new* young lot. Everywhere I meet them—they are the American leaders and lawmakers of tomorrow. I am deeply impressed as I talk with them by their sincerity, their directness and their capacity for devotion. These are the men of tomorrow—the bosses and law-makers. These are the men who will be and are making the United States.

Yet you and I know that the majority of our criminals are boys and young men. The average age of men who are inmates in prisons and reformatories is under 26.

American youngsters are no fools. They don't follow the hypocrite or the lukewarm. They are furnaces of strength, fierce interests, and urgent dreams. They want to be recognized. They want credit. They crave to stand out. They want desperately to be a part of doings.

What are we doing for them and about them? The problem is not juvenile delinquency, but adult indifference. The time to stop delinquency is before the boy becomes delinquent . . . at an age when most adults consider them too much bother.

The farther I go in years, the boy I was draws closer to me. With each passing birthday I see more of what I am in what I was.

I was born at Grassy Point, New York, of second generation Irish stock, the second of five boys, my brothers being John, Phil, Tom, and Bill. My schooling began at five years of age, and included High School and a year's course in a commercial school.

The things we boys took for granted in a small town would be privileges beyond purchase to our city lads. We had open fields, hills, streams, trees, animals, birds, fenceless spaces. We had fishing and swimming and plenty of space to mark out a baseball lot. We had coasting, skating and the big popcorn or candy-making feasts around outdoor fires.

We had the blessing of needed work. You can't live in the country without going miles to school or market, without tending furnaces, clearing walks, caring for chickens, horses or cows or other stock, and knowing a garden with your knees.

My father was killed by a horse when I was ten. Mother was left a small insurance policy and a half interest in a little schooner that carried bricks 30 miles down the Hudson to the big city.

Maybe we five sons didn't feel *responsible!* And therefore *important.* I ran errands and did chores until mother bought a small business with her last $1,000. Then we really had responsibility. During the summers I also worked from 3:30 to 11:00 A.M. as a machine boy in Morrissy's brickyard for less than a dollar a day.

Hardship? No, it was a prideful achievement to a boy with the stirrings of manhood in him to be pulling his weight and to be needed. I still found time to be the local waltzing champion, and at eight I was carrying a torch in a "Bryan-for-President" parade, and I never missed church. I took a confirmation vow never to drink or smoke, and I've kept it.

Perhaps the two greatest blessings I had in boyhood were a

fierce love of my parents and a deep devotion to my religion. These are woven in the fabric of the man that boy was. On every election day my whole life through I've gone to the graves of my mother and father and prayed.

A few years ago I saw an inter-church world survey of statistics in cities of over 300,000 population, 52.7 per cent of which were non-church going people. In rural areas the percentage was even higher. What has happened to us?

Speaking as a father and a churchman, I ask you, what can we expect of our boys when more than half of our homes are religious jungles? It is not going to be easy in the years ahead to keep and to build our democratic way of life. Are we to expect the men who take our places to do it without God? Only a vast religious awakening can give full value and unassailable dignity to our lives.

Every boy needs a leader. One reason so many become criminals is because they follow the wrong leaders. A boy has far more idealism than some people suspect. He will work. He will take rules and follow them—and even keep in strict training. He will struggle to qualify at great personal sacrifice. If he is convinced, no fooling, there is a job to be done, he will *give*.

Anybody can collect a gang of boys and throw a basketball up in the air. But when you build on a church you give a boy identification with the power of God Almighty. When you take him into a club or a purposeful group you build stability and the sense of *belonging*.

No doubt your church has a Cub pack and your Legion Post has a troop. Maybe it takes care of 20, 30, 60 boys. We also have, thank God, Boy Scouts, Big Brothers and other great organizations. But do *you* see to it that there's room for every boy in the neighborhood? Groups for the fellows too old to join a youngster group? And a pack for the little chaps in their most tender and impressionable years?

Beyond games and entertainment, skills and crafts, there must be projects to achieve at every age level. Goal after goal can be set up and won. Tomorrow's men must feel the elation of tough, worthwhile constructive *doing* . . . some eyesore cleaned, some foul spot in the community righted, some needed job done, some vital equipment earned, or a structure built. In being part and parcel of the community he helped to better, the boy will give a piece of his raw love to that spot and the people in it.

Every man can take on one boy, even form a group of 5 or 10 boys. Nightly they roam the streets and lanes longing for companionship and acceptance. Many are from broken homes. Many never heard of God. Many see their elders living and dying without God or with just enough of the church to get married and buried in.

Each of us can teach at least one boy the glory of God and the excitement of doing. Lots of people overlook that joy completely in the idea that if a man is smart enough he can find ways to live without working. Maybe an individual can, for a while, but a nation, never. The trend has become to do as little as we can and get as much as we can. Perhaps that is a far-swing of a pendulum. And it had better swing back before our red-blooded boys sicken and rot.

But there's a right way and a wrong way. Without respect for God there can be no respect for each other, past animal urges. There's a God to be honored and served because His Spirit is in us and our own spirit claims honor and service.

Tomorrow's manhood is at your elbow. Can you put out your hand and take hold of him? He's knocking at the door that is *your* future. Will you open it to him? With God in your heart and in your welcome? No man or woman, aware of our dangers today, should be able to sleep soundly without giving some share of time to our future men, individually and collectively.

Every Kid Has His Hero

by DOAK WALKER

How does sports competition build outstanding citizens? Doak Walker, a famous football all-American at Southern Methodist and now a star halfback for the Detroit Lions, tells the heart-warming story of the boyhood influences which guided his life.

I HOPE THAT PARENTS won't discourage their youngsters from participating in sports just because of the publicity given to a few athletes who went off the beam in recent years. For every disgraced athlete there are thousands who, through their character and sportsmanship, are a wholesome influence on the youth of America.

I'm no one to preach a sermon, but I would like to reminisce on what my athletic experience has meant to me.

My father once told me: "Play football as long as you enjoy it, Doak. Play clean. When it's no longer fun, stop playing."

I'll probably always be a kid in my love for football. (I also believe that the professionals play ball because they like it. The pay helps, but the desire and love for the game is the main factor.)

As a boy I had my heroes. One was Harry Shuford, a great triple threat star for Southern Methodist from 1933–1935. In my grade school English class I wrote a theme about Harry, who, I pointed out, was great not only because of his ability, but because he had ideals and gave up individual honors to boost his teammates. I wanted to be like Harry.

My dad has always been a hero to me. As football coach at North Dallas High, he started tossing a football at me when I was 18 months old. When I was 3, I made my first trip to the high school locker room and immediately fell in love with the leathery, sweaty, locker-room odors. In the equipment room I put on a pair of football shoes, and clopped triumphantly around the room.

By the age of 6 I had learned to drop kick a ball over the clothes-line in our backyard. My sister, Pat, would retrieve the ball, with our dog, Jakie, barking after her. More often, though, my kicks wobbled to the side and into mother's rose bed.

There was plenty of time for athletics in my young world, but my parents made it clear to me that sports were not the most important thing in life.

God had top spot in our family. We said the blessing before every meal and prayed together for many things—problems of the day, our family and friends . . . world peace.

Both mother and dad taught Sunday school in the Westminster Presbyterian church. I can well remember slipping out of my junior Sunday school room and into my father's class for older boys . . . to listen intently to his down-to-earth interpretation of Christian living.

Since it wasn't possible for me to have dad as my high school football coach, then I'm glad it was Rusty Russell. Rusty not only built strong teams, but his coaching program was aimed at promoting ideals and creating life-long friendships. One fall he had us camp together in the gym for two weeks before school opened. We practiced on the field, ate together in the school cafeteria and slept in the gym camp style.

It was during one of these nights that our squad got together and spent a lot of time and thought working out a set of football objectives. The seven rules we drew up included emphasis on sportsmanship, hard but fair play, learning to think, personal conduct on and off the field, knowing how to take defeat and the importance of scholarship.

Bobby Layne and I were co-captains of our high school team that year. Bobby, one of the closest friends I ever had, went on to Texas University. A year later I went to Southern Methodist.

The college game which I will perhaps remember longer than

any other was the one we played against each other back in 1947 in the Cotton Bowl. At game time both Texas and SMU were undefeated and untied. Bobby and I had been playing together since Junior High; now we would have a chance to match wits against each other in friendly rivalry. Layne had already become recognized nationally as one of the best passers in the game.

I did what I always do before the kick-off of every football game, I paused for a moment and said a short prayer—I prayed for Bobby, for all the players and asked that no one be hurt.

Texas kicked off to us. In a few quick plays we scored a touchdown and led 7–0. Then Bobby got his passing wizardry going and it was soon 7–7. Later in the game we scored again and kicked the point to make it 14–7. Bobby's passes netted another touchdown, but the all-important extra point was missed. We won 14–13.

It was one of those very exciting, rugged, but clean games that make competitive sports so stimulating for youth. Victories are wonderful and this one made me thank God for the exhilaration of just being alive. But you can't win them all, and the defeats, believe me, are good in teaching humility.

Bobby Layne and I now play professional football on the same team, the Detroit Lions. On Dec. 21, 1952, came a great thrill and victory for both of us. Bobby's passing paved the way for us to meet the Cleveland Browns for the professional football championship. We won the title game 17 to 7.

Every man has a right to work out his own life pattern and personal convictions. I have never been ashamed of my complete faith in God. It means too much to me. I do not drink, although I wouldn't ever try to force my conviction about it on others. Therefore, it was no problem for me to turn down a $50,000 radio offer from a beer sponsor. I'm not crusading against beer, but I don't see how alcoholic drinks can help me get any more fun and satisfaction out of life than I do now.

I wouldn't be human if I didn't say that I've loved the excitement of football. But the things that have meant most in the long run are the friendships gained, the sense of values learned, and the hope that perhaps in some way I've measured up to my boyhood idol, Harry Shuford.

Along the way have come some wonderful awards which I hope I have deserved. But, putting first things first, I'll never value anything more than this note from my mother.

"I have been proud of you as a football player," she wrote me one Christmas, "but I am more proud of you as my son in the home."

With Trust They Climb

by FLOYD STARR

*A delinquent boy who had stolen cars arrived at
Starr Commonwealth For Boys. The very first week
Founder Floyd Starr sent him on an unusual errand,
with the shrewd knowledge of boys that, for forty
years, has produced good citizens out of many errant
youths.*

HARRY DROVE OFF alone with my car and the five dollars I had
given him to buy his supper. He was to meet me after I had returned from an appointment. The fact that Harry was new at
the Starr Commonwealth for Boys—and had gotten into trouble
with society by stealing cars only two months before—did not disturb me.

Like the thousands of other boys who have come to the Commonwealth in the past years, Harry was not a bad boy. He was
old for his 16 years, intense, with a shell of hardness about him,
yes—but he was not bad. I trusted him.

Right at the appointed time Harry appeared with both the car
and the change from the five dollars.

On the way home from Bay City, Michigan, where he had
driven me, Harry said, "Uncle Floyd, I would like to ask you
something. You trust me, don't you."

"Of course I do."

"But I don't understand why. Don't you know what I've
done?"

"Harry," I answered, "I don't know what all you've done; I'm
interested in what you will become."

"But I think you should know why I came to Starr Commonwealth," he persisted. "I lived in a home where there was nothing
but drinking and fighting and swearing. One day I came home
and saw a big crowd of people around the house. Then I saw

165

them carrying my mother out on a stretcher. My father had come home drunk and beat up my mother and cut her with a knife. She was taken to the hospital and my father is in prison.

"I was so unhappy I didn't care what happened. So I joined up with a gang and we got to stealing cars. I have stolen cars. That's why I was sent up here and now you trust me with your own car. I don't understand."

"Harry," I said as we drove along in the night, "that's all in the past. . . . Everything will turn out all right."

Most of the boys come to Starr Commonwealth because of youthful mistakes or broken home situations which created social and emotional problems in their lives. Like 90% of the others, Harry did turn out all right. Our goal has been to teach them to accept responsibility, to make wise choices, to win the respect of others, to cultivate things of the spirit and generally to become happy, useful citizens.

Starr Commonwealth began with two boys back in 1913. My original purchase was an old farm with one ramshackle barn. Today we have 2000 acres, including a 40-acre campus, and more than a dozen fine buildings—all thanks to the help and prayers of a great many people who believe in what we are trying to do.

Located just three miles from Albion, Mich., we house a total of 165 boys in 12 cottages. Each cottage has its own dining service, its own housemother. Emphasis is on cleanliness, affection, consideration for others and the qualities representing the best in a home atmosphere. Suitable dress and good manners are observed. They contribute to self-respect and improved conduct.

No boy is ever accepted unless he enrolls voluntarily, and all faiths are represented. Average enrollment is two years, at the end of which period the boy is usually ready for placement elsewhere. Our alumni are in all branches of the Armed Forces, in industry, the sciences and all professions.

The program of education (our standards meet all state requirements), coupled with exercise and work, is aimed at developing a vital, spiritual philosophy of life. Believe me, the boys can give us elders lessons in the practice of faith.

Several years ago David, one of our most active youngsters, asked me, "Uncle Floyd, have you done anything about having the plan drawn up for the new school house?"

I told him no, because we didn't have any money.

"But," said little David, "we prayed about it. I think we ought to get the plans drawn up so that you will have them ready when somebody comes along with the money."

After that comment I called in an architect, had him draw up a set of blueprints, and then put them away in my desk drawer. Some months later a representative of our school was calling on a woman in Grand Rapids who had been a small contributor one year but had not renewed. The woman said, "Is there some project about the school that would interest me?"

"We do need a new school building," our representative answered.

"Well, call Floyd Starr on the phone and ask him if he has plans drawn for it," she said.

Thanks to little David's faith, I was able to pull the plans from my desk and send them on at once.

The lady of Grand Rapids took them to her own architect, found it would cost $100,000 to erect the building—and gave us the entire amount.

One boy came to us whose community and State agencies had despaired of helping him. Today, the church where he has been pastor for several years has the largest youth congregation in that city.

Starr Commonwealth is a private enterprise. It receives neither state nor federal aid, its work advances entirely through private contributions. But we do have a special source of "outside" help here.

Like the tragic experience when Howie had come back from a trip and brought in an antique revolver he'd found. He meant no harm with it, intending to use it as a souvenir to decorate his room. In cleaning it the inevitable happened and the bullet pierced his intestines in five places.

The doctor asked me if we had ever had a death in this school.

"You had better prepare for it now, then, because this boy cannot live."

I said, "I will start the boys to praying. We will call in another Physician who will help in this case."

Each house took two hours to pray, around the clock, for 24 hours. At the end of the day Howie was still alive. The doctor said it was remarkable, but that he couldn't live another 24. At the end of four days the doctor was touched by our faith but told us we were dedicated to a hopeless case.

At the end of a month we were having a meeting—a prayer meeting—when the door opened and in walked Howie, just as healthy as ever.

Yes, God's help has always come when we needed it most.

That Extra Boost

by BOB RICHARDS

> *The story of a delinquent boy who became the Olympic and World champion pole vaulter. What chance remark by a girl helped change his life? What source of energy enabled this athlete-minister (also an Associate Professor at LaVerne College) to rise from a sickbed to make his winning jump?*

PEOPLE OFTEN ASK me if prayer "works." I'm not sure whether they are asking me as a pole vaulter or a minister. It doesn't really matter as the answer is the same. Through prayer I have done things that otherwise would have been impossible.

Two of the best jumps of my life have come as a direct result of prayer. Once in Finland several years ago, I was sent to the hospital with a strep throat two days before the big meet. All Thursday and Friday I lived on a diet of penicillin and nothing else. Saturday morning my arms were so tired I could hardly do a push up. Nevertheless, I had been asked to make an appearance and attempt to compete.

Up to the time they put the cross bar into position, I was praying for strength. I cleared the bar at just under 15 feet, the highest jump of my life to that very minute.

Again in 1951 I found myself worn out, depleted mentally and physically just before the Chicago Relays. Was it wise for me to fly East to a meet in which I didn't think I could offer my best? With the question came my immediate answer . . . the expense money and tickets. So I went.

The plane left Los Angeles at 8:30 in the morning and arrived in Chicago at 7:00 that night . . . just time for me to make the event. Instead of sleeping on the flight, I spent the time in prayer.

That night I barely missed the World's Record. My jump went down as 15 feet, 4⅞ inches.

To me, those are answered prayers. And I don't mean God giving me the edge over the other fellow—for I never pray for victory and I always pray for my opponents as well as myself.

What I do mean is that prayer is our point of contact with a very real power within, that releases the energy necessary for us to turn in the highest performance of which we are capable.

Is pole vaulting important enough to command that power?

Everything and anything is.

It's like leaven. Once you contact it, it infuses every activity. In my case the sports field *has* been important. It has given me a passport with youth throughout the country . . . and it has introduced me to the qualities we must all humbly seek if we would live like champions.

Youngsters are demanding, practical. "If I learn to pray," they say, "If I learn to contact this power, if I accept the discipline that is required . . . where am I?"

Then I can show them that the qualities that have made great champions have made them tremendous not only in athletics, but in life itself.

Dean Cromwell, for 40 years track coach at the University of Southern California, when he addressed his Olympic team headed for London in 1948, told us straight, "If you can't win fairly, don't win."

He reminded us that a clean, fit body and a clean, fit mind were essential. It would require work and discipline to render each man a fit vessel to fulfill our prayers. In that degree, God would help those who helped themselves.

"Like the two little girls who were afraid they'd be late for school one morning," Cromwell said. "One had an idea. 'Let's stop and pray.' But the other had a better idea: 'Oh, no. Let's keep running and pray as we run.' "

His team ran and prayed and they weren't late ... they came back covered with Olympian glory.

The champion who relies on a Power greater than himself dares to believe he can do ever better. Because he is aware that the Power is not his own, he puts no limits on it. Thus records go on being smashed, men run faster, jump higher, until they are *proving* that this power is limitless, bounded only by what each individual believes he can do.

Dutch Warmerdam, a man who recognized the power of prayer, was told that a pole vaulter would never clear 15 feet. In four years, between 1940 and '44, Warmerdam did it 43 times.

Faith and confidence, as well as hard work, turned tragedy into victory for Glenn Cunningham. As a kid Glenn was badly burned saving his brother from a schoolhouse fire. His legs received the worse burns and healed slowly, covered with stiff ugly scar tissue. For a while no one believed he would walk again. With infinite patience and faith he began teaching himself ... working behind a plow ... until he could take a few steps. Then walk. Then trot. The training was long and arduous. The scar tissue never disappeared from his legs. But Glenn Cunningham became one of the greatest milers who ever lived.

Here you can offer proof positive to young people that the qualities of discipline, faith, prayer, carry them up the path they want to travel. I know that well for I needed to find it out myself.

As a kid in Champaign, Illinois, I ran around with a gang that I suppose was tougher than most. We fought daily, swore a lot, stole fruit now and then. I don't think we ever stopped to wonder where all this might lead.

Then, because some girl in high school made a crack about wanting a "Christian boy friend" it suddenly occurred to me that I hadn't been to church in 10 years. That high school girl, believe me, was a true worker for Christ. I didn't dash off at once ... not by a long shot. But one Sunday morning weeks later, when I was reading comics and listening to the radio, I had a sudden overwhelming desire to go to church. I didn't stop to ask myself why. I didn't even stop to put on my tie. I just went straight to the Church of the Brethren that I remembered passing in the neighborhood.

Here the minister, the Reverend Merlin Garber, began telling me about this other path, the one of discipline, faith, prayer. He told me where it led. It sounded good. Five of the fellows in our crowd later went to jail for holding up a gas station. It wasn't hard to figure which was the better way.

That, I suppose, was my conversion. But understanding didn't follow immediately.

There's no telling how long I might have floundered about if a friend of mine, a young preacher, hadn't told me a story about his first sermon.

Charlie was a young man who was pretty sure of himself, proud of his self-sufficiency. When an older preacher warned him that his first sermon might be tough, Charlie just laughed.

"But, Charlie," said the older man, "it might. Words just might not come. If that happens try taking a Bible phrase and hold fast to it. Repeat it until God stabilizes your mind and you get the blessing and inspiration *from* Him."

Independent Charlie just laughed again. "I won't have any trouble." But he did.

Faced with his first big audience his mind went blank. From nowhere came the old minister's words. He had said, "until *God* stabilizes your mind and you get the inspiration and blessing *from Him*." From those words Charlie drew his strength. He got his help. And that thought began to help me.

Maybe my mistake, too, was being too sure of *myself,* too proud of my self-sufficiency.

That was the beginning of my understanding, an understanding which gave me the earnest desire to become a minister myself; without that I'd probably have gone right on following my own will.

Each one of us has to catch up someday with the wisdom of Paul the Apostle, who admitted frankly that the good he wanted to do he could not, while the evil he didn't wish to do, that he did ... *until* he found he could "do all things through Christ which strengtheneth me."

The answer doesn't lie in any change outside the individual. The first change has to come within the heart of man ... his concept of himself, his concept of God and prayer. Where man has failed God *has* provided an answer. Where we are weak He is strong.

The history of the greatest champion who ever lived, Jesus, has proven that, once and for all. And Jesus invited us to follow "the Way, the Truth, and the Life."

Many of Jesus' victories were major ones. Certainly He dared to do the "impossible."

His advice would apply to any athlete today. Christ insisted:

On clean living ... "the pure in heart."

On hard work ... "no man that puts his hand to the plow and looks back is worthy ..."

On faith ... "whatsoever ye ask, believing ..."

On confidence ... "Fear not, little flock, it is your Father's good pleasure to *give* you the Kingdom."

Certainly He came through when the pressure was on. Instantly and before multitudes He healed the sick, fed five thousand, raised the dead. Then He instructed those who followed Him to contact that same power.

"Follow thou Me ..." "Greater works than these shall *ye* do." He told us that the Kingdom of Heaven was *within* us, that the power of a champion was there, available to us all.

Graduate from a Park Bench

by HARRY CLINTON EVA

Harry Eva, when fourteen and alone in the world, slept fitfully one night on a park bench in Boston Common. Before morning he made a promise to God. The result—Harry Eva started a remarkable venture of faith that has helped thousands of boys.

I WAS STILL IN KNEE PANTS when I first met, in a most personal way, the problem of homeless boys.

My mother and father had come to the United States from Cornwall, England. They settled in Vermont, and before I was 14 years old, they had both passed on, leaving me penniless and without friends.

I worked my way to Boston, and only later did I discover—tragically—how lucky I was to land a job right away as cash boy in a grocery store.

During this period of tight employment around the turn of the century, my $5 a week salary seemed like a lot of money. By the time I got my first pay envelope, I had exhausted all my money—except for one nickel. With $5.05 in my pocket I would have felt like a rich man except that my room and board came to exactly $5 a week.

My room was five flights up and about the size of a small closet. In it was one bed, one mirror and a chair. There were no windows and the landlady required me to keep the door shut.

One day at work the boss told me, "Look here, Harry, you're going to have to do something about your clothes. Your elbows are coming through."

I reached into my pocket and pulled out my nickel. "I've kept this ever since I started to work," I told him. "It's all I have. I didn't dare spend it."

My employer turned away without a word, and I thought he understood. But that Saturday there was a blue slip in my pay envelope. I had to ask my landlady what it meant, which was a mistake.

"It means you're fired ... canned ... through," she told me. "And as of this moment, I want my rent in advance."

"But I'll get a job and pay you by the end of the week," I said.

"You'll do just one thing," she said. "You'll get upstairs and pack your things."

It was a cold January night. Since I had never been on the streets of Boston after dark, there was panic in my soul when I left my landlady's house that evening. I had no place to go except Boston Common. There, on a park bench, I huddled with my overcoat wrapped closely around me and my personal belongings in a bundle under my head.

I was afraid of three things: that I would freeze, that I would starve and that one of the flotsam and jetsam characters that floated around the Common would kidnap me, like an adventure from Dickens.

I had been brought up in a puritanical, Christian home, and I don't use the word puritanical in any but the historic sense. In those days we didn't just drop into church for a half hour on Sunday. "Church" meant a two and a half hour service in the morning and long devotionals in the evening.

But, as usual, with this strictness went a deep appreciation of prayer and a thorough founding in the workings of faith.

These blessings were my only solace as I faced my three fears that night on the Common in Boston. Each of the thirty or forty times I awoke that night, I repeated a promise that if God protected me, I would devote my whole life to homeless boys.

When morning arrived at last, I was glad I hadn't spent my nickel. It bought a loaf of bread—the only food I was to have for eight long days. I broke off little pieces and ate them—just

enough to keep me from starving while I made the rounds looking, unsuccessfully, for work.

On the morning of my eighth day in the park I saw the most
important piece of money that has ever come to me in my life. It
was a penny, turned sideways in the snow. My first reaction was
to buy a roll or a bun; but then it occurred to me that perhaps I
should buy a newspaper.

In the male help column was an ad: *Boy wanted, cafe work*.
That meant food! When I arrived at the address—it must have
been 5:00 in the morning—there were 28 boys lined up outside
the building making applications for the job—I made the 29th.

When it came time for my interview the proprietor asked me:

"Do you smoke cigarettes?"

"No."

"Do you shoot craps?"

"Pardon me, sir. I don't know what 'craps' means."

The man looked at me with startled eyes and said: "You have
a job."

I still had in mind my promise to God to start a home for other
homeless boys. Since I was able to get my meals at the cafe, I put
aside three-fourths of my salary of $6 a week. I did the same with
subsequent jobs too and in nine years I had saved four hundred
dollars.

Saved penny by penny $400 seems a lot larger than it is. Na-
ively, I went around to churches and organized charities trying
to give my money away to establish my dream shelter.

But no one would take the money under my conditions. Some
even laughed at the idea of starting a home where boys could
come with no qualifications except that they were homeless and
needed a friend.

This must all have been part of God's plan, because as time
went on I still had my $400 and began to realize that God in-
tended *me* to found this shelter.

I went to New York and rented an old store. The landlord not only helped me set up the first home, but gave me a job selling umbrellas during the day to ease the drain on that first bit of capital. Immediately I went down to Union Square and found six stranded and homeless boys. By the end of the week I had twelve boys. We took turns sleeping on chairs, on the floor and—only occasionally—on a bed.

By that time I was faced with a decision. I needed money. I could either start a campaign to raise funds or I could try something I had long been anxious to attempt: stepping out on God's promise. He had said, *"Take therefore no heed for the morrow: for the morrow shall take thought for the things of itself."* * I felt that if this work were within God's plan, He would be more interested in it than I, and would somehow supply our needs.

Fifty-one years have passed since that first day and over 46,000 boys have known our Home. We have had to move to larger quarters, of course, and next year we hope to move still again, this time to a building that can house 200 boys at once.

When we were still working with our original $400, I would come home from my job and do the housework with the boys: the cooking, the scouring, the mending. We have help in this now, but I do not consider any work I have done more important than these scullery chores.

Willie Thompson came to our Home from one of the worst New York tenement districts. Lonely, familyless, he had run away and was wandering the streets when we found him. At the age of 18 he enlisted in the Army, giving as home our address: The New York Home for Homeless Boys, 462 East 158th Street, New York City.

In August 1950 he was sitting by his machine gun in Korea, protecting the withdrawal of his platoon. Refusing to retreat, he held the enemy at bay single-handed until killed. To him went the Congressional Medal of Honor, the first Negro to win the nation's highest military honor since the Spanish American war.

*Matthew 6: 34

We are very proud of Willie, and others who have gone out from the Home to live useful lives.

Today, while New York sleeps, we search the streets, the parks, subways, and water fronts for the stranded boy. When we find him, we don't ask questions about race or creed, we just give him a hearty welcome, a clean bed and meals until we are able to find work for him.

We are the only free home for boys in New York. Yet I have never asked for money, nor have I needed help when it didn't come. Once we were sitting down to supper when young Jimmy was asked to say the blessing. We had only potatoes and cabbage for supper and Jimmy said, "But gee, what's there to be thankful for?"

"Why we can be thankful for our potatoes and cabbage. We can be thankful for all the good meals we've had in the past."

At just that moment the doorbell rang and Jimmy answered it. He called out a few moments later that it was a package too large for him to carry. I went to give him a hand and found a sixteen pound ham that the delivery man had left. It was from Mrs. Theodore Roosevelt.

Later, when I recounted this story before a group of club women—where Mrs. Roosevelt was present—someone asked from the audience: "How did Mrs. Roosevelt know that you needed help at just that time?"

I started to answer that there was no way of her knowing, but Mrs. Roosevelt interrupted me.

"I would like to answer that question," she said. "I did know of Harry Eva's need. I knew because something inside told me." She paused, pointed to the audience and singled out women here and there . . .

"And every one of you can hear that still small voice too if you put yourself in tune with God."

The Fourth R

by ALEXANDER CAMPBELL

*How do you teach reverence and religious truths to
lively grade school youngsters? Reverend Alexander
Campbell learned the hard way when he started
Campbell Hall, a church school, outside of Hollywood, California.*

IT STARTED BACK IN 1940 when a motion picture director admitted
to me, after church one Sunday, a vague dissatisfaction with the
lack of roundness of his child's education.

"Why," he asked, "can't you teach the Fourth R—Religion,
along with Reading, 'Riting and 'Rithmetic? Right in school. So
it's an everyday part of learning and not a Sunday special."

Why not, indeed? Schools, however, were not in my line. At
least that's what I thought. But the seed was planted and it grew,
along with my church, St. David's Episcopal Mission in North
Hollywood. By 1941 we were a parish and our Sunday School
had overflowed until we needed a branch in another part of the
Valley.

The demand also was growing for a church school. From past
experience I was convinced that where there is a real need, somehow God provides.

And so, with little more than a group of enthusiastic parents,
and a few eager teachers, we opened the doors of Campbell
Hall School in 1944 in the one-room building which housed our
branch Sunday School. Our first teachers were recruited through
an announcement made at the chancel steps one Sunday morning. Our seventy-four pupils came from homes where parents
believed in that Fourth R.

Keeping our expenses to a minimum, we made our school
available to children of parents from all income groups. Children

whose fathers worked in an aircraft factory mingled casually
with those of film stars. They represented all faiths. Clearly the
demand was not for the teaching of a creed, but for the teaching
of universal truths.

Each morning we would conduct a twenty-minute chapel service to open the day, twenty minutes based on the inspirations and
great teachings from the Old and New Testaments of the Bible.
A blessing preceded each meal—to establish an habitual Thanksgiving for the source of our plenty. All teachers at Campbell Hall
were actively affiliated with one of the Christian denominations
and were expected to teach spiritual and ethical values along with
academics.

The immediate fruits were startling. Some of the children were
not accustomed to the thought of God. Some had only connected
Him with their weekly visits to Sunday School. Their interpretation of spiritual truths was completely literal.

Stevie, 6½-year-old son of screen star Dana Andrews, showed
a marked interest in any and all of the stories from the Book of
Genesis. While watching a weekly televised Bible program that
has won great interest among Valley children, he kept predicting
coming events to his grandmother. At the point, where Cain slew
his brother Abel, Stevie nudged her and said with supreme confidence and authority, "Now God shows up."

There was then, and there is now, a constant challenge in un-
folding truth to these young minds, and my preparation for those
chapel talks has been one of humility and listening prayer. It is
not "my" truth that I must show them . . . but the truth that God
is. Not "my" conclusions that I must offer, but the spark that
must be struck which will set them seeking, in the church of their
own denomination.

Stories, like the adventure of Joseph and his brethren, capture
their imaginations. Everything they could imagine happening
to Hopalong Cassidy happened to Joseph as a boy. And Joseph,

armed with nothing but unwavering loyalty to the spirit and a supreme trust in God, became "prime minister" of Egypt.

One boy had been sent to us laboring under a heavy cross of defiance and belligerence. The "why" of it didn't matter, but lightening the load did. Our staff noticed his habitual use of profanity as well, and nothing they, nor our fine principal, Miss Mildred E. Hawks, could say seemed to show him what reverence was. But the story of Joseph did.

At Campbell Hall he made his first contact with chapel . . . and with Joseph. Something in that story touched him deeply and from it he caught his first vision of God. Here was a way of life he could accept. It robbed him of none of his fire and spirit. It made him neither a weakling nor a sissy. Instead it would translate his talents into channels worthy to become "father unto Pharaoh" . . . and shortly he became a leader in our school.

There were other fruits, too. Interest in church attendance increased, sometimes among the children only, sometimes whole families began going again to their own church. If they had none, the doors of St. David's were open to them.

At Campbell Hall there developed a loyalty and a school spirit that have, on the whole, become passé among so many youngsters. Muffet Beery, daughter of actor Noah Beery, heard about Campbell Hall from playmates. "Muffet just kept organizing until she got here," said her mother when she delivered her daughter to our care.

Nor did the spirit stop with the children. Between parents and teachers, banded together in a council, there was complete cooperation and harmony. Our pupils are in excess of three hundred.

Today education is available to every young American. But academic studies alone have not proved enough to give all of them a proper outlook on life. Those are simply the tools. Somewhere they must learn how to use them. *Somewhere they must learn stewardship along with skills.*

Someone has said: "Christianity has not been tried and found wanting. It has been found difficult and not tried." But in leading these youngsters to the Fourth R as a daily part of living and learning, they are not finding it difficult at Campbell Hall. Like the leaven of old, it is working, through their education, helping to build a stronger youth to serve a stronger America.

Handicaps
Can Be
Your Greatest Assets

Let Not Thy Left Hand Know[*]

by ROBERT CHRISTENBERRY

The transition from civilian-to-army-to-civilian status has always been difficult. Bob Christenberry tells here of the particular help he found. It carried him to success as manager of New York's famous Astor Hotel and guides him today as New York State Boxing Commissioner.

THE DAY a fellow ships home after a war should be thrilling. But I was a frightened lad of 20 when a big transport pulled away from France in 1918. I wasn't facing forward. I hung over the ship's rail looking at the foreign shores. Somewhere there in France was my right arm.

I yearned to go home and crawl in a hole. But I knew I'd hate myself if I did it. Yet I just couldn't lather up any more *effort*. For a peace-loving people, we Americans have seen a lot of warring. It appears not unlikely that we'll see more. My share of war was over. But if ever I was scared stiff in battle, I was twice as scared at the thought of living and what was ahead.

Just as bad, if not worse than lacking a limb, was the realization that I was ignorant. Hauling me smack out of a quiet Southern town in my teens, the Army had whisked me through New York, over the Atlantic Ocean and a slice of Europe. In each mile of it I had felt more and more the intellectual barefoot boy. Languages, speed, different customs and ideas, morals and ethics, responsibilities, wealth, the effects of one person's mistakes on another, of one nation's importance to another—all left me feeling an incompetent, bewildered, untutored fool.

When I arrived home I would be faced with the problem of

[*]*Matthew 6: 3*

185

how to find a job. Could a fellow really wise himself up, really enough to be part of a complicated world?

And supposing such a dream were impossible, how could I keep from being a semi-invalid? Could I live a full man's life?

All around me were men charged with the excitement of going home. Yet I knew most of them were as frightened inside as I was and as full of questions about an uncertain future.

When I went below to turn in early that first night on shipboard, I was jumpy. I dug through my kit until I found my own special sedative, the book my grandfather put into my hands the night before I went into service: his Bible.

As Grandpa had told me to, I had turned to it often, when home and plain living were an ache inside. I pored over it that night, with the ship's nose heading toward the States, and my home town of Milan, Tennessee. And I fell to remembering Grandpa. I could see my Grandfather, the minister of our town, standing straight, as he spoke the words of God. He had always been absurdly partial to me, probably because I was forever in a peck of trouble.

He died while I was overseas. When I opened his Book after that I told myself his hand had smoothed the pages and his eyes had traveled the words. The memory of him steadied me. That first night sailing home I'd have given most anything to be able to talk to him: "Grandpa, how do you lift the load with one hand?"

Back home, I found his answer everywhere. In his room, his chair, his church, his town. The memories he had left were messages of what he had stood for. The conviction grew that he had given me all the answers when he placed his Book in my hands. I took to rereading the Scriptures, sitting in his study. The Holy Words were strong. They were not for those seeking the easy way. Over and over He said: "Fear not."

And very deep those words of His penetrated my heart. What

had I to fear? Paul's words have given courage and confidence to so many and they made me a man again: *"If God be for us, who can be against us?"* *

One day when the sun rose, I stood up ready to live . . . to take the first job that was offered me . . . to get books and study so that I might prepare for better and better jobs. I was no longer afraid. And not being afraid, I was no longer self-conscious. I forgot the empty sleeve and the missing arm. The less I thought of it, the less anyone noticed.

The day came when I got an offer of a job in Florida. Before I left I went up to Grandpa's study again. I remembered how many times I'd burst in on him when I was hurt or in trouble, knowing so well that he loved me enough to help, forgive, advise, and make me *want* to be somebody special. Often he said to me: "You have a Father in heaven who loves you more than I do, Bob boy. Never forget it, and learn to go to Him for anything, no matter how bad you've been."

It seemed like the last needed lesson to recall as I headed off to Florida to face the world of business and the urge to climb upward. From then on I've had no hesitancy to ask my heavenly Father for *anything,* large or small. Or to thank Him. And the more I talk to Him, go to Him with problems, do things to please Him, the more truly I feel a son of God and very much at home in His world.

My prayers, most of which Grandpa had taught me, became as necessary as food. Mingling with others who were seeking to know God better was strengthening; church and Bible classes and spiritual discussions were nourishment, and lifting up my voice in the hymns of praise and love brought joy.

But best of all was *sharing* the faith that did so much for me. Passing it on. Proving it to people. Urging them to prove it to themselves. At first I was like some excited prospector running,

* *Romans 8: 31*

announcing: "Look! Look! Gold. I've *found gold!*" Only to find some folks would smile and say, "Poor guy's had a lot of trouble and he's a little teched." Others say, "Oh, he's tapped a small pocket, perhaps. But the gold's all played out long ago." Or some shrug and say, "Gold's not much good these days; no market, you know. But thanks just the same. Wouldn't be worth hauling." Gold or Faith—oddly enough—are not easy to give or share.

One learns not to speak of it much. I seldom mention it at first to the many handicapped people who seem to seek me out to get a job. They've been told over and over again in their painful days about God. I am about the only kind of human being who can dare to be tough with them.

"I don't care *what's* the matter with you," I shrug, and wag my empty sleeve at them for emphasis. "You have a brain. Nothing wrong with your mind, is there? Those are the only people my heart aches for. As for *you,* how *good* are you? What can you do? What have you got to contribute to the world? If you're competent, that's all that matters. And I'll give you a job or help you get one."

When delivered with a smile, there isn't one of them who doesn't sit up higher and smile back.

But there are times when it's called for to speak of faith.

I stopped in at my favorite haberdashery recently for a sweater I needed. The shop owner, who had been ailing, was quite plainly on the verge of collapse.

"Sam," I said. "What's wrong?"

"I'm a sick man, Mr. Christenberry." Then, unable to speak further, he lowered his face.

"Sam," I told him, "I'm going to send you to the Greatest Physician in the world, and right this minute. Your boy can do up my sweater."

The man lifted his eyes to mine.

"Down in the basement," I said quietly, "is your stock room.

You go down there and talk to your God. Tell Him all your troubles and fears. Ask Him to help. After all, if He created you, He can take care of you. You stay down there in quiet, and listen to Him."

Two weeks later, a big box was on my desk. The card inside read: "A new hat for you, from a friend you made a new man of."

I stopped in his shop later to thank him. He *was* a new man. But I expected him to be. The help never fails for those who go to God with an earnest and seeking heart, "as a little child."

Am I not a walking proof?

Anyone Can Start His Own Business

by C. RODNEY DEMAREST

> *He prayed for sight, but the operation left Rodney Demarest blind. "Prayer doesn't work," he said grimly to himself afterwards. But this young man was to learn that prayers are answered in unexpected ways.*

"IF WE OPERATE IMMEDIATELY," a prominent eye specialist told me in 1940, "you have one chance out of a thousand to retain your vision."

His words left me, at eighteen, sick, very frightened and terribly alone. I had heard about great dramatic answers to prayer. Could it happen to me?

In a few days the operation was performed. A week later the bandages were removed. My long-shot chance hadn't come through. All was darkness.

"Prayer doesn't work," I told myself grimly. I was through with it, and sharply questioned the existence of a God who could let such a disaster happen.

From then on I resolved that whatever I accomplished would be done through my own personal efforts. This business of turning to a Supreme Being for strength and guidance might satisfy the holiness boys, but it wasn't for down-to-earth situations and people, I figured. My parents were wonderful in their understanding and encouragement during this period, but I was determined to act entirely on my own.

An attempt at selling life insurance was soon abandoned. Other ventures failed. Feeling as I did that the world owed me a lot, I became more and more bitter.

Then pneumonia caught up with me, and next a complete nervous breakdown. Lying there helpless on a hospital bed in my world of darkness, I admitted to complete defeat. Life often has to knock people flat on their faces before they get any vision. In this despair once again I turned to God and asked for strength and peace of mind. If He couldn't help me now, nothing could.

In the months of slow convalescence that followed, I saw dimly how prayer was answered. For me, it was by doing the next thing that came along, no matter how small or unimportant. I can see now how each little action was part of a Master Plan.

In 1942, I obtained employment in a defense plant as an inspector of radio equipment. It was a job that seemed to lead nowhere, nor did it last long.

During 1944 and 1945 I attended Stamford Business College where I mastered typing, learned dictaphone transcription work and Braille shorthand at the rate of 120 words a minute. My course also included general business subjects with emphasis on letter writing and promotional work.

But my efforts to find employment where I could utilize this newly acquired skill and knowledge were unsuccessful. All my recent training seemed for nothing, and I was no better off than before my siege of pneumonia and a nervous breakdown.

The difference was that this time instead of plowing on ahead bitterly, I stopped and took stock. Perhaps it just wasn't in the cards for me to get a job. What could I do then—start my own business? Why not!

I hadn't any money, but my parents were willing to loan me $400. This was enough to rent a one-room office in the center of Stamford, to purchase several desks, rent a typewriter and have a telephone installed. Meanwhile, I had figured out four different categories my new business could cover.

First: I intended, personally, to act as a public stenographer—taking dictation in Braille shorthand from salesmen and small business men who did not require or could not afford a secretary of their own.

Second: I would rent desk space on a monthly basis to anyone who required a central business location, but who could not afford or did not need a private office of his own.

Third: I could start a daytime telephone answering service.

My fourth and final service was to offer mimeographing, multigraphing, Robotyping, and printing which I arranged to broker at a 15% commission. At the time, no other Stamford firm offered this variety of services.

Significant to me was the fact that I was able to put into play all the knowledge and abilities developed out of my past jobs. Prayer had led me to certain types of work that seemed a waste of time then—now it all fitted into place.

I typed out and mailed my own promotional letters, advertised and solicited by telephone. At first, the response was so poor that it did not even meet my basic operating expenses. My funds at the end of three months consisted of ten dollars. It was necessary to borrow an additional hundred dollars to keep going.

It is at this point where most small businesses go under. Many are given up too soon when an extra effort might make the difference. I was determined this wouldn't be my cause for failure—if I was to fail.

Again the faith and confidence born of prayer sustained me. In July, 1946, three desks were rented and over a dozen telephone answering subscribers signed up. Also, an increasing number of business men came in to dictate letters and have other material composed for them.

By January, 1947, I was meeting all expenses, drawing over $60 a week for myself, and had paid my debts. At this time, my brother, Russell, became interested in my enterprise and offered to join me as a partner. He invested funds equal to my own holdings.

Within three months, we negotiated to buy out the only letter shop firm in Stamford, merging it with our own growing business. Then one morning the telephone rang and the voice at the other end inquired, "Are you set up to produce and mail 110,000 letters each month?"

Without hesitation, I assured him that we were. An appointment was made to discuss details, the contract was granted to us and we have been doing this work steadily ever since.

This new undertaking, of course, called for great expansion. My father and mother offered to put more money into the business and join with us. We then incorporated as the Demarest Associated Services, moving into larger quarters. Since then, we have added an entire printing plant to our organization.

We now occupy the entire first floor and basement of an office building and, as of April, 1953, have twenty full-time and six part-time employees. Our answering service includes 110 subscribers; we have a 120-line switchboard to handle the calls. Last year we did $100,000 worth of business, marking the sixth straight year of steady growth.

Thus my life is full and complete in all respects. Blindness has not impaired either my social or business activities. I have a wonderful wife, a young son, and recently we moved into our own home.

I have learned that nothing is impossible if God's help is sought through prayer. There is no catastrophe imaginable which could serve to alter or disturb my unshakeable conviction of the ultimate good and righteousness of God's loving ways and His infinite scheme of things.

Certainly blindness is a small price to pay for such knowledge.

By Wheelchair to the Stars

by HARRY DOEHLA

Told at the age of 17 that he would never walk again, Harry Doehla let bitterness and self-pity consume himself for two years. What was the dynamic principle that changed this defeated lad into an unbeatable personality and resulted in the founding of the Harry Doehla Greeting Card Company?

THEY SAY THAT at some point of his life, every man knows despair. I knew it at the age of 17.

Just after high school graduation I had been stricken with what was diagnosed as rheumatic fever. The day came when I knew I'd never walk again. I was crippled. *Useless.*

That last word jabbed worse than all my pains. It began to do to my heart and mind what the disease had done to my legs and arms.

I had earned ever since I'd been able to run about. My parents were textile workers. When they were married my father made $8 per week. Yet together they worked and saved and managed so that we had a spotless little home and a wholesome family life. They had been so proud of their boy; ambitious, energetic, eagerly planning to earn his way through college and become a chemist.

Those dreams were no longer mentioned. Every penny my folks could manage went to my endless care and needs.

At last another tough fact had to be faced: my mother must go back to work. I must learn to take care of myself alone all day.

Alone all day. Seventeen. Eighteen. Seated in the kitchen in a wheelchair made by my father, my noon meal left within reach, bitterness grew in me like a rank weed with self-pity the far spreading roots. The minister came to call regularly—he soon learned not to probe my bitterness, but he left me things to read.

And I read once that perhaps the most human moment of Jesus Christ's life was when He cried out: "My God, My God why hast Thou forsaken me?" I know it's an echo of Old Testament fulfillment—but it's still a human link between the Man Jesus and everyone of us who feels like crying out the same desolate question.

What had I ever done to deserve this . . . and on and on and on . . .

And I read "Whom He loveth He chastiseth," and tried to figure sense out of that. The minister and I argued about it.

"Sure it's hard to understand," he told me. "But if you don't love a person or even an animal you don't bother to train it, do you? All parents chastise the children they truly love. They wouldn't take the trouble with some cantankerous kid they aren't responsible for. And—you see—the Lord is our Heavenly Father. Whom He loveth He chastiseth to make us take a big step forward—to teach us the next lesson to be learned."

"Tough to swallow," I shrugged.

"Yes. But I have a feeling that the bigger the soul, the bigger the test. Doesn't that make sense?"

Days later it began to make sense.

And so, above all others things, as I dipped again and again into the Bible, a certain thought brought me up sharp: *"Of myself I am nothing; with God all things are possible."**

I decided not only to believe it but work it.

And I do. More and more through the years. The start, however, as is often the case in spiritual growth, was slow and arduous.

But at that time I decided with God's help I could at least do *something*. The worst thing in my long list of Job-like miseries was the sound of my mother weeping in the middle of the night. She did not guess how little my own sleep was, nor would I let her know. Often in the daytime she voiced her continual fear—

---

*See John 5: 30 and 15: 5; Matthew 19: 26; Mark 10: 27.

what would become of me if she and father became seriously ill or died?

Well, with God's help, I could do something to make money— to ease her fears—perhaps even enough to keep her home.

I tried typing. I tried to write short stories. I bought a multigraph machine on time but earned little more than the payments. None of these things was successful. It looked at times as if everything I tried was a failure.

Some visiting friends, whose nephew was a polio victim, told us of how he painted black and white Christmas cards and sold them. They urged me to try, and told me where to get the stuff and how to go about selling them.

Well, I was no artist. It took me six months before I did one card good enough to sell for a nickel. I painted 8 hours a day and I have a very crooked and gnarled right hand to show for it. My circulation was so poor and the cramped position of painstaking work with a fine brush left my hand knotted in spite of exercising the fingers half the night to ease the arthritic pains.

One day in moving across the kitchen floor, I somehow fell off my chair and toppled to the floor. I couldn't rise. I struggled and sweated and wept with impotence. And on the kitchen floor I battled again the wave of black bitterness that I'd only recently conquered. Hours passed. If I ever prayed in my life, I prayed then . . .

Eventually, the postman came on his late morning round. Our mailbox was outside the kitchen and when I heard him come I yelled for him. He came in and picked me up. And we chatted. I just *wouldn't* let him see how humiliated I felt. So I got to joking to hide my feelings.

"Gosh, Harry," he said, "you've got what it takes. Whenever I get to feel like whining and grousing, I think of you. Man, you've got courage. And mark my words, nothing can stop you."

He left before I could answer. It was a left-handed compliment.

If anyone thought he had troubles, he could remember poor hapless Harry, huh? No—that was bitterness. I mustn't think bitterly. I blessed him for the word of recognition and praise when I really needed it most.

It helped, at that, when I let it—as I went back to the grind. Trying to paint, and reading every self-help and inspirational and religious and philosophical book I could get hold of. My inner growth was slow—groping—but I kept at it because I *had* to have a deep faith.

I earned, that year, $800 with my hand painted cards.

If I could double that!

But my hand wouldn't last forever. Already my right hand was getting unusable.

So I decided on mail order selling. I studied books on it and planned an almost reckless plunge. We took a $2800 mortgage on our little home and borrowed $1600 from a friend who believed in me. That was a total of $4400.

Prayer? We *all* prayed! The whole house vibrated with the feeling—*with God all things are possible* . . .

I got cards on credit and made it a terrifying challenge to myself by ordering *12 thousand* box assortments to retail for $1! So, I'd *have* to get rid of them or we'd all be broke. Our money was used for sales literature (copy for which I sweated out without help), shipping supplies and postage.

I contacted churches mostly—after getting directories of the various denominations. I did all this by mail, still working in the kitchen.

I sold not 12 thousand, but 19 thousand $1 greeting card assortments, that year. From then on I built up my mail order business.

And I'll never forget the first time I realized that I had done a million dollars worth of business. By then the money wasn't the vital part of life. I'd long since been able to relieve my mother of any hard work, and to surround my parents with every comfort.

What mattered was the excitement of living and doing. My life has been like a fairy story. The oddest "coincidences" are *not* coincidences but God's wondrous workings. There has been, through the years, a strange supplying of whatever I needed or wanted. For example, my hunger to make music became almost an obsession, but my right hand couldn't function. One weekend a friend called me up like an excited boy to come over and see an organ he had just bought. And I almost wept with joy at the Hammond Electric organ on which the right hand plays the melody with *one finger,* the left hand on the lower keyboard fills in, and the feet supply the bass.

I still have a full rich life ahead. Whatever is in it, I know I can accept. Whatever God sends me I can take without bitterness or loss of faith. I know *of myself I am nothing—with God I can do all things.*

I can even thank Him for the privilege of poverty and pain that forced me to find Him and myself.

No Time for Yesterday

by MARGARET SCOTT

Evelyn Haynes retreated to Huckleberry Mountain in North Carolina where she expected to die. What happened, as told here by Author Margaret Scott, changed not only Evelyn, but the whole community.

A CHECK FOR $300 when you are ill and broke is usually mighty welcome, but to my friend, Evelyn Haynes, it meant the knell of doom. An insurance company, acting on a doctor's report, was paying off on *total disability*.

Following spinal surgery, Evelyn had been unable to walk, her vision was double, her speech crossed. At 30, this young Rollins College graduate felt she could only wait for death. Evelyn then conveyed to her mother, Mrs. Mary Belle Haynes, her desire to return to Huckleberry Mountain in North Carolina, where as a child she had spent so many happy summers.

Mrs. Haynes, a teacher at Rollins College, owned a stretch of woodland and meadow on the side of Huckleberry Mountain in the Blue Ridge. She had conducted a girls' summer camp there, later sold the site. Now the property, run-down and tax-ridden, was back in the family on a foreclosure.

There was scarcely a cabin with a whole roof, no plumbing, no transportation. The property was more than a mile up the mountain from the crossroads at Uno, eight miles from Hendersonville. But there were the tall pines, the laurels, the cool spring and lovely streams; the little mosses and fantastic toadstools that might have been designed by Disney—or God. For neighbors, half a mile or so either way, they had the lean, blond mountaineers who speak to everybody and talk to nobody.

There in peace and quiet, Evelyn Haynes let her spirit take over and literally waited on the Lord. She did whatever small thing she was able, though the lifting of a finger was a large proj-ect in itself. But in her active mind, she wrote and planned and prayed.

Then slowly, miraculously, her vision steadied, her speech cleared, her hand moved. One day, she walked again. With each returning faculty, she increased her effort, deepened her prayer, widened her plan. One part of the plan, at last, became fixed. Whatever her new found future might hold, she decided, it must be here on Huckleberry Mountain where her faith and life had been renewed.

She had less than no money, since she and her mother were deeply in debt. But she had faith, friends and a growing two-fold idea. She would rebuild the camp at Huckleberry as a summer retreat for creative artists, writers, painters, sculptors—a place where people could come for a fresh start, or renewal of courage. She also wanted to help her proud, penniless mountain neigh-bors.

As the summer camp idea took hold, the mountain people helped. They cleared brush, planted fields, restored roofs and re-paired floors, taking for their labor, notes payable after the season began.

For a staff, Evelyn simply invited people. Dr. Edwin Osgood Grover, writer and vice-president emeritus of Rollins College and Vivian Larimore Rader, writer, poet and teacher, were among those accepted. When the camp opened, there was a distin-guished staff but not a single paying guest. Notes for repairs were due at the end of that first week.

Then on Sunday some student artists, who had read of the proj-ect on a college bulletin board, arrived and registered as the first guests. Their money was sufficient to meet the first repair bills.

Today Huckleberry has a busy summer season, with accommo-dations for 50 guests and a staff drawn from all over the country. There is great freedom, yet great orderliness in the colony; the feeling of accomplishment through faith is in the very air. As one woman artist put it, "It's Evelyn Haynes. Her conviction of ultimate good in all things does something to you."

But the summer camp is only one aspect of Evelyn Haynes' plan. Her year-round project was to help her neighbors. The big art studio near the road is really theirs. Here the mountain children come, twice each week, to study modeling and ceramics, to work with the beautiful red clay. The finer arts of spinning and weaving have been taught by a succession of European displaced persons sponsored by Evelyn Haynes and Huckleberry.

Most of all, the children are learning economics from Mis' Evelyn. Everything with these mountain folk is home grown, home made. The children in flour sack dresses and patched jeans went barefooted to the one-room country schoolhouse. But recently a big bus came to take them to the Combined School and they were becoming ashamed of their clothes, their absence of pocket money.

So, at Huckleberry, Evelyn set up a special economy. Each child is paid for attending classes regularly; a dollar a week for top achievement. Ten percent goes to their church, ten percent in a special investment fund. When the child has five dollars, he can invest it in a pig, or chickens, to make more money.

A store was set up with good, second-hand clothing which Evelyn requests through letters from all over the country. These items are sold cheaply. Thus, no child is taking charity and each youngster can *select* a wardrobe. A good sweater for ten cents, shoes for twenty. The money goes back into the school fund. Nobody gets rich but nobody begs.

How earnestly the children take their budget was demonstrated when Evelyn found a nine-year-old girl earnestly regarding a small child's sweater. Finally she stated her problem. It had taken 80 cents to purchase her own needed clothes. This sweater would fit her little brother. It cost ten cents, just what she had left for the church.

"Mis' Evelyn, do you suppose the Lord would mind if I spent His dime this week? Willard's awful cold."

Evelyn looked at the gaunt, solemn eyes which at 9 years had already known more sacrifice than many at 70.

"I'm sure He'd trust you for a week," she said.

At Huckleberry, too, the first public library in Henderson County was started. Now, in addition to the library rooms at the camp, books are sent out in boxes of 50 and placed in crossroad grocery stores. Every six weeks, the boxes are switched so the people up at Locust Valley can read the books previously enjoyed by the folks down at Chimney Rock. The sheriff's department has volunteered to take over part of this work.

Now, fully recovered and driving her own car, Miss Evelyn negotiates the mountain roads in a big, lumbering, surplus army vehicle. Sometimes she sounds a bit breathless as she transports children, books, and visitors many miles in a day. Most of the visiting artists know nothing of her past history. She is too much interested in the present, too hopeful of the future, to mention it.

The Man Who Couldn't Talk

by CONSTANCE DE HAVEN

> *"I haven't spoken for six years," the patient wrote on
> a slip of paper. Came the answer, "If you can breathe,
> you can talk." An unusual story by Author-Musician
> Constance DeHaven of how faith and science can
> make an unbeatable combination.*

HIS HOSPITAL CHART READ, "John K.—unemployed seaman—age
54—Laryngectomy. Patient has not spoken for six years."

As I waited in the corridor for the nurse to bring him out, I
wondered what type of man he would be ... a smallish timid
man, probably furtive and defeated.

To have lived in unbroken silence for six years would surely
leave its mark on a man. I knew nothing about him except a brief
outline from a Social Service worker. Six years before he had been
rushed to Bellevue Hospital, for an emergency laryngectomy,
which is an operation for the removal of his larynx. Overnight he
became a mute and a public charge. He had no family.

They sent him to Welfare Island where he had spent the past
six years wandering around hospital grounds in a grey flannel
bathrobe.

Today they were sending him to a hospital for speech disorders
for his first lesson in articulation without a larynx. They asked
me to accompany him there and back.

The door of Hospital Room 14 swung open and out stepped
John K. It was hard for me to conceal my astonishment. John K.
was a powerful man, with the vigorous step of alert expectancy.
His eyes glowed with excitement. I had not seen such enthusiasm
since I took my nine-year-old nephew to his first baseball game.

Small wonder—for this strong bulk of a man had not walked a
city street since they took him off his ship, gasping for air, six
years before.

He shook my hand until I thought it would break off at the wrist. He reached in his overcoat, pulled out a pad and pencil and, with his shaking hand, wrote in large letters on the memo pad four of the most heartening words in his life: "*When do we start?*"

"We're off," I said.

Down the elevator—into the November sunshine. We darted through traffic across First Avenue. A bus pulled up.

"How much?" he wrote on the pad. "A dime," I said. The act of dropping the coin in the box made his face light up with soundless laughter. Frantic, hurried people were pushing us. John K. seemed not to notice them as he swayed, balancing himself as if he were on the deck of a boat.

We got off at 18th Street. A hesitancy came over him as we neared our destination—a protective shyness against the possibility of a major disappointment. A vague uneasiness assailed me. I knew his case history had recorded his long resistance to this experiment. Seized with a terror that I would not find the right words to keep him moving on, I breathed a quick prayer.

"Listen," I fairly yelled at him, "you don't quit a ship in a storm when it's so close to port." For a moment he grappled with an impulse to flee. Then abruptly, he lunged into a terrific stride.

Breathlessly, I ran alongside of him until we reached Irving Place. As we stopped a black cocker spaniel stood at the curb. The dog was carrying a large paper package in his mouth, his body tense with the dignity of accomplishment. His eyes beseeched our approval.

John K. whipped out his pad. "He's got a job—he feels important," he wrote.

"You bet," I answered. "We've got the green light—hurry," I said hoarsely, for I was close to tears.

We walked in the busy hall of the hospital. John K. nervously wrote out the answers to certain questions at the reception desk.

I pointed to a sign on the wall. John K. smiled as he read the slogan, "Slow and easy does it." He squared his shoulders and started for the elevator. When we reached the fourth floor, he stepped out with a strange urgency. There, panic seized him again. He gazed as if hypnotized down the length of the tiled corridor. It was as if he could never escape the narrowing walls.

"So you're John K.," a huskily pleasant voice, with a peculiarly persuasive quality, called after him. John stopped. A smiling young man was swinging toward him, with outstretched hand.

John K. gripped his hand with fraternal eagerness. He knew instinctively that here was another man without a "sound box" who had learned to talk!

"My name's White," the man continued with that odd rounded sound as if he were talking through a small megaphone.

Furtively John K. pulled out his pad. "I haven't spoken for six years," he wrote.

"That's a long time," said White, "but you can breathe—can't you? And if you can breathe, you can talk. I wouldn't tell you so if it were not so. Come on, what are we waiting for?" he finished. He linked his arm in John's and strode towards the classroom.

I sat on the visitors' bench for two hours waiting for the first lesson to finish, wondering if the promise of speech would be fulfilled. White's words rang in my ears, "I would not tell you so if it were not so." I remembered similar words from the Master Himself. The positive quality of conviction that restored a man.

Idly, I picked up a little booklet. On the cover I read, "I shall pass through this world but once. Any good thing, therefore, that I can do, or any kindness I can show to any human being, let me do it now. For I shall not pass this way again."

Quite suddenly it came to me that that was the secret of White's exuberance. I know a little about White. He was a man whose faith had helped over a thousand muted voices. Eleven years ago, after losing his own power of speech, White felt sorry for himself and was a burden to all who knew him. Through the insistence of his wife he went to a doctor who was practicing a new type of rehabilitation which consisted of using the natural body tissues to produce sound.

Mrs. White's faith in him and her determination not to heed her husband unless he used his new-found voice, brought results. Today, except for the huskiness, it is impossible to tell that anything is different about this man's larynx.

This experience developed an inner core of belief in White which had much to do with his decision to help other mutes in the capacity of a remedial speech teacher. White found that when reasoning, sympathy, and getting tough failed in his rehabilitation work, he could often get results by appealing to a man's faith. "God has provided man with a substitute for a 'voice box,'" he would say. "But God won't help you unless you help yourself."

As John came out of the classroom, I saw him pull his diaphragm up, then expel his breath as if he were emptying his lungs. His mouth was rounded in a sort of oh, and as he exhaled, he made a strange grunting sound. He was shaking with excitement. It was the first sound he had made in six years!

From that moment on, his progress amazed all of us. At the end of a week he was counting up to 10. "Slow—but *not* easy," he wrote on his pad. On the tenth day I called for him as usual.

Out on the street he seemed withdrawn from reality. Suddenly, he looked at me searchingly, as if he hoped I would understand. Then, with a superhuman effort he sucked in his breath, letting it out in short gasps—he articulated four words:

"I'm on my own."

I watched him dart across First Avenue towards the bus stop— reach in his pocket for a dime, wave wildly at me with his hat—as if he were taking off on the most thrilling adventure of his life.

"So long, John," I whispered. "Slow and easy's done it!"

How to Strengthen
Your Personal Faith

The Echo

by LOUIS B. MAYER

> *There is always one persistent echo throughout your
> entire life. Louis Mayer will never forget the day his
> mother took him into the mountain valley—and
> what she made him shout at the echoing walls.*

EVERY MAN in the world is given moments of light and words of
truth. They do not always come at expected times. But once seen,
once heard, they return again and again. In moments of danger,
of temptation, of pain or sorrow or fear, in times of triumph and
high endeavor these tokens move as a pillar of cloud by day and
of fire by night.

They do not forsake us.

My mother was a gentle woman of simple faith and love of
God. It never entered her heart to doubt that prayer was part
of everyday life and that God was a very present help in trouble.

One day when I was a small boy I got into a fight at school, as
boys will. My recollection is that the result was a draw, but I may
be giving myself a little the best of it. It is most often the loser
who is bitter and filled with resentment and vengeance, and I remember distinctly that I was sore in mind as well as in body.
When I got home I went about muttering threats of what I was
going to do to my opponent when next we met, and it must have
been that my vocabulary had been partially, at least, acquired
from the older boys at school who thought profanity a sign of
manhood.

My mother didn't seem to be paying any particular attention
and went on about her work in her usual serene manner. I was
surprised, however, the next day when we were out in the country on a family picnic and she called me aside. "Louis, come here
a moment. I want to show you something," she said.

Now that part of the country near New Brunswick, Canada,

was in a beautiful valley, with tall, rugged mountains towering on all sides, perfect for echoes. My mother took me over to a little clearing that faced the mountain wall.

"Now, Louis, say what I heard you say yesterday."

I began to feel embarrassed.

"But I don't remember saying anything wrong," I protested weakly.

My mother was never one to dodge an issue.

"I do," she replied. "You said 'Damn you!'"

I had to nod. I could keep nothing from my mother and she knew it.

"Yes, I remember now."

She touched my arm gently.

"Say it now," she commanded.

I repeated it, as quietly as I could.

The words rolled back with startling volume in the echo.

My mother smiled patiently.

"Louder, son. Say it louder. Whatever you say, you must be willing to say as loud as you can, to shout it for all to hear."

I didn't want to do this very much. But it did not occur to me to disobey my mother. Gentle as she was, she carried the authority vested in her by God where her children were concerned. So I faced the mountains and shouted at the top of my lungs, "Damn you!"

Right back it came, like thunder. Like a voice from heaven it denounced me.

"Now," said my mother, "try it another way. Say 'Bless you!' instead."

I took a long breath and yelled, "Bless you!"

Back came the benediction. "Bless you," strong, clear, welcome.

"Which do you prefer, my son?" my mother said. "It's entirely up to you. That is the way life is. It always returns to us what we say to it. If you shout at it and at your fellow man, 'damn you,' life and your fellow man will shout it right back at you. If you say to life, to humanity, 'bless you,' then your life will be an echo of those words, 'bless *you.*'

"Choose ye whom ye shall serve, Louis. You have that choice. As long as you live you will have your choice. Every day, almost every hour, in some way a choice will be presented to you. It says in the Bible, that before you this day is the choice, blessing or cursing. I tell you now, my son, that life will echo back to you what you say to it as surely as you just heard this echo here, and the choice is yours what you shall say for it to echo."

At that moment, though of course I was impressed by the amazing illustration, (and sometimes later sneaked out to that spot to see if I could change the law and get the echo to come out wrong, though it never did), I don't suppose I realized that my mother had given me a light, a moment of true inspiration. Like every human being, I have sneaked up on life at times and tried to see if I couldn't break the law of the echo, but I have never succeeded, not once.

As the years went by, that law was confirmed in my experience. The wonderful hope of the lesson became more and more present in my thoughts. The words came back so often, a guide, a reminder. This situation, this moment, this experience, this decision, this person, will echo back to you what you say to it. Back to you will come your own words, and beyond that your own thoughts. What you do now to this man will come back to damn *you,* or bless *you.* For many years it has refused to leave me and though I have not always been obedient, it has checked and led me often.

Just a few years ago I had a bad accident when some stablemen put the wrong bridle on the horse I was to ride. The fall was almost the end of me. For many weeks the doctors had little hope and my fate was in the balance.

As I lay on my hospital bed in pain and misery I seemed to hear my mother's voice again. *"You will have your choice as long as you live."* And I began to meditate and to ponder and to wonder what I should give the law of the echo to give back to me. I said to myself, "I am not afraid to die, but I want to live." That last word echoed back to me. Live *Live*. It was strong and clear. So I began to give out that word all the time. Live. It multiplied into life, into strength, into power.

The doctors called it the will to live, making a fight of it. They said I was a "good patient" and that I never gave up and that it made all the difference in the result. But I knew that I was getting back the exact echo of what I had put in, and that was all I could get. If I put in hatred, meanness, revenge, I would get them back. If I tried to speak love, kindness, forgiveness, they would be returned to me. If I said Death, it would come back; if I said Life, it would echo in my experience.

God bless you.

God bless you.

A simple rule, but to me it has been a pillar of cloud by day and of fire by night.

Code of a Sea Raider

by FELIX VON LUCKNER

> *Von Luckner is the swashbuckling German sea com-*
> *mander of World War I whose exploits are legend-*
> *ary, and who greatly aided the Americans during*
> *World War II. Here is perhaps his most amazing ex-*
> *perience.*

IT TOOK BEATINGS, broken bones and nearly seven years as a jack-tar before the mast to knock some sense into my thick head. I went through hurricanes, shipwreck and plague during which time the fo'c'sle became as familiar to me as charts to an admiral.

This first quest of mine for adventure taught me my biggest lesson.

I wasn't really a bad kid. Big for my age, awkward and thirsting for adventure, yes. My idea of education was to get out on a windjammer and taste the salt spray on my lips.

My school instructors voiced a unanimous prediction: "it's no use; the boy doesn't learn. There's a devil in him."

If I had a devil in me, I thought to myself, it must be a sea devil, by Joe.

One day, I read a book that made my blood race. It was the story of Buffalo Bill, American hero and adventurer.

"What a man!" I exclaimed. "Indians, buffalo, outdoor men ... I must get to America and join Buffalo Bill."

My mother who was kindly and wise tried to calm me. "You'd be no good to Buffalo Bill until you can discipline yourself. It's foolish to run off blindly. God has a way of working these things out if we but listen to Him."

But I was foolish. While only 13, I ran away from our home in Dresden, Germany, determined to find Buffalo Bill.

In Hamburg, an old sea captain named Peter Breumer found

me wandering along the waterfront and took me under his wing. When he saw he couldn't discourage me from going to sea, he helped me find passage on the Russian ship Niobe as a cabin boy. One of his parting gifts was an old family Bible.

"Read it often, boy, and think of old Peter," he said. "You'll find you need it."

On the Niobe I found that my duties were to clean the pigsty daily. The captain was a brute. He kicked me often because I smelled like a pig. Everyone called me "Pig."

For food I had to go around and eat what the sailors left on their plates. They said that was the way pigs were fed.

During a storm I climbed aloft to help furl the canvas. A sudden gust of wind blew the sail out like a balloon—and me into the sea. The quartermaster, entirely on his own, lowered the boat that rescued me. From the captain came another beating.

So this was the life at sea! "You put yourself into this fix, by Joe," I said to myself. "You're nearly 14 now, Felix, so you've got to take the punishment like a man." At 14, too, I was the size of a grown man.

Ironically, the discipline that my mother and school couldn't teach me, a brutal captain beat into me.

Instead of landing in America, the Niobe docked in Australia. My quest for Buffalo Bill was off to a slow start. I jumped ship, then wandered from job to job—assistant lighthouse keeper, a member of a traveling band of Hindu magicians and finally to the Salvation Army. The kindness of these devout people touched me, and I was an enthusiastic member for a number of months before again resuming my search for Buffalo Bill.

During my next voyage I experienced some of that comradeship of the sea for which a sailor will endure many a hardship. Perhaps it was the sight of old Peter's Bible, which I had kept with me and read faithfully, that brought forth a remarkable experience from an old salt named Jack Blomquist.

Near the end of the century, off the coast of Brazil, Jack and his entire crew had been stricken with yellow fever. Weak and gaunt, he lay dying in the fo'c'sle.

Suddenly he forced himself upright. "I'm just quitting on life," he said to a bunk-mate. "None of us will live unless we force ourselves to." But his friend was quite still and turning black.

Jack's feverish eye fell on a book nearby. Anything to hold onto, he thought, reaching for it. It was his family Bible, canvas-bound and over 80 years old.

At first, the verses he read were blurred. Then, as the words penetrated his wasted body, hope and strength began to replace despair.

"The Lord is my rock and my fortress ... and my strength," he read.

There seemed a vitality to the very touch of this Bible!

Jack was the only one of his ship to come out alive, and he did it through sheer faith and will power.

"By Joe," I said to myself after hearing this tale, "that's something." I thought with a pang, of old Peter and my family. From then on the Bible had new value to me. It seemed almost as if God had His finger on me, seeing to it that His Word was in my hands from the start.

But my quest for Buffalo Bill still possessed me. After years of false starts, I finally arrived in San Francisco in 1895. Buffalo Bill, they told me, was 1800 miles away in Denver. I had no money, but owned a stout pair of legs, so I started to walk the railroad ties to Denver.

Often there were stops at farms for temporary jobs to earn enough for food and shoes. Several times short hops on coal cars were provided, but mostly it was slow plodding—a short right step and a long left, from tie to tie, mile on mile.

Finally—Denver. Excited and nervous, I asked directions to Buffalo Bill's place. A woman answered my knock.

"Is Buffalo Bill here?" I stammered.

"No, he isn't."

"I'll wait."

She gave me a long, doubtful look. "You've got a long wait, lad. He's touring the world."

I couldn't believe my ears. Had I sailed 12,000 miles and walked nearly 1800 more for nothing? What fantastic bad luck was this?

When, as a prodigal son, I returned home after seven years, the amazing truth came out. At the very moment I was looking for Buffalo Bill in Denver, he was visiting Germany and a guest of my father in our own home. I never did see Buffalo Bill.

A man's dream, or an answer to his most heartfelt prayer, so I found, is seldom beyond the horizon. It is often at his hand, if he but looks for it.

Wish You Were Here

by IRENE DUNNE

> *"How can I tell others what religion brings to my life?" once asked Irene Dunne. This great actress then found a way to do so, stressing what, as a mother, she would never do without.*

AT AN EVENING PARTY in my home several years ago, a fascinated group gathered around Clare Booth Luce (now Ambassador to Italy), who held her audience, not by brilliant discourse on politics or the theatre, but by her eloquent statements on her personal religious convictions.

An elderly gentleman smoked his cigar and listened quietly. When the party broke up, he turned to me and, shaking his head admiringly, he said, "You see, she's just too smart not to be on the safe side!"

I was amused, but later on, as I went about emptying ashtrays and putting out lights, I thought again about my guest's remark. What he doubtless meant to say was, "She's too smart not to be on God's side." How hard it is for most of us to talk about our religious feelings, I mused. But to tell others about them, to share your treasure, is so important, for surely the best way to keep your religion is to give it away freely.

Now I am no theologian, no scholar, not even a writer. I ask myself, "How can I find a simple, uncomplicated, sincere way of telling others about the richness, satisfaction, and joy that my religion brings to my life, so that they, too, may desire to open the door and let God in?"

Then it occurred to me it was something like seeing your friends for the first time since your return from a wonderful trip —let's call this a heavenly trip. You had such a glorious time, you've already sent post cards, saying, *"Wish you were here."* If you have the gift of words, your description of the place will make them want to go.

Even if you have not the gift, they will note that your trip has refreshed and restored you; your step is buoyant, your heart is light. The place where you have been, and still reside in secret, has done so much for you that all who come in contact with you will yearn to go there too. They want their cup filled to overflowing as is yours.

And the wonderful part of this heavenly trip is that everyone can go. Of course, the trip will entail sacrifices. Pleasures nearer home may have to be foregone; perhaps what may seem like valuable time will be taken away from the office or from social engagements. And the journey may take a long time. It all depends upon the person and the way he chooses to go about it.

For my own part, I can recount for you no dramatic stories en route. I did not, like Saul of Tarsus, suddenly awaken to find myself already in the Heavenly Place. Nor did tragedy or affliction force me to be towed in, or sirened in by ambulance, as has happened to so many. Neither did I have to search long and hard for the right road as did Thomas Merton who tells about it in "The Seven Storey Mountain."

No, I was placed on the road at an early age, and it was straight and narrow and pleasant, though I suppose I made a few detours here and there and from time to time I took more rest than was necessary.

I was born into the Catholic faith at Louisville, Kentucky, and there was schooled by the Sisters of Loretta. Early in my youth I began to study voice and piano. I can remember attending early Mass, then going to a nearby Baptist Church to sing in the choir. I took my religion entirely for granted.

On the opening night of my earliest musical show years ago, I was observed from out front, making the Sign of the Cross before my entrance. I had no recollection of this whatsoever. That's how automatic, yet so much a part of me, my religion was. The process by which I began to be happily aware of its enormous benefits to myself and others and to consciously try to practice it in my daily living, has come about very slowly, but I hope, just as surely.

Folks often ask me wonderingly how I have managed to keep my balance in the tinsel world in which I have lived. It is no wonder that those who are suddenly smothered in unaccustomed luxury and adulation are sometimes inclined to lose their sense of values and are tempted to play God themselves. Bishop Fulton Sheen says: "Twentieth Century man who thinks he is a God has to be psychoanalyzed to find out why he feels like the devil."

In my own case I had the good fortune to be kept on the beam by the prayers of my saint-like mother. My father, a river steamboat man who became a United States Supervisor of Steamships, died when I was very young. Mother and I moved to Madison, Indiana, and I studied at a musical conservatory in Indianapolis.

While on my way to East Chicago to take a job as teacher of music and art in high school, I stopped to visit friends in Chicago. Just by chance I read where the Chicago Musical College was holding auditions for young singers, the winner to receive a scholarship. I tried out, and to my astonishment—won. This encouraged me to try to become a singer in the Metropolitan Opera Company in New York City, and shortly Mother and I were on our way to New York.

I never did get to the Metropolitan, but the decision started me on my career. Throughout my working years in motion pictures, Mother's steady faith has been an unfailing source of strength to me.

Her death a number of years ago was the most shattering personal blow I have ever had to bear. My Mother's presence and her prayers for me, like my religion, were something I had possessed all my life and taken too much for granted. How alone I would have been at that time if she had not pointed the way to another Comforter who would never leave me!

It is not alone in the crises of life that God has sustained and

strengthened me, but also in day-to-day living problems, the un-
ending decisions and petty annoyances. Most of us have grave
responsibilities to our marriage and our children. I, for one,
wouldn't have the nerve to attempt to bring up my daughter
without God's help. To do so would seem to be the most incredible egotism!

Out of my heart and my own experience, I know that God has
infinite treasure to bestow. The joy and peace of mind that accompany love of God and faith in Him, are beyond the power of
words. Because of my religion, I know that I have lived a richer,
fuller, more satisfying life than would have been possible without it.

With all its hardships, the journey *is* worthwhile. Faith is
a wonderful resort. How I wish you were here—if you've
missed it!

Almost the End of the Earth

by SYDNEY R. MONTAGUE

This famous author, and former Canadian Mountie, has spent many snow-bound months in the remote areas of civilization. The mystery of a misplaced box made one such winter vigil an unforgettable experience.

A COMPANION MOUNTIE and I were to patrol and open up unknown Eskimo territory.

Our commanding officer had carefully briefed us. We were not traders; we were not missionaries. We were representatives of law and order and material progress. Although we might consider our new charges, up there at the entrance of the Hudson Strait, to be pagan, it was not our function to sow doubts in the minds of the natives about their spiritual beliefs. We were to explain that the white man was different but that this difference did not make the Eskimo, or Inuit as we call him, wrong.

Corporal Nichols and I were put ashore at Port Burwell, an island near the southern tip of Baffinland. With us were landed crates and boxes containing the "makings" of a house, our stove, pots, pans, and beds; our supplies of canned goods, salted and preserved foods. For fresh meat we were to hunt as the natives instructed us, for white man's ways of hunting are of little use in the place which the native calls "Killinik-Kusak," meaning "almost the end of the earth."

The Canadian Government is solicitous of the welfare of their men who volunteer for duty in these Arctic areas. They understand that two men, alone together, may well get on each other's nerves. Companions are carefully paired, and the men's taste for relaxation studied.

But sometimes the best of plans go wrong, and we were to dis-

cover that a certain large crate had not been unloaded before the
S. S. Bay Rupert sailed away and left us.

Nick and I built our dwelling with the natives lending a hand.
Some had never seen a white man before, others had only been to
a Hudson's Bay Company Post; some had talked with sailors
whose ships passed through broken ice floes during the few
weeks of semi-thaw.

We made patrols by dog team into the vast windy barrenness
where, some day, if our mission proved successful, meteorological
survey and airplane service might follow us. With natives we
hunted and explored the sea coves in Kayaks and Omiaks. On
one such expedition our Omiak (a native sailing vessel) was
crushed in the ice. When starvation seemed about to claim us, a
native killed a polar bear—on its meat we survived and got back
to our outpost.

The dark of winter closed in upon us. Corporal Nichols was
setting dough for our bread one day as I emerged from the store-
room.

"Dick, I can't find the books." I reported.

"I've checked the inventory; they're not here," he said. "I suppose they were in that box they forgot to take off the ship."

Remembering the fine selection of volumes the Government
had provided for us and the hundreds of long snow-bound nights
and days ahead of us, I was stunned.

"You mean there's not a single thing to read?"

"Only the labels on those cans, Syd."

There was nothing to do but make the best of it. For a while
I amused myself by making a dictionary of Inuit words, using
the backs of the can labels to write on. One of the native boys
had a name that I could not pronounce; so I rechristened him
"Tommy." From Tommy I learned of the Great Spirit.

He told me that the Inuit native has no corresponding term for
"I." There is no ego; everything and everyone are One, the lesser
one contained within the Greater ONE.

From Tommy, I heard that the native considers sleep a little death and that he may awake from unconsciousness a different spirit from the "one" who lay down to rest. With Tommy, I saluted the Great Spirit of the Aurora Borealis.

Once Tommy and I were on patrol when a terrific blizzard came up. We built an igloo with our snow knives and prepared to wait it out.

"Why does not the white man pray to his God for the blizzard to pass, and that we are not lost?" Tommy challenged me.

We knelt together on the fur-covered snow bunk of the igloo, Tommy speaking to the Great Spirit as man to man, I repeating the prayers as the white man prays. Eventually, the blizzard did cease, and we found our way back to camp.

To pass the time Corporal Nichols and I invented many extra chores indoors and spent much time going over our equipment. During one such session I began to clean out my duffel bag when I came across something that made me let out a whoop!

"Nick!" I shouted. "Something to read . . . I've found a book!"

The Bible which I discovered had been put there by my mother who packed my clothes before I left Montreal for this particular expedition.

I had never read the Bible much before, though my experience with prayer goes back to my infancy.

When my sea captain father emigrated to Canada, I was carried from England, on a cushion, too delicate to be taken even into Mother's arms. Until I was four, I could neither stand on my feet nor walk. Then, quite suddenly, with no determining cause, I did both. I was as excited as my parents. Strength grew and I became restless. While still in my teens, I took off from home to see the world.

When I returned, years later, in the full trappings of a Royal Canadian Mounted Policeman, my mother's handsome head tilted to one side as she looked me up and down.

"It's my Syd! Grown so fine and strong, like a miracle. But

that's what I prayed for. I'm really not surprised, just very grateful, and happy."

So that winter, near the Arctic Circle, we read the Bible which Mother had packed for me; we read it from beginning to end, and even the "begats." It was awkward, too, for we could not both read it at the same time and neither of us enjoyed reading aloud.

During a terrible blizzard which lasted thirteen days without letup, I separated the books of the Bible and bound them individually with paper that had come as wrappings. Then, I, for one, began to study what I read. Later on, spurred by Nick who was a fair scholar in several languages, we tried translations. The days passed, hardly counted.

Presently, I found the Bible was really a textbook for living. And for the first time the verses of Genesis took on meaning.

When we had first arrived, I realized that the Eastern Eskimo, or Inuit, had a much stronger, more trusting belief in the Great Spirit than I, with all my Christian training, my disinterested attendance at Sunday School, and the proud day my mother saw me confirmed.

But in a police post of the Arctic wasteland, now abandoned because of a geographical position too rigorous for the ways of modern white men, I found deep satisfactions in religious truths.

Before Mother passed on, I was able to tell her I had learned to understand what she meant by true prayer—the deep desire.

I had always been fascinated by the phrase, "In my Father's house are many mansions ... " Of course, Tommy, the Inuit, explained it in his primitive way, which I, with all my schooling, had never understood before. . . . The Great One dwells in the soul spaces of billions of human beings—many mansions certainly. We are all houses of God.

Pony Express to Jet Plane

by BRONCO CHARLIE MILLER

> *The youngest man ever to ride the Pony Express,*
> *Bronco Charlie passed his one hundredth birthday*
> *in 1949. Here's his story covering America's growth*
> *from covered wagon to jet plane, as he tells it to*
> *Gladys Shaw Erskine, his official biographer.*

I'LL NEVER FORGET the time I first rode the Pony Express, for all it happened back in 1861. In Sacramento, California, that was.

I was only 11, when a wild galloping horse come down the dirt road with empty stirrups flapping. It was the Pony Express, and the saddle was empty on account of the rider having connected with an Indian arrow. My father tossed me into the saddle, the menfolk standing around cheered, and I was off with the mail.

That ride was one of the longest I ever made, for all it was only to Carson City, Nevada, because Indians were all around and you never knew when an arrow would whish down from the rim rock above and you wouldn't be riding no more.

I was mighty scared and I sure needed the strength of God through that long, dark night. But I got through, although on a later ride I was chased by a band of 10 painted Bannocks and got two of their arrows in me, and still carry the scars.

When I got back to Sacramento the Pony Express put me on that run regular. There was an oath I had to make when they swore me in. They handed me a little leatherbound Bible, the kind they gave to all the riders, and a six shooter. I was told to use the Bible all the time, and the gun only in case of necessity. I took this oath:

"I do hereby swear before the Great and Living God that, while I am an employee of Russell, Majors and Wadell, I will use no profane language; that I will drink no intoxicating liquors; that I will not quarrel—and that I will conduct myself honestly—"

Old man Russell built an empire on such practice. People felt they could trust a man with a business built on Bible ways.

I rode for the Pony Express for the last five months it was alive. That was history in the making. We carried the last messages of Buchanan, news of the election of Lincoln, and of the firin' on Fort Sumter. They reached the Pacific in seven days and 17 hours, and to think that I have lived to see the Air Mail, sort of heir to the Pony Express, you might say, carry the mail across the continent in less than 17 hours!

This was in 1879 and the railroad was running by then. I took the iron horse and landed in Medora, North Dakota, where I went to busting for a French Marquis. There I was taught a lesson by a young man I ain't never forgot.

This day I had under me an outlaw roan that the other boys had given up as plumb loco. I was riding this roan pretty hard when right in front of me, I see this young man, mighty erect in the saddle, and he raps out like an officer, "Don't be so ugly with that horse!"

I was so surprised I didn't answer back.

He says, "If you had half the sense that horse has, you'd know that two positives never got along. If one is ugly, the other has to be kind."

I quieted down, and suddenly that ornery, bucking bronc of mine was just as still as I was. What this city fellow said made sense. And I ain't never forgot it.

"What's your name?" I asks.

"Roosevelt," he grins, "Teddy. What's yours?"

And later still, Buffalo Bill Cody saw me ride and allowed as how I might be one of them—join his Wild West Show.

"I'm taking the show to England," he says, "for Queen Victoria's Jubilee. Want to come along?"

We arrived in New York, ready to sail, and I don't know which was the bigger show—the easterners staring at us, in our six gallon hats and chaps; or us looking back at them, all done up in stiff collars and store-bought clothes. Why, they looked like a bunch of tenderfeet, for sure. And I reckon we looked to them like wild mavericks.

But you know, we was all just people—just folks—the trouble was we was wearing different brands, and we sort of bristled up.

When we come back to America, after showing to kings and queens all over Europe, I got married and settled down for a while.

It was then I got interested in the Salvation Army. They was having a hard time, getting stoned in the streets and all—and at first I wasn't making it any easier for 'em myself.

Then, one night, I stumbled into a meeting—and they was so gentle and kind that I took the oath. Later on, I spoke for them on street corners but mostly I talked from horseback.

So there I was busting sinners to wear a spiritual halter. Folks come to see me out of curiosity, but they'd stay to listen—and I meant every word I said.

There was plenty of talk about my preaching—folks saying I need more learning and different churches wanting me to wear their brand. But, some way, I always figure as how religion weren't a question of education, or brands, or which church.

I've seen covered wagons grow into jet planes in my 104 years. I've seen America really come busting out as the greatest country in the world.

Things have changed a lot except what always counts most— like meaning everything you say and do, right from the heart, and trying your best to live by the word of the Lord.

Healing Techniques For Sorrow, Fear and Worry

Why Laughter Has Power

by BOB HOPE

> *Says Bob Hope to a wounded soldier getting a blood transfusion, "I see they are giving you the old raspberry, son." It is all a part of the famous comedian's philosophy that laughter not only helps change despair to confidence, but also provides a spiritual value.*

ONCE WHEN I was in Shreveport, Louisiana, a minister offered me his pulpit for a sermon on "God and Hollywood."

Hastily I explained that in my business, success was measured by "yocks" versus "boffs." When that just confused him I said, "You know, yocks . . . little laughs . . . and boffs . . . great big ones. And if I got up there in your church I might still, unconsciously, be trying for those boffs."

We let the matter drop. But afterward, during a nightmare, I found myself in a pulpit and the laughs were rolling down the aisle shaking the dignified old rafters. I told a friend of this dream.

"And what would be so wrong about that?" he wanted to know. "Laughter has a spiritual value. An Englishman named John Donne had that pegged over 400 years ago. He said, 'Religion is not a melancholy, the spirit of God is not a dampe.'"

He had a point. Certainly I knew that laughter has a constructive power. I have seen what a laugh can do. It can transform almost unbearable tears into something bearable, even hopeful.

Overseas in 1944 with USO Camp Shows Frances Langford and I saw it lift a whole ward at the service hospital in Pearl Harbor. We were working our way up a long aisle when a nurse touched my arm.

"That boy near the end in the very high bed. They pulled him out of a B-17. Herbert hasn't spoken a word for weeks. If there's anything you can do . . .'

As we got to that end of the ward I winked at Frances. "Okay, boys," I said. "Frances Langford is going to sing you a song . . . and Herbert," I pointed to the bed where we could just see a white face, bandages covering the eyes, "Herbert, this is for you."

Frances approached the bed slowly, beginning her song . . . "Embrace me, my sweet embraceable you." An unnatural stillness settled over the entire ward. One of those that doesn't feel right, too hushed and breathless. All you could hear was Frances' low plaintive song, "Embrace me, you irreplaceable you . . ." And then, just as she reached him, her voice broke off.

In two steps I was beside her looking at Herbert. Where his arms had been there were only short stumps.

For several seconds we all just stood there stunned. No one moved. But the part of the mind where habit and involuntary reaction holds sway provided me with a diversion.

A couple of guys laughed, bless 'em. On I rushed trying to build that chain of laughter while Frances regained her composure. But the miracle was Herbert. Herbert spoke, *for the first time in weeks.*

"It's all right, Miss Langford," he said. "Don't worry about it."

Laughter binds men together in a kind of secret free masonry.

Hear it sometime travel around a circle . . . then notice that, however large that circle may be, it is a closed one.

For a brief few hours in 1944 I met 15,000 Marines of the 21st. Division at Pavuvu. They were on their way to the invasion of Peleliu. We were doing a routine series of camp shows on the Pacific Islands.

When an officer suggested the unscheduled stop he said, "We'll have to fly you over, a few at a time in small planes, and land you on a road. There's no airport. But it'll be worth it to them."

As we circled for our landing such a shout arose from 15,000 throats that we could actually *feel* it like a cushion of sound under our wings. We were from home! We were the promise of laughter ... today. Tomorrow, and they knew it, they were staging a little show of their own and 40% wouldn't come back.

We laughed and clowned as we landed. But looking at those faces I knew how Charles Lamb must have felt when he "jested that he might not weep."

Later back in the States, my wife and I at the dedication of Oak Knoll Hospital, walked into a ward to be greeted with that same laughter. One of those explosions that happen between old friends.

Voices kept yelling, "Pavuvu! Pavuvu!" Dolores was a bewildered outsider. But I was in. It was the 21st. Marines ... or what was left of them.

Laughter can sometimes appeal beyond reason, prejudice and cynicism.

In a jungle I heard the jokes of padres lift G.I.'s spirits into wanting the fearlessness and gaiety of the men of God, where no amount of solemn approach would have inspired them.

And I have heard a minister devastate a profane agnostic with quiet wit.

It happened at a very swank club one night. After a pointless and slightly blasphemous story the comedian noticed that all eyes were suddenly fastened on the collar insignia of a big, silent man at the end of the table.

"F'r crissakes," blustered the story-teller. "Are you a chaplain?"

With a light smile and deliberate emphasis the chaplain replied. "Yes, for *Christ's* sake, I am."

Laughter can return a sense of proportion to a troubled mind, for it erases self pity, self justification, self importance.

But perhaps the most important thing laughter can do is to bring back the will to live—and, when the time comes, give us the courage to go with good cheer.

I've seen the ones who aren't going to make it—American boys smiling their way right up to St. Peter's gate, and I've got a hunch they're holding a sure pass. Like one youngster who was stretched out on the ground getting a blood transfusion. "I see they're giving you the old raspberry, son," I said.

"It sure feels good," he laughed. "The guy who gave this must have been tax exempt or raised his own beef. It's strong stuff."

Before I had gotten 20 yards he had gone his way, smiling.

My young brother Sydney passed on 5 years ago and, for quite a while, he knew he was going. Someone with a very long face and a "religion of melancholy" had urged him to "prepare to meet his Maker" . . . to "petition Providence to provide for his poor little orphans."

It took the whole family and his five kids to convince him that "the spirit of God is not a dampe," here or hereafter, except for those who choose to have it so.

Every gay thing, every joyous or humorous or good thing that came to our attention we offered to my brother as proof of the infinite wisdom and kindness of God. When he went, he went smiling—and trusting. And, we had done such a good job for him that we had healed ourselves of much of our grief.

A comedian can't take much credit either, because people insist they are funny. You become a habit—a laugh habit. Sometimes people laugh at me before I open my mouth—even when they can't see me. Mention the arrival of someone they've laughed at before and they relax. They drop their strain. They expect to laugh and so they do.

They depend, too, on the laughmaker to stay the same. They want new jokes but not too much change. I don't think they've ever forgiven Charlie Chaplin for abandoning his big shoes, cane and derby hat. When I go into a service hospital they expect me to louse up the joint. To go on being me. No sympathy. They want me to walk into a ward filled with guys harnessed to torturous contraptions and say, "Don't get up fellows."

When I come to a Christmas party if I notice the lone star atop a pathetic Christmas tree I'm supposed to say, "Don't tell me a Brigadier General is running this show too."

So I say it. And when people wonder how a guy can go on and on like that . . . well, the answer is that the results themselves keep you up. You can't possibly not do it. The power works both ways. You are sustained by *their* laughter.

Nor does the power belong exclusively to the professional funnyman. There is a kind of geniality that brings mirth, and confidence. Bing Crosby has that. If there are two kinds of people, people who lift and people who lean, Bing is a lifter. Geniality might be defined as strength to spare.

The power of laughter lies in its ability to lift the spirit. For laughter cannot exist with clipped wings. It cannot be dictated to. It must be spontaneous and free as the air you breathe. Thus it is a special property of free men in a free land who are able to laugh at anything . . . or anyone . . . especially themselves.

Face Up to Fear

by JAMES L. KRAFT

Where can one turn when troubled, in danger, homesick, or apprehensive? The late James L. Kraft, famous founder of the company bearing his name, discovered the answer in his own lifetime of rich experiences. Here is one of the last published writings of this outstanding businessman.

THROUGH THE DARKEST moments of human experience it has been plain, to those not blinded by their fear, that God is in this world, and that man's extremity is God's opportunity.

Within the memory of millions of us is the stirring story of an event which occurred during World War I, at the desperate time when the Germans stood at the very gates of Paris. Many will recall that it was the virtually hopeless assignment of a courageous Canadian regiment—the Princess Pat—to hold back the enemy long enough to give Parisians a few hours respite.

They stood bravely for a time, but eventually the regiment broke, and began the inevitable retreat.

Then something happened. A small thing, so stupendous in its effect that it turned the tide of battle!

That evening the American papers announced that the German army was on the run and that the Princess Pat regiment was the spearhead of the attack. The account concluded with the statement that the regiment had been led into battle by a man on a white horse. No name given.

It happened that Brigadier General Gunn, leader of this famous regiment, had been a long-time friend of mine. After the war was over, I went to see him.

General Gunn and I sat together before a great log fire in his living room. Finally I said, "Tell me about the man on the white horse!"

He started. "How did you hear about that?" he asked.

I mentioned the single line in the newspaper dispatch.

"Well," he told me firmly, "the man was there all right. There is no question about that. I saw him, riding straight through the lines of German fire. Nothing touched him. I shouted to my men: 'Follow the man on the white horse!' They did. And you know the rest of the story!"

"General," I asked him, "What became of the man on the white horse?"

"I don't know," he answered. "He was there when we needed him. Then he was gone!"

There was that in his voice which made me know that he would have written that phrase, "He was there when we needed Him!"

All adults will remember an historic incident of World War II. It is called, most often, the Miracle of Dunkirk—that fateful day when the entire British Army, defeated and put to rout, huddled on the beach of Dunkirk at the mercy of the pursuing Nazi forces.

That day the Archbishop of Canterbury asked all of England to pray that the men might be saved. All of England did pray.

The English channel which separates Dunkirk from the shores of England is never a quiet body of water. But on that day, so the record reads, the waters of the channel were unusually still.

The whole world knows what happened. With God's help, the people of Britain rescued their men from certain destruction. It was an operation that attests to the triumph of faith. He was there indeed when they needed Him!

Here is still another example, a graphic account given me by a member of our company then serving on the Admiral's flagship. The scene, Salerno Bay in Italy.

Our American fleet moved to a point inside the bay and beneath the powerful enemy guns on the heights of Salerno. A terrific storm arose.

The waves were so high and violent that a conference was

called on the Admiral's ship to debate whether the entire fleet should retreat to wait for a more favorable time.

Withdrawal, however, would necessitate the ships moving out of the bay under full fire of the enemy guns again. So it was decided that, in spite of unfavorable conditions for landing, zero hour must be 4 o'clock the next morning.

The chaplain on the flagship asked permission to call the men together for prayer. "We have written record," he said, "that God has stilled the waves before. The need was perhaps no greater on the sea of Galilee than on the shores of Salerno!"

The Admiral said, "You're giving God a big order. This storm is scheduled to last about 48 hours more. But if you want to try it, go ahead!"

The men on the flagship did pray—they prayed hard. And they asked for just one thing—that the waves be stilled.

By 4 o'clock the following morning—zero hour—the stormy sea was like glass. The landing was made without loss of life . . . and the rest is history!

Corroboration of the details of this story came to me much later in Ernie Pyle's book called "Brave Men." He too was on that flagship off Salerno, and his dramatic account of the episode concludes with the statement that a miracle took place that night.

If we are to endure through our own personal extremities, without fear in our hearts, then we must plant, in its stead, faith. We must learn that daily prayer nourishes and waters that plant of faith whose flower is victory.

We have God's promise never more beautifully stated than through the prophet Isaiah: *"Fear thou not; for I am with thee; be not dismayed; for I am thy God; I will strengthen thee; yea, I will help thee, yea, I will uphold thee with the right hand of my righteousness."*

The Reason Behind Tragedy

by MRS. WARREN GREGORY

"Your baby is not normal," this mother was told.
Suppose it happened to someone you loved?

BUSTER WAS BORN in January, 1951, a premature baby. All seemed normal until I took him to our Buffalo doctor three months later for a routine check-up.

I can't describe what happened during that visit. Later, I carried my child out of the office, while certain words floated through my dazed mind: "It's hopeless . . . he's mongoloid . . . treatment is useless."

Somehow I managed to get into a cab. The driver, a graying, weather-beaten man, spoke gently:

"Lady, I know you've just left the medical building. Can I do anything? Are you sick—is it the baby?"

I nodded. "No one can do anything."

He started the cab, talking over his shoulder. It took time before the words penetrated: " . . . only 20 years old and a good prize fighter. Yeah, me . . . then was paralyzed from the waist down. When I heard them washing me up for good, I started to talk to God like He was right in my hospital room. Lady, I'm telling you He's right here in this cab with us now."

I closed my eyes and tried to imagine God sitting on the other side of the seat. All I could see were Buster's wide eyes staring at me solemnly.

The driver's voice sharpened into victory. "I found out that the way you think sort of decides what happens. Look at me . . . I'm driving this cab and my legs work fine . . . Hope you don't mind my talking to you like this, lady, but you gotta have faith. My wife and I will pray for you both."

When he helped me out of the cab, the driver told me his name was Willie Cunningham. Willie, known throughout Buffalo for his big, gentle heart forever had my gratitude for his comforting words that day.

Warren, my husband, and I shared our heartache that night on the phone with our families in Indiana. We faced the decision of either sending Buster away to an institution, or keeping him at home with the possible danger, doctors explained, that he would destroy our normal family relationships with our other two children, Patricia and Kenneth. What should we do?

When Warren and I were married in 1948, we both felt then that love, energy and determination were all we needed to make a successful marriage. Although reared in a religious atmosphere, it had never seemed important to me until now that we have more basic beliefs to fortify us.

Our first move was to take Buster to an Indianapolis specialist. Upon arrival, I called my sister-in-law, Mrs. Anthony Ackermann, who has a true working Christian spirit. "Will you take me to church before we see the doctor?" I asked.

The two of us went to a small Lutheran Church in Edgewood, a suburb of Indianapolis. We entered the sanctuary and knelt on the first bench. I wept openly and without shame.

Looking toward the front I concentrated on the round stained-glass window, depicting Jesus at Gethsemane. I repeated His statement, "Come unto me, all ye that labor and are heavy laden and I will give you rest."*

When we left I had more peace of mind than ever before in my life. Today, whenever I falter, courage will return to me if I will concentrate on the Image of that window.

The Indiana doctor confirmed the diagnosis with this difference: "Your son is a high-grade mongol and will not destroy your family. He will learn slowly, will make social adjustments and will be able to work." We felt as though we had been given the

* *Matthew 11:28*

world and I returned to the church and offered a prayer of thanks.

But our joy lasted only until we took Buster to another doctor in Buffalo. He told us we would be wasting our time to work with *any* mongoloid child. We couldn't continue to run from one doctor to another. Nearby was St. Rita's Home, a Catholic institution to care for children whose minds do not develop. It didn't matter what denomination we were—or none.

When we took Buster to St. Rita's for an examination, the Sister Superior tried to hide her astonishment. "Why, he is strong, alert and active!" she exclaimed. Treatment was prescribed.

We did everything possible to help bring a miracle of love and faith. My step-mother and I went to church daily to pray. Both Warren and I studied the subject of mongolism and all types of treatment. I joined the Eggertsville Community Church and had our children baptized.

We contacted a new organization, The Association for the Help of Retarded Children, where we became members. Once I started sharing my experiences with other parents, scarcely a day passed when I didn't find someone to help.

When Buster was five months old, he had a sudden heart attack. For three weeks he was kept in the hospital, then allowed to come home again. Helped by an oxygen tent, he began to improve rapidly. We took him to a wonderful specialist in Boston, Dr. Clemens E. Benda, who assured us everything possible had been done.

Another heart attack followed two weeks later. This time we cared for our son at our home, which fairly vibrated with quiet activity and prayer. But Buster was failing: his breathing became more and more irregular. Then, as the night wore on, Buster slowly, with little struggle or pain, slipped away.

It was all over. Months of exhausting efforts, huge expenses and continuous prayers—all to no avail for his life. Buster's death created in our lives an emptiness—you would expect despair and bitterness to rush into this void.

Instead, marvelous things have happened. Our whole family somehow has been knitted closer together because of Buster's short life. My father spends time raising money for the fine work being carried on at St. Rita's. In fact, our whole family is contributing. My husband goes with me to church affairs and together we discuss my Sunday School lessons and church sermons.

In our Eggertsville Community Church a children's worship center was donated in Buster's name. Other parents have since contributed to this in memory of their children.

Recently two more memorials have been offered in Buster's name by members of our families: one to St. Rita's Home and one to the Bethesda Lutheran Home in Watertown, Wisconsin.

As for me, I have had a complete spiritual rebirth. God is as real to me now as He is to Willie Cunningham, the cab driver. I teach Sunday School, and have been appointed Recording Secretary for the church council. My activities continue with both St. Rita's and the Association for the Help of Retarded Children, where I share my experience with similarly grieved parents who have retarded children. The more I seem to give, the more help and strength I receive.

I also feel that Buster gave new insight to several doctors who now see some hope in "hopeless" cases through proper care and treatment. Doctors can warn parents of the suffering they may face. But they can't predict that such suffering is sometimes the best thing that can happen to a family. I know ... and so does everyone who knew Buster.

He was a little baby who lived for only seven and a half months. But look at the lives affected by him. God can use his children in wondrous ways.

When Life Seems Grim

by RALPH MORGAN

*Are you facing a personal loss, panic, heavy bur-
dens? Read the formula for shedding self pity, offered by a distinguished actor.*

I HAVE ENJOYED many of the good things in life, for which I am
very grateful. But, like most others, I have also encountered what,
to me, have been great tragedies. There is no man or woman living who does not face catastrophe, loss, panic, heavy burdens and
the terror of buckling under.

Recently my sorrows and reverses piled up on me to such an
extent and my future ahead looked so grim that life had almost
no meaning. Yet, when everything seemed to be completely dark,
a thought came to me:

"Why don't you try something that you have always believed
in, but never used? Why don't you really try to love? Right now,
start loving everyone with whom you come in contact—the milk-
man, the paper boy, the postman, the man at the service station;
yes, and the trees, the flowers, the birds, every living thing.

"And tomorrow when you awaken, vow to yourself that you'll
love more than you did today."

I tried, and it worked. The returns were unbelievable. Gone
were the depression, the self-pity, the lack of good in my life. My
world changed almost overnight. There is nothing mysterious
about it. All that is needed is an honest effort.

Let me give you a specific instance. You are an actor, like myself. You're standing on the stage ready to go on and play your
part. Another actor comes off-stage and says, "What a terrible
audience. They're sitting on their hands. There isn't a smile in
the whole crowd."

Don't you believe it! Say to yourself that it isn't true. Tell yourself: "I love those people out there, and they love me."

Go on the stage with that thought sincerely and deeply in your mind, and see what happens. You will be amazed.

I've proven it. I've seen it work. And if it works for me, it will work for you—for the salesman, for the businessman, for the mechanic, for the housewife, for each and every one. And when it works for you, you will feel exalted with a great hope that becomes a conviction.

You will also know that one of the great commandments, "Love thy neighbor as thyself," was not an idle request, but that it was given as a guiding principle which will bring the Peace of God which passeth all understanding to each of us. I love this verse of John Greenleaf Whittier's:

> *"Then brother-man, fold to thy heart thy brother,*
> *For where love dwells, the Peace of God is there;*
> *To worship rightly is to love each other;*
> *Each smile a hymn, each kindly deed a prayer."*

I suppose every individual, deep down in his heart, believes that he has a formula or recipe for the healing of the nations, which, if adopted, would bring lasting peace to the peoples of the world. This cannot be accomplished until the great majority of us has found peace individually.

My formula is a very old one, as old as man; yet it has rarely been tried, except by comparatively few wise people. Of one thing, however, I am sure: it never fails when sincerely applied. This entire solution is embodied in one word, the word which I believe has been more abused than any other in the English, or any other, language—Love.

One word, four little letters; yet, that little word carries within itself all the power there is in Heaven and Earth! If you honestly apply it, you will see something happen that will appear to you to be a miracle. But it won't be a miracle. It will be the natural operation in your life of The Great Law that governs the universe.

Biggest Room in the Company

by LEN LESOURD

> *One of America's largest corporations hired a pastor-counselor and opened another kind of power plant.*

JACK ADAMS, a machine operator for R. J. Reynolds Tobacco Company in Winston-Salem, North Carolina, sat brooding several years ago over the death of his son. The boy had been killed by a truck while crossing the street.

"Why don't you see the new counselor?" a friend finally urged. "Clifford Peace is his name. Nice guy . . . easy to talk to . . ."

Several days later, Jack Adams strode into the 20-story main office building of the company and found his way to Room 110. On the door it read: Pastor-Counselor.

There was a restful atmosphere inside. A pleasant-voiced girl welcomed him to the reception room, where he could see into two other rooms, one the counselor's office, the other, a small chapel.

When he entered Mr. Peace's office a few minutes later, Adams sat down and gazed stonily at the relaxed, smiling face of the counselor.

Suddenly, Jack clenched his fist, drew back his arm and struck out hard at an imaginary force. It was an unexpected, violent action, but the counselor's face didn't flick a muscle.

"You know what I'm doing?" Jack snapped. "I'm striking at God. If He were a man I'd punch Him in the nose just like that." Then he loosed another vicious swing. "That's what He gets for taking my son away from me!"

"I'm sorry about your son's death," Clifford Peace said gently. "Would you care to tell me more about it?" He did.

Patient and skillful listening unraveled the man's fuller story, finally exposing a hidden sense of guilt mixed in with his grief. Feeling that God had killed his son in punishment for his own

245

past family neglect and disloyalty (and having this constantly "rubbed in," as Jack said, by a nagging wife), he had become hostile toward God.

Gradually the pastor-counselor helped the troubled man to identify and to deal with his confused emotions. "But the big day," said Mr. Peace, "was when he found relief from his sense of guilt. Feeling a radiant sense of God's approval. he could then affirm Him, as a friend. The rest was easy."

It was during later visits that Jack Adams* began stopping for a few moments in the small chapel next to the pastor-counselor's office—a quiet and beautiful little sanctuary, a sort of haven for troubled hearts and a stimulant to right thinking.

"Here's the real power plant in our company," Adams admitted on coming from the chapel one day. These words were music to Clifford Peace, because to him this chapel was a dream come true.

The 42-year-old counselor was hired to fill a position that Board Chairman, the late James A. Gray and company President John C. Whitaker, visualized soon after World War II. Although the Reynolds organization is large (over 12,000 employees), a fine personal relationship has been built up through the years between management and workers.

Working conditions had been improved, free medical care made available, pensions, insurance and many other material benefits provided, yet the company officials were aware that many of its people, like others in the nation, had deep emotional needs that must be met. Supervisors were encouraged to be even more sensitive to these needs. Another answer was the sending of *Guideposts Magazine* to all employees. Hiring an ordained minister to serve people on the job as pastor-counselor, and installing a chapel were the latest steps taken in this program.

---

* The names of Mr. Adams and Mrs. Lester in this article and certain unimportant facts in connection with their case histories have been altered to protect the real persons from embarrassment.

The choice of Reynolds executives for the job of Pastor-Counselor was Clifford H. Peace, who came from his ministry at the St. Paul's Methodist Church in Asheville. He had grown up on a North Carolina tobacco farm and his temperament fitted his name.

His qualifications included two degrees (one with a leaning to psychology and the other in theology), three and a half years spent as an Army chaplain, extensive counseling and "grass roots" experience working, while in school, with highway construction crews and in the harvest-fields of the West.

After being only a week on the job, Clifford Peace presented the idea of a meditation chapel to President Whitaker. This request was considered by the Directors who gave enthusiastic approval. Plans for such a chapel were drawn up late in 1949 and work started soon after. Clifford Peace, meanwhile, approached his new job with a quiet dedication and restraint that quickly began to win those with whom he was to work in the company and community.

Counseling cannot be forced on people. "How am I to get those with personal problems to my office?" he asked himself.

This problem was partly accomplished by company announcements and explanations. Mr. Peace realized he could not serve the people adequately unless they knew him and he knew something about them. So only two hours a day were allotted for office counseling for the first few months, while he visited each employee at his job the rest of the day. Countless invitations to speak on his work came from company and community groups. Soon workers were coming in to see him regularly.

By the end of 1950, basic construction had been completed on the chapel. Gothic in design, the woodwork is dark walnut in finish and the walls covered in tapestry of royal blue, with gold colored symbols meaning "Victory." In the center of the cathedral-glass window is the figure of Christ at prayer.

On December 29th the Board of Directors assembled in the

chapel for an opening ceremony. During the simple service, the executives knelt for prayer.

Fred S. Hill, company Treasurer, walked out of the chapel with filled eyes. Later he explained to the pastor-counselor how moved he was that such a chapel was available to all for private meditation and prayer. Private meditation was one of his greatest sources of inner strength in coping with a declining health situation which he alone knew.

The chapel continued to mean a great deal to Fred Hill right up to the night, less than a month after its opening, when he died quietly in sleep.

To workers, the chapel is a quiet place where they may go during the working day, either directly or in relation to their visits with the pastor-counselor. To Clifford Peace, it is a holy spot which he visits several times a day to kneel by the side of a person who has requested him to do so. In the early morning he goes there alone to pray for company personnel, naming one by one those whose intimate burdens he knows and shares.

The first time Mrs. Lester, a company clerk, appeared in his office months ago, she was almost hysterical.

"My husband left last Friday night on a fishing trip," she began. "He's sent me word that he isn't coming back. There is another woman involved—and I know who she is."

She jumped from one detail of the story to another, with little regard for sequence.

"The Lord knows, I have my faults," she admitted. "I have a quick temper and I know I have nagged him some . . ." After a moment's hesitation, she said, "I'll do my best not to repeat my mistakes. I want our marriage to be a success, and for us to make a good home for our little boys."

As the woman started to leave, Mr. Peace led her by the open door of the chapel. She stopped and looked in.

"Would you like to go in and sit down for a while?" he suggested. She did so.

How much patience and faith did Mrs. Lester have? What of her little boys—with Christmas only a week away? The counselor considered these and other aspects of her problem seriously, aware that any hasty action on his part might simply make the situation worse. The husband would probably welcome retaliatory steps from his wife, because it would help him, while hard pressed, to justify his own action.

When Mrs. Lester came out of the chapel, there was calm on her face; her hands were relaxed by her side.

"I know how helpless you feel in this situation, Mrs. Lester," the counselor said. "I believe that your husband still loves you, regardless of what he has done and said. But it may take weeks or months for him to realize it fully enough to come back. Prayer is the best weapon we have. Let's make the most of it."

Mrs. Lester took a long breath. "I will try ... and thank you ... I feel better."

Clifford Peace and Mrs. Lester began a persistent prayer campaign. After several more visits, it was observed that she was becoming increasingly considerate of others, and more active in her church. She didn't denounce her husband or the other woman although the temptation must have been great.

One afternoon several months later, the pastor-counselor was completing a report of his 18 months of counseling. There had been some heart-warming results. Failures too. Yet failures, the counselor mused, can often become successes in ways that only God can see.

At home, the pastor-counselor's devoted wife probably had dinner ready. Three lively daughters were waiting to romp. He started to rise from his desk when the office door opened.

In walked Mrs. Lester—*and Mr. Lester.*

Arm-in-arm they stood there, beaming at him happily. "We decided, Mr. Peace, that you should be the first to know. We're back together again and happier than we have ever been before." Mrs. Lester was unable to hold back the tears.

"We would like to begin our marriage again on a new basis. Could you perform some kind of service for this, here in the chapel?"

A reaffirmation of the marriage vows. What a wonderful idea! In the quiet atmosphere of the chapel, the two joined hands as they reaffirmed their holy vows to love and cherish each other till death. The cares of the day slipped from the counselor's shoulders. Experiences such as these have hallowed the very walls of the little chapel.

The lean, leathery foreman, who came in one morning to meditate, best described it. "This is a mighty little room," he said. "But it is the *biggest* room in the company!"

Is Your Health Bankrupt?

by DR. HOWARD WESTCOTT

> *One case before Dr. Westcott seemed hopeless. "Is*
> *there anything else I can do?" the doctor asked after*
> *all normal procedures had been tried. What hap-*
> *pened then was pure inspiration.*

How MANY PEOPLE ever consider that the lack of certain qualities
—such as, balance, common sense, tranquillity—affects the physical state of the human body?

Man continually marvels about the perfection of God's crea-
tions—mountains, rivers, the sun and stars—often forgetting that
in himself God has achieved His most complicated and perfect
creation.

One of the most distressing phases of medical practice is to
watch the gradual destruction of this perfect work of God by the
deliberate abuse of mental, physical and spiritual equilibrium.

How? Through fear, worry, anxiety, hate, selfishness, suspi-
cion, jealousy and lust, to mention a few.

Let me cite a striking example of the harmful effect of fear on
body function. A very intelligent young lady was a victim of severe bronchial asthma. She received medical attention in hospitals, from private physicians, and at analytical laboratories. There
were periods of temporary relief, but she was quite desperate
when she found her way to my office. Through friendly conversation I learned gradually that she was much afraid of tuberculosis, since she felt it ran in her family.

After uncovering this submerged fear (not expressed voluntarily), I was able to prove scientifically to her that she had no
tuberculosis. Thus her fear of lung disease (asthma) was not
necessary, and her symptoms were cured. Now, after two years
of freedom, she is married and about to have her first child.

Fears, both real and imaginary, are a scourge on the face of this
earth and affect the lives of many of us. There is only one way to

lick them and that is to bring them out in the open where their weakness is apparent.

Did you ever hear of people being sick because they hated someone? This is not uncommon.

A society woman married a Social Register man for money. The man came to realize that he had been taken in, and I suspect learned several other things about his wife which hardened his heart. He found his solace in dogs.

Now it happened that dogs were the lady's pet hate, and the irony of their hold on her man made her introspective and vindictive. It was not long before she noticed pain in her chest, shortness of breath, palpitation, and then dreaded insomnia which, of course, led her to me.

Tests showed absence of any heart disease, but clinically she is an invalid because of her fear for her heart—actually brought on by the events as outlined to you. In my humble opinion, she could cure herself by letting love replace her hate and thus give her something worthwhile to live for.

How do I explain the fact that fear, hate, worry and jealousy destroy the human body? I believe that man alone has a soul, and that many souls are incomplete or inadequate until God has touched them.

Keeping right with God to keep well reminds me of another experience I had recently. A fine-looking prosperous man in his middle forties came in for a general check-up. He looked downhearted when I found him to be quite perfect.

Then rather sheepishly he told me that for several months he had been impotent and was hoping I would find a reason for it. I soon discovered that prior to this he had indulged in indiscretions and was quite apparently suffering from a guilt complex. In the presence of his wife who trusted him, the terrible shame of his unfaithfulness set up a nerve block which was the cause of the trouble.

The cure was as plain as the cause but much harder to face, I am sure. I do not know whether he confessed to his wife or to God, but I know that absolution from his sin was the cure of his disorder.

There has often been doubt in the minds of most men as to whether or not God does, or Christ did, perform miracles. Since the 7th day of January, 1945, I have not the slightest question of these miracles!

On Jan. 2, 1945, one of my patients asked me to visit her husband who was in very poor graces with her at the moment. She was a dressmaker and he a head-waiter at a large hotel. As you may guess, he had done considerable drinking over New Year's and arrived home in an intoxicated state.

He vomited strenuously and complained of an acute pain in his stomach, which could have been due to his drinking. But to be sure, I took a blood count. In two hours he was on the operating table. A ruptured stomach ulcer was sewed up and the patient was treated for peritonitis by all known measures.

Things did not go well; the patient developed an acute ileus and on the 7th of January was almost comatose. He was just able to recognize me when I came in for medical consultation. No care had been spared. What could I do?

I could not leave him without a silent prayer to God for help, and to cure him if it be His will. I had hardly finished my prayer when he looked up and said, "Please help me, Dr. Westcott."

I comforted him, and turned to go and inform his wife of the hopelessness.

Suddenly I had a thought ... an inspiration. Why not try pituitrin? I made the suggestion, but both resident doctors said it would not work. Nevertheless, I wrote the order and it was given.

Within 10 minutes from the moment that pituitrin was given, the man was relieved of congestion. In 12 hours the course was definitely changed. Today he is symptom free, belongs to A.A., and is still working at his job of head-waiter.

For my money, that was a miracle!

How to Help Yourself
—By Helping Others

I Found America's Heart

by ANTHONY CUCOLO

> *At the age of 16, immigrant Anthony Cucolo was*
> *wheeling 800-pound loads of cement. One simple act*
> *of kindness changed his life. Tony tells here what it*
> *takes to rise from laborer to boss.*

I HAD JUST PLACED three 100-pound bags of cement on my wheel-barrow. Before I could move them, the foreman hollered out:

"Eh-h you! The new boy, there! Let's get a better load'n that."

He walked over and started piling more bags on. Four. Six . . . eight. That was 40 years ago. I was big and strong for my 16 years —but not that strong.

I began to have pains at night. Sometimes cramps were so bad I would break down and cry, "God, please help me." I hadn't thought America was going to be cement and pains in the back.

In my home town of Summonte, Italy, we had a magic phrase, "quando vado in America . . . when I go to America, then everything will be well."

I had arrived clutching my entire fortune of 15 lire (worth $3.00), ambitious to become a contractor like my father back in Summonte. But while I dreamed of becoming a great contractor, with million dollar jobs, the job I actually got, paid $1.00 a day. And left me in pain.

Twice my father sent money for my return to Italy. Yet somehow I could not leave . . .

Then one day we went to Thomaston, Conn., to put a side-walk around a private house. That night, after hauling cement as usual, I again could not sleep. Tossing, trying to find the key to my dreams, I again cried out, "God, show me what I should do."

A day or so later, as I was about to load my wheelbarrow, the foreman called me. "Eh-h you, Tony. Come here."

Silently I walked to him.

"Tony, boy, you want a vacation with pay?"

The foreman was laughing, but went on to explain: The woman who hired us to build the sidewalk thought the work too hard for me. She said she would pay for my time until the job was finished.

I never learned the lady's name, but her act of kindness to a stranger was a turning point for me ...

We really labored in those days, coming to work at 6, not stopping till noon; by then the men were weak, touchy. In Italy, my father always called a stop at 10 for bread. Maybe, I thought, we could do that.

I got permission from the foreman. The old timers told me I could get a big bag of day-old bread and some "second-hand cake" for 10 cents. Some of the men couldn't even afford two pennies for the buns and the rest of us would chip in for them.

What started out as my attempt to repay an act of neighborliness, became the answer to my question, "God, show me what I should do." Because with these breaks, our spirits responded, our work improved.

"You know," I said during one of these breaks. "I think the rolls are just as important as the cement on this job. If I'm ever boss ..."

My next move wasn't to a million dollar job, but I did make foreman. And we had our rolls. And our work was good. I thought I had discovered something big enough to risk chucking my foreman's pay and going into business for myself.

Business cards, two shovels, two picks and a custom—stopping for bread—were my equipment. One shovel and pick I swung myself.

My first contract was to build a curbing 300 feet long at 14 cents a foot. I was as enthusiastic about making that $42 contract as any of the larger contracts that have come since.

And then, many years and many contracts later, there came the news that New York State was inviting bids on the dangerous

Storm King By-pass. It was a million dollar job ... maybe more.

But I wasn't sure we were ready for it. We would have to operate on a shoestring, and the mountains were so extremely hazardous only two other companies even considered the job.

I kept repeating the prayer I had made that night, long ago, in pain in my room ... then entered my bid. We were awarded the contract!

It would not be true to say that I was not worried. A job of this size requires a lot of credit and cash. The biggest single expense was a new Northwest Shovel, a huge, 60-ton machine.

Then, at dinner a week after work began, the foreman called excitedly. "Boss, the Northwest Shovel went over the cliff."

A 200 foot drop! I jumped in my car, trembling. "God, I hope you guide me."

"How's Ray?" I asked the foreman as soon as I got to the job.

"Okey, he jumped in time."

"What about the gas cap?"

No one had thought of it. A fireman ran down and removed it. Afterwards, the damage was assessed as fairly light and work proceeded almost immediately.

The fire official commented. "Good thing someone thought of removing the gas cap. Otherwise the whole thing might have blown up." And our contract would have blown up with it.

Now, even though I'm a contractor, I have often been kidded about my lack of mechanical knowledge. The point is, how could I have ever thought about the gas cap simply on my own?

Without help of this kind, and without teamwork from the men and our neighbors, we might never have finished this first million dollar job.

Today, I have a sign on my office door at Suffern, N.Y. It is in memory of the unknown lady who first showed me the ways of neighborliness—in memory of the hours spent with my men over coffee and rolls.

"Help to live," the sign reads. "It makes a better neighbor."

We Are Borrowed Timers

by GUYER THOMAS

> *You have to be dead three months before you can join the Borrowed Timers. A story of an amazing organization and its accomplishments, written by Guyer Thomas, the founder.*

ONE NIGHT AT DINNER on a California ranch many years ago, I was suddenly startled by a thought.

"Why, all three of us should be dead now!" I exclaimed, looking around the table.

It was true. Ethel Mason was a victim of arthritis and beyond medical aid. Mrs. Parker had incurable heart trouble. I, a civil engineer, had an extreme stomach disorder. Doctors had given us all but a few months to live, but for each the appointed time had passed.

We all stared at each other, and each expressed a different thought:

"We're living on borrowed time."

"I wonder how much time we do have?"

"What shall we do with it?"

I pushed aside my usual milk-and-cream dinner as we discussed excitedly our state of health. Some months ago all of us had arrived at the ranch from different localities—discouraged, doomed. That we were strangers, sharing a common disaster, comforted us, and now the successful strength of joined forces opened a new outlook. We formulated plans—daring plans.

Soon after we met, I had ventured a new thought in the midst of one conversation about our desperate ills.

"Prayer is a powerful thing," I had said hesitantly. "I'd like to know how to pray better. Can either of you help me?"

Without embarrassment, almost like children, we began to practice praying out loud together.

As those first days passed, our spirits rose, and we found new interests in the ranch. Now came the discovery that we had out-prayed our death sentences.

"Why couldn't we help others who are waiting for death?" we asked each other eagerly.

That's how the Borrowed Timers started, back in 1936. The three of us went to San Diego and established quarters in a large house where members could live and work. Membership is open to those told by a competent physician that their days are num-bered. Ninety days after the death sentence has passed those per-sons may come into our group.

As one wit summed it up: "You have to be dead three months before you can join."

Only those with contagious ailments are unacceptable.

The troublesome problem was how to find means of support for the group. One night, discouraged, I sat down by the fire-place, watching the dying embers and pondering the needs of the group. Everyone else had retired.

I formed a prayer. The logs in the fireplace meanwhile dark-ened except one central portion that continued to glow—in the form of a perfect cross!

I rubbed my eyes and looked again. There, in the fireplace, was the answer to my prayer. But what did it mean?

With rising excitement I began to pace the floor. I recalled that one of the young boys in our group had a chemistry set. In it was some luminous paint!

After pulling out the set, I began mixing these chemicals. Then in the early hours of the morning I made the first Prayer Re-minder Card—a glowing cross marked out on cardboard to hang on the bedroom wall.

Since then we Borrowed Timers have made and sold millions of these now familiar cards (with a blue Crusader Shield, and the Sallman picture of Christ).

It was decided at the start that all Borrowed Timers would have to work at something. Abilities and skills are pooled; so are both good and bad body parts for efficient management. The undamaged body parts work to make a living for everyone, while the damaged parts are pooled in such a way as to make the most efficient self-care possible.

We insist on amusing pastimes on the theory that there is more health in a good laugh than in a hatful of pills. And romance is no stranger to our group.

Betty Dale, for example, was an attractive girl who had spent 15 years in a wheel chair with infantile paralysis. When she came to our group, doctors had just informed her that it would soon be necessary to remove both of her legs in order to give her an added year of life. This was in 1942.

Betty had other ideas. She married Donald James, a soldier who happened to see her picture in the local newspaper. He decided he would like to meet her. Then in 1948, instead of not having any legs, Mrs. James had six of them—her own and those of twin girls, Betsy and Bonnie. Today she holds down the full job of a farmer's wife.

Whenever there is a bogging down in spirit, much can be gained by placing these "down" people together and assigning everyone some special task so that each can aid his companions. This builds the will to live through the feeling of being important.

Many have asked what is our secret. Well, we accept the possibility of death calmly, resolving to make every day useful, thereby to discover the self-helping outlet of helping others.

Through all-important prayer comes the humility to make the personal adjustments necessary, and to begin life anew from any level.

The Chapel of the Good Thief

by REV. A. R. HYLAND

> *The convicts built it themselves. A pick-pocket even
> designed a slug-proof collection box. Here is a proj-
> ect of trust inspired by the Rev. A. R. Hyland, chap-
> lain of Clinton Prison in Dannemora, N. Y.*

I STOOD AND WATCHED the men in grey march by.

It was late August, 1937. I'd been at Dannemora under a month, and I couldn't fathom the dense apathy of the men. The day was grey. The uniforms and the faces of the men one after another, were grey. Three thousand social outcasts! My heart was grey.

I had come to them young and full of hope. I had been ordained less than 10 years prior and had only two assistant pastorates behind me. But I had dreams and hopes . . . which had met with stony indifference.

The prison was called the Siberia of America. It is a "maximum security" prison, housing mostly hardened and habitual criminals, long-term recalcitrants. In the years between 1920 and 1930 turmoil was rife in all our prisons across the country. The revolt in Clinton Prison in 1929 had only brought on sterner measures. As a result these lethargic men who so puzzled me were resigned to even a more trying, vigorous ordeal in living than their predecessors knew.

As Chaplain I was director of social programs and libraries. I had met an almost insolent contempt for any suggestion I made.

I went to my makeshift Chapel to pray once more for inspirational help. It was an old smelly auditorium, used for movies, school, hospital and place of worship for all creeds. Directly over the mess hall, the steam of cabbages, potatoes and beets hung over the place. From the day I had first knelt there I had dreamed of

263

having a real Chapel—something distinctly set aside for the worship of God.

That morning when I preached, words seemed to come in answer to my prayers. I spoke of the fact that Christ chose to associate with "Publicans and Sinners" and to die with criminals. One was Dismas, a penitent thief who asked for forgiveness. "Remember me, Lord, when you come into your Kingdom," Dismas said on his cross.

And Christ, to whom no sin is unforgivable except the lack of any desire to be forgiven, answered: "This day thou shalt be with me in Paradise."

So a thief, a convict publicly executed for his crimes, was the first Christian we know about to get into Heaven.

That night two prisoners came to me and asked to be heard at Confession. During the week that followed, six more came. One, who had once been a choir and altar boy, offered to serve Mass for me the next Sunday!

Soon, many men of other faiths came to me. Each explained he had felt my past helpful attempts had been something of an act. Now, however, it was clear I felt a convict was not only redeemable but a could-be Somebody. Like St. Dismas.

I seized this opening. A man can be, with God's help, pretty much what he chooses, I told them. No one is lost until or unless he feels himself lost. Some of the greatest saints were great sinners. But God could not help those who fled Him.

With the first little group, I talked of Dismas and my hope of a prison church with him as patron saint. The idea of a Church of the Good Thief grew almost faster than I could keep up with. The men offered to do all the work, and permission was granted by the authorities.

In one corner of the North Yard, an old dairy barn was being demolished. All around was a new prison high wall, but there remained just inside, the old prison wall, also due for demolition.

I went to the men, announced we might have the site and asked if they'd help with the demolition job. The stones could be reshaped for our church, the barn lumber reclaimed and reused.

"Wasn't Christ born in a barn?" one old criminal roared. "Why it's a natural! It's given us for His Church."

That did it—enthusiasm sparked. Volunteers signed up by the scores.

I wrote letters by the dozens: to old college mates, to every friend—and they to their friends. My father, in whose hardware company in Chateaugay, New York, I'd often worked, helped. Everyone helped. Dollars, time, instruction, advice and legal help were given, and even relatives and friends of the prisoners helped. Journalists publicized it.

One of the convicts was an artist of considerable talent. He wished to do a painting of the Good Thief on the Cross. Another inmate offered to pose, grew a beard and went unshorn. He was secured to a cross by ropes and elevated on a small keg. The keg was taken away and our artist bemoaned the light, the tools, the brushes and canvas. The organ played. I recited my breviary, a guard stood not far off, while the poor crucified wretch sweated and panted, a look of such real anguish on his face that the finished picture has been commented upon everywhere for its realism.

Some of the gifts took our breath away. Two Jewish theatrical brothers who prefer to be anonymous presented a $25,000 organ. A contractor furnished all cement needed; a lady donated roofing material. Money, from silver to large checks, came from all faiths, all walks of life.

The convicts, however, with their work and their fast-growing spiritual rebirth, were the true heroes of that swift and amazing monument to God. The first time a scoffing inmate spoke of the church workers as "black sheep that had become the padre's little woolly lambs," there was a free-for-all fight that nearly brought on punishment. After that, criticism was not healthy.

My doubts and illnesses were cured as I gave over calmly and watched criminal forgers forging iron instead of checks, stick-up men raising scaffolding and joking about it, hoist guys hoisting lumber. A man who specialized in high explosives (for blasting safes and vaults) offered to mix the chemicals for laying tiles. He was hospitalized with calloused knees and chemical burns but he laid a wonderful floor.

A pickpocket designed a slug-proof collection box which rang a bell, sounded a siren and set off a record that yelled: "I've been robbed!" Our decision not to use it dashed his spirits until he grew absorbed in designing the background of our Baptistry.

Our church—and its history-making inaugural—is a thing of wonder. But if by any chance, I considered that this alone was the Dismas project, I was startlingly mistaken.

The clearly important part of the project is the result in men's rehabilitation. Eighty-five per cent of these convicts are as fully restored to normal living, holding jobs better than they ever originally hoped for, as if the past had not been.

The first who made this clear to me was a prisoner who left, paroled on the day of our dedication. He is a Protestant—an active and ardent one. He has a job, a car, a home, and for the first time, a family. What's really important, he has been a salutary influence in his union, and he now brings up his children in his church.

How To Build
A World Brotherhood

God Sings Through Me

by ROLAND HAYES

*The hisses pouring from the crowd seemed like ar-
rows of hatred aimed at his heart. Yet Roland Hayes,
famous American singer, faced the hostile audience
with composure. Here is an unforgettable story, rich
in significance for everyone.*

THE FIRST GREAT turning point in my life occurred when I was a
teen-age boy working in a window sash factory in Chattanooga,
Tennessee.

I always sang during my work, because it was as natural for me
to sing as to breathe. The factory owners didn't generally allow it,
but when they discovered that the men worked better when I
sang, no one stopped me.

Somehow my singing came to the attention of other people, because one day I was invited to sing in a church choir. It was there
I met Arthur Calhoun, an educated Negro musician, and he invited me to his home where for the first time I heard the music
of Caruso and Melba on phonograph records.

I have never been able adequately to describe what happened
to me when I listened to those records. It was a religious conversion, for a door seemed to open, revealing to me the dim outline
of the purpose which is now my whole life. I knew suddenly that
my goal was to become a great singer, but it went deeper than
that. I felt God entering my life majestically, and I sensed that He
was choosing me for an Almighty mission.

From that moment on, I realized that I dared not depend on
others to help me. To achieve my goal and to discover my mission, I must take chances. Against all advice I quit my factory job
and set out to become a singer.

The next years were full of disappointments and setbacks as I traveled from city to city, but inside me a bell rang steadily in my heart. My singing gave a purpose to life. Finally, I arrived in Boston where I became a page boy in an insurance company. Every day I carried my music to work so I could sing at my desk when not busy. Again my employers did not interfere; in fact, many times the executives would open their doors to listen to me.

My mother, who lived with me in Boston, was the most wonderful human being I ever knew. One evening she came into the room where I was singing and said to me. "Roland, what did you say?"

"I was singing, Mother."

"But what did you say? I couldn't understand the words. Roland, when you sing, say the words so that everybody can hear and understand them."

Here was my mother, who never had a minute of schooling in her life, urging me to pronounce my words distinctly. To her I owe my clear diction.

For several years I sang in and about Boston during free hours, but I felt I would never really arrive until I had given a recital in Symphony Hall. To accomplish this, I took another great gamble and planned a recital in this famous hall. I had to guarantee the manager four hundred dollars. I laugh now when I think of the way I went about it.

I took the telephone book and picked out two thousand names, trying to select wealthy Back Bay people who I hoped might become patrons of my concert. Then, in my spare time, I pounded out two thousand letters on an old typewriter asking each person to buy two tickets at a dollar and a half each and explaining what I was trying to do. I was trying to get a hearing.

The letters began coming in with amazing speed. The life insurance company where I worked took half of Symphony Hall. On the night of the concert seven hundred people were turned away, and I cleared two thousand dollars. Success had arrived.

But shortly after this triumph, I woke up one night and began to pace the floor. Why this strange restlessness? Suddenly I felt His spirit in me. My mission in life, obscure until now, became clear. Our race had a contribution to give the world, and somehow I had been selected for a special role. My singing had been given to me as an instrument to promote better racial understanding.

Since then each night before commencing my concert I pause a moment. With closed eyes I stand quietly facing the audience and pray, "God, please blot out Roland Hayes so that the people will see only Thee." Thus, I become a channel through which God's spirit flows to uplift the audience and create in them understanding.

This power of the spirit over any force was well demonstrated to me one night years ago after fame had come to me. I was out walking when for some reason five men set upon me. They cursed me, then started to attack me with a brutal lust. I felt the weight of their intense hatred, not so much for me as for my whole race.

Helpless, I knew that resistance on my part would only further incite them. Then I realized how to be a match for them. I could bring to bear a power that no evil could withstand by turning inward into God-consciousness, the most powerful force in the world.

Relaxed, with eyes closed, I asked that the spirit of Christ flow through me into the hearts of these misguided men. I felt my soul lifted high above their hatred and passion, and I was looking down upon them in compassion and pity. One of the men lifted his pistol to crash the butt end down on my head. Suddenly a bewildered expression spread over his face. His poised arm dropped. The power of God-consciousness entered each of the men, and hatred and violence left them.

This experience further convinced me that my mission in life was not only to work for a better understanding of my race, but for a greater understanding among all peoples. It was this desire that influenced my decision to tour the world. As a result of this tour, I had an opportunity to achieve my greatest triumph of God's spirit over hatred and discrimination. This occurred many years ago in Germany.

My scheduled concert in Berlin coincided with the period when the French Army was policing the Rhine with Negro troops from their African possessions. German indignation was high. I remained in Prague until just two days before the concert. The American consul there received several angry letters protesting my singing in Berlin, asking if an American Negro was to insult the spirit of Goethe, Schiller and other great German writers by singing plantation songs from the cotton fields of America.

I was worried about this storm of protest. The American consul in Prague advised me not to go to Berlin, but others suggested that my singing might do much to improve racial understanding in Germany. I decided to accept the challenge since I owed everything to taking just such chances. This was no time for the easy way out.

Slipping into the city incognito, I remained in my hotel room, leaving only for a stroll at night in the Tiergarten. On the night of the concert I took a closed taxicab with my Negro accompanist to Beethoven Hall.

The Hall was packed. At the given hour I walked on the stage with my accompanist. The stage itself was white with light, but the deep hall looked like a black cave. At my appearance a barrage of hisses, like arrows of hatred, shot out of every corner of the hall. These angry missiles seemed to be aimed at my breast.

It was a terrifying experience. I fought back the panic that threatened to engulf me. Then I remembered Him. With hands clasped before me, I stood there, praying that Roland Hayes might be entirely blotted out of the picture, that the people sitting there might feel only the spirit of God flowing through melody and rhythm, that racial and national prejudices might be forgotten.

When I do this sincerely, the audience instinctively senses what is happening. But this was the hardest audience I have ever faced. I stood there in the curve of the piano, my head up, my eyes closed, letting the spirit do the work.

The hisses continued . . . two minutes, three, four, five on to an interminable ten minutes. I stood in silence. Then slowly the noise began to die down. Was the spirit taking effect or were they just getting tired? The answer would come when I began to sing.

Without turning my head from the audience, I told my accompanist to play Shubert's "Thou Art My Peace." It begins softly, almost in a whisper. As the clear notes of the piano playing this song floated out over the audience, it fell silent. Then I began to sing.

I then continued with the scheduled concert even singing two French songs that I had originally included in my program. When I finished, they began to applaud, stamping their feet, their hatred forgotten. Soon they were swarming over the stage, shaking my hand and congratulating me. Never did I receive an ovation that meant more.

The victory was no personal one. It was God's victory over prejudice and intolerance. He sang through me and won the audience. I was fortunate in that I could be the instrument of His power and glory.

Jack-Hammer Diplomats

by JOE SCEPPA

> *In front of United Nations Headquarters in New York is a tunnel which had to be blasted out of solid bedrock. Workers on this project—college man and immigrant, Christian and Jew, black and yellow man—often compared their problems to those of the United Nations. Joe Sceppa, assistant superintendent of the heavy construction crew, tells what he learned down in the hole.*

ONE DAY one of our timber cutters was down in the hole shoring up a span of pipe to run into the United Nations. A big diesel shovel was working near him, and this cutter didn't like the way the bucket swung out over his head. Once in a while the shovel operator had to balance a ton rock on the teeth of the bucket. If that rock slipped and fell, it would have crushed the cutter on the spot.

"Swing that load out the other way!" the cutter yelled above the noise of the drills. When nothing happened he got mad.

I don't blame him for getting mad, but I do blame the way he settled the thing. He just ups himself into the cab, pulls the operator out by his lapel and starts in on him. We had to pull them apart and bring them both in for coffee, till they settled the thing on some other grounds than who was the strongest.

Later we got to talking about how this was like the United Nations. We did a lot of talking about the UN down in the hole. The big guys up there in those plush conference rooms sometimes have the same problem as the shovel operator and the cutter: they can't get their work done for arguing about how it should be done.

People from those offices would come around, ask us what it's like building the UN.

"Do you know how big this job is?" they'd say. And mostly we didn't answer. But when we grabbed ten minutes for coffee . . . there's nothing better than coffee around an oil drum fire . . . we'd talk about whether this job was different.

In many ways all heavy construction's the same. You know you'll work with mud and rock. You work with drills and your hands throw a plunger that dynamites tons of rock at a time.

I've been a heavy construction man for over 15 years around New York. Whenever visitors come from out-of-town, I can take them almost anywhere and say, "I built that." The 6th Avenue Subway, the Midtown Tunnel, Natural Gas Lines—I've laid miles of conduits and I know the secrets of New York's underground life.

New York is my city, was my father's before me. He came from Italy half a century ago to work on construction crews, building, like I do. He's an American now, and he gave me New York; his city belongs to me, because I helped build her.

When I started working on the UN, it was the same mud and rock, the same noise of dynamite and drills, but somehow the job promised to be different. Of course, some of the men up there in those conference rooms might be putting on a big act. Maybe they were shouting for peace and dressing for war.

They could come down here in the mud, those men in the conference rooms and, by watching us and by knowing a little about the land the UN is built on, they might get a few ideas.

They tell me that the ground between 42nd and 48th Streets is blood ground, and during the Revolution, British soldiers had a warehouse at the foot of 45th Street, and the Liberty Boys fought for it on a midnight in 1773. Three years later Nathan Hale was hung on the same spot where the UN building stands.

But it was blood ground more recently than that. I remember the slaughter houses that stood on the UN ground. Cattle boats sailed up the East River and in a good week one house could kill 3,000 head.

The stink was pretty bad, and nobody wanted to live there, so the ground that wasn't bloodened by sudden death was covered by tenements where death was slower. The whole area was slums —tough, saloon, leadpipe slums, and the old timers tell how sometimes a steer would break loose and run wild in the streets, getting even with men.

We brought in wrecking crews to tear down the slaughter houses and gashouse slums. Underneath them, hidden by layers of pavement, were the secret arteries that keep New York alive— steam pipes, sewer lines, water mains, gas pipes, signal conduits, electric and telephone lines and wire cable so complicated that New York had to draw up a special map to keep us construction men from cutting them. We had to tear up these arteries; and stick 'em back just right, so you couldn't tell there'd been an operation.

But digging up old lines was only the beginning. Under this part of Manhattan is about 80 feet of solid bedrock called Manhattan Schist. Just a few generations ago it would have been impossible to work in this tough rock.

But today, we have drills that bore down and explosives that shatter from the inside—one hand plunges a lever and we go down through this bedrock to build foundations for the United Nations. Then came the shovels that scoop up nine cubic feet of broken rock, and the heavy trucks with vertical exhausts which haul the rock away.

Like I say, I wasn't sure my job was important. But I noticed something: The more I put my own back into the UN, the more important it became to me.

I think the delegates must have felt the same way. Every morning they would come from all over the world, many of them wearing long robes or turbans or different shoes from ours, to watch the shovels and trucks. I like to think about them maybe sitting down over a cup of coffee, trying to solve their differences, like we did. And we've plenty of them.

In the first place, there was every kind of person working in the hole: college men and immigrants, Jews and Christians, black and yellow men. They all put their sweat into this job. If we couldn't keep harmony on this job of building the very foundations of the United Nations, we certainly couldn't expect these people in different dress to do any better. Every man has a right to gripe. That's only human. But we solved these gripes over coffee; we let people spout off, but we didn't settle our problems on the basis of who's strongest.

The delegates seemed fascinated with the idea of building the UN on solid rock. I hope they realized that just as it takes drills and dynamite to build in rock, it'll take hard-cutting tools to blast away at some of their old ideas and policies that have led to war after war.

As the verse in the Bible says:

"He is like a man who was building a house, who dug deep and laid his foundation upon the rock, and when there was a flood, the torrent burst upon that house and could not shake it, because it was well built."

Overalls Can Fit All Men

by FERDINAND M. ISSERMAN

> *The Jewish Rabbi from Temple Israel, St. Louis, Missouri, was asked to handle burial services for his good Christian friend. A story of hope and promise for the future.*

FOR MANY YEARS I have been spending my vacation near the same lake community in northern Wisconsin. Of many friends made in the little community, none were closer to me than Ray.

Ray was a sportsman who loved the out-of-doors, who liked to go in a rowboat after the day's work was done and, as the sun was setting, cast with a fly-rod among the weeds. And how still he sat when the deer came to drink of the water, that he might observe them, and then see their white tails disappearing in the brush.

He was a basically religious man. People who seek out such experiences are bound to have souls free of bigotry and narrowness. Such was Ray's soul.

He was a simple man, the driver of the school bus. It is not a minor position in such a rural community. Annually the parents of the children vote for the bus driver, and year after year Ray was elected because his neighbors had confidence in him, in his steadiness, his sobriety, his conscientiousness, and in his sense of responsibility.

While the children were at school, Ray used to do carpenter work for the people in the town. He was handy with his tools and had considerable skill as a craftsman.

Besides his overalls, Ray, I believe, had one suit of clothes. This suit he wore on Sundays and on important occasions. Otherwise he wore his overalls. When Ray walked down the main street, everyone knew and respected him. He called the banker by his first name, and also the owner of the town department store. He knew the postmaster, the forest ranger, the physician, the druggist. He knew everyone and everyone knew him.

In 1949 when Ray was ill, I went to call on him. As I left I felt that I wanted to bless him, but hesitated, not knowing whether the family would be embarrassed because of our different faiths. I did not know what the reaction in the community might be. To my great regret, I remained silent.

Just as I was ready to return to St. Louis, Ray died. When I called upon his wife to express my sympathy, she said, "I know that Ray and you were friends. Our minister, the pastor of the Presbyterian Church, is in Nebraska on his vacation. Would you take charge of the services for Ray? I am sure that would be his wish, too."

I was touched by this invitation from a simple woman in great distress, who believed that in her great sorrow my ministry, whatever the faith, would be a comfort to her and her dear ones.

A Protestant minister in a nearby town and I discussed the details of the service, and I successfully urged him to take part in it along with me. I soon found that the people in northern Wisconsin were very much like the people in our city. I also discovered that there were no mysterious rites demanded by the Presbyterian Church—that with the exception of one or two prayers which contained definite references to Christ, there was little difference between it and the services of Judaism on behalf of the dead.

Services were held on a weekday afternoon. The stores on the main street were closed and almost half of the population filled the seats in the Presbyterian Church to bid Ray farewell and to express appreciation for his life. In the big city, he would have been one of 10,000 men whose passing would have been ignored. In the small community he had walked with head erect, an equal among his peers, evidence of the glory of American democracy.

Both the minister and I offered a prayer. There were two hymns from the church choir, a violin solo, Scriptural readings and a few words of tribute. Everyone seemed to take it for granted that I, a Rabbi, who had known Ray, a Christian, should have officiated at that service.

I have since discovered that, while not an everyday occurrence, the circumstance was not uncommon. My good friend, the Rev. Hampton Adams of St. Louis' Union Avenue Christian Church, told me that he once performed a similar function for a Jewish family in Frankfort, Kentucky, there being no Rabbi in that community at the time.

When the wife of a former Christian police-chief died, Rabbi Thurman was called in to officiate at the final services. And, when Louis P. Aloe, after whom the Aloe Memorial Plaza in St. Louis is named, died in the summer of 1929, no Rabbi who knew him was in the city at the time. The family called in the Reverend Ivan Lee Holt, then pastor of St. John's Church (now Bishop Holt), to be the officiating clergyman at the services.

My experience in Wisconsin seems to have become a part of the American tradition, part of the American scene. This has produced interfaith confidence and interfaith fellowship, unknown in any other country. It is one of the noblest expressions of American civilization.

Bridges of Song

by CONRAD THIBAULT

*What happened when one of America's outstand-
ing concert singers tried out for the choir in a small
community church—and was sized-up doubtfully by
the minister, who did not recognize him.*

ONE SUNDAY recently while singing in an Episcopal Church, I
noticed that the person seated next to me was looking at me
oddly. "Something wrong?" I asked.

"I thought you belonged to another church and were here only
as a guest today," he queried.

"That's right. I belong to the Catholic faith."

"How is it that you know this ritual so well?"

"I've learned the rituals of almost all churches," I answered.
Then I explained that I give many concerts a year in churches of
all faiths, proceeds of which go to church needs.

It is a small contribution, because I love to sing in churches, and
if my singing can further God's work and help promote interfaith understanding—so much the better.

One unforgettable experience occurred several years ago when
I read of a minister in Corona, New York, who was rebuilding
his church literally with his own hard labor. He even made and
hauled the concrete blocks, and did the plastering and carpenter
work.

Interested, I drove out to his church. It was a week-day afternoon, and inside the church I found the minister in work clothes,
painting the walls. He was short and stocky, a simple man of
Italian descent with a face of great calm and peace.

His complete humility impressed me deeply. Anything you
could do to help a man like that was doing a favor for yourself.

When I introduced myself, his face lit up with a warm, friendly smile of welcome. Yet I knew my name meant nothing to him. I was just another of the friendly people he had met in the neighborhood.

"Can I help you with the choir?" I asked.

"Sure," he said. "We don't have too many voices right now, but you don't need much experience. Do you sing or play the organ?"

"I sing a little," I told him.

When I arrived at their first rehearsal several days later, the minister had a slight look of bewilderment on his face. "I'm sorry," he said, "but I don't believe I got your name right the other day."

I told him again.

"That's what I thought you said," he continued, "but the other choir members thought I was joking when I told them you were trying out for the choir."

We had a wonderful time rehearsing and planning for the first service. When eventually held, it was one of the finest experiences of my life. The minister's quiet humility and keen sense of humor were combined in his truly moving message.

What touched me so greatly, even more than what he said, was what he had done. Not only had he built most of the church, but the walls and the very atmosphere of the sanctuary seemed permeated with his love and beauty of soul.

I heard recently that he made his church available to people of another faith in the same neighborhood, worshippers who were temporarily without a church of their own. Perhaps they, in turn, will catch the spirit and keep the chain growing.

It is on this personal level that people can build bridges of understanding around the world. Anyone with love in his heart and a desire for service can use his abilities for this effort.

Why A
God-Centered Home
Insures Your Happiness

Message To The Betrothed

by BISHOP FULTON J. SHEEN

> *Why does it take not two but three to make a marriage? What are the two greatest words in the vocabulary of love? Married couples of every faith will find fresh inspiration, and practical help, in this penetrating article by a great churchman.*

IT USED TO BE, and it perhaps still is, a tradition of the sea that captains go down with a ship. Until a generation or so ago, everyone recognized there was one ship a person ought not to leave, even when he thought it was sinking, and that was the home.

A recent survey shows that in 30 of the large cities of the U.S., there was one divorce for every two marriages, which means roughly that 50 per cent deserted their ships despite the orders of the Great Captain: *"What therefore God hath joined together, let no man put asunder"* (Matthew 19:6).

These divorce figures prove that the most beautiful word in our language has been distorted by the lie of Satan, so that what we call love today is nothing more than a confused mixture of sentimental pathos, disguised egotism, Freudian complexes, frustrated living and weakness of character.

I am not concerned with the divorces, but with the articulation of the doctrine of Christ on marriage which is clear and irrevocable: *"Whosoever shall put away his wife and marry another, committeth adultery against her. And if the wife shall put away her husband, and be married to another, she committeth adultery"* (Mark 10:11, 12).

For that reason, all Christians vow in the marriage ceremony that they will love one another until death do them part.

For someone to say two years after marriage: "I gave my vow at the altar, yes, but since I am in love with someone else, God

would not want me to keep my vow," is like saying: "I promised not to steal my neighbor's chickens, but since I fell in love
with that Plymouth Rock, God would not want me to keep my
promise."

Once we decide in any matter that passion takes precedence
over truth, erotic impulse over honor, then how prevent the stealing of anything once it becomes "vital" to someone else?

For your wedding you stand at about the only place in all the
world where contracts and vows are still regarded as sacred,
namely, before the altar of God.

The lover's language is never temporal nor promiscuous. There
are only two words in the vocabulary of love: "you" and "always." No one ever said: "I will love you for two years and six
months."

Hence all love songs have the ring of eternity about them: "till
the sands of the desert grow cold" and "forever and ever." True
love "alters not when it alteration finds."

The jealousy which has been instinctively inseparable from the
beginnings of your love is a denial of promiscuity and nature's
vanguard to monogamy.

But there is still more profound reason for the unbreakable
character of your marriage. Have you ever noticed that Sacred
Scripture nowhere speaks of marriage in terms of sex, but always
in terms of knowledge? For example: *"Adam knew Eve his
wife: who conceived"* (Genesis 4:1): *"Jephte's daughter knew
no man"* (Judges 11:39): *"Joseph knew her not"* (Matthew
1:25). And when the Angel appeared to Mary to announce her
Motherhood, she asked: *"How shall this be done, because I know
not man:"* (Luke 1:34). And didn't St. Peter say: *"Ye husbands, likewise dwelling with them according to knowledge"*
(1 Peter 3:7).

Why does Scripture speak of marriage in terms of knowledge?

Because that is precisely what marriage is: the knowledge of
the mystery of your own completeness.

If your marriage were only a question of flesh, it would have little more sacredness than the relations of animals, promiscuous and transitory. But once it is regarded as a knowledge of the mystery of your completeness, it follows that its ties are binding through life.

The union creates a unity, and the unity is born of the fact that physically only one person can communicate the knowledge; therefore, a bond is created with that person which is as enduring as life. The woman can never return to virginity, nor the man to ignorance.

Two persons revealed to each other the inner secret and found the completeness of life. A new relationship is established; that of responsibility toward the other for solving the riddle of life and since the change induced in one another is life-long, the responsibility is life-long.

Only when you stake your eternal salvation as a guarantee of your fidelity to your vows does your life become bonded at the altar, sealed with the seal of the Cross, and signed with the sign of the Eucharist which you both receive into your souls as a pledge of the unity in the Spirit as the foundation of your unity in the flesh.

It takes more than two to make love. It takes three: you, and you, and God.

May your marriage be faithful, happy and long. And as you thrill to the joys of one another's companionship, and are cast into ecstasies of love's delights, often ask yourselves these questions: If a human heart can make you so happy, what must be the Great Heart of God. If the spark of love is so bright, oh! what must be the Flame!

God Love You.

My Friend God

by ELAINE ST. JOHNS

> *To six-year-old Kristen, people were either "close to God" or they "didn't know about God yet." a tender, moving story of what parents can learn from a child's faith.*

MY DAUGHTER, Kristen, is a thoroughly joyous being who inhabits a small tanned body and inspects the world curiously through unperturbed blue eyes.

During her day of play it is very hard to tell when she is my daughter and when she is somebody else—Brave Heart, Gretel or Hoppy.

Every so often, because of her high regard for the truth, and to keep the record straight between us, she reassures me.

"It's only a 'pretend,' Mommy," she confides. "I'm really your little girl, Kristen."

But she has one special friend with whom no liberties are taken. That is "my friend God."

She introduced Him into our daily living when she was five. Sitting on the living room floor in a pool of sunbeams, Kristie seemed absorbed in crayoning. It should have been a quiet Sunday afternoon. But the radio had been nudged higher and higher so the Head of the House could hear the ball game above the noises that her brother, Koko, and I were making.

Suddenly over the din Kristie's voice rose.

"My Friend God wants me to have peace," she pleaded.

In the abashed silence that followed, Kristie didn't even look up. She continued her art work.

Since then, I, who introduced them, have been humble before their ripening friendship. Humble, too, before the unfailing simplicity with which she approaches Him.

288

Where did she get her facts? She got them from the usual sources . . . Bible stories we read at home, Psalms we say together, from the little Sunday School where she and her playmates learn hymns. But the interpretation is strictly her own.

She has found that her Heavenly Father is always around, a thing she cannot truthfully say of her earthly parents. She is sure He created all things good and beautiful, hence He is a powerful ally, fully capable of assisting her with any problem. He has never let her down.

Take the matter of her red wagon. Did we, or did we not, lose it? One day it is there in its usual place, the next day it is gone.

We search diligently in all the possible places on our four acres. We ask Koko. We ask Grandma. We have done our best but we do not find it.

"Well," advises Kristie matter-of-factly, "We'd better ask God."

And because her blue eyes are fastened trustfully on mine, I sit down on the stone wall beside her and we ask. But I'm afraid it won't work.

Suddenly we are prompted to look in the coal shed, an un-heard-of place for the red wagon anytime—especially during summer months.

We go to look. It is there. We hug each other, rejoicing.

Scrambling into the wagon and pushing off with one foot, Kristie says, "Thanks, God."

Her Friend seems to have taught her a simple, infallible rule for brotherly love. Some of Kristie's playmates have noticed that her nurse-companion, Rose, is a Negro girl and have pointed out gleefully that her jovial friend from the telephone company is a "fat Mexican."

"Are Negroes and Mexicans close to God, Mother?" she asks.

That's how she sizes them up. People are either "close to God," like George Washington who never told a lie, or Hopalong Cassidy who used his smoking guns to save a widow's ranch . . . or they are people who "don't know about God yet," like cattle rustlers or a man she saw on the street who was quite drunk.

She has good-natured tolerance for those of us who "get away" from God temporarily by losing such human things as tempers or self-control. For there are times when she herself is not on the very best of terms with her Friend.

"Some days," she explains thoughtfully, "I just want to do what I want to do. I don't *want* to listen to Him."

These are very unpleasant days, crammed with tears and punishments, and I am always grateful when she has had enough and creeps quietly into her room to "get close" to Him again. I do not know if she talks to Him, or listens to Him, or prays. These matters are between her and her Friend.

On the adult plane where we scientific parents dwell, all this could be charming fancy well laced with coincidence—except for one fact. Like the mountain climber who does not know the quality of the rope until he has fallen, so with my daughter's faith in her Friend. For she fell off the side of a mountain, and her rope held. Actually though, it was a small mountain.

But she had her bad spill while carrying a small glass bottle. A razor-sharp fragment from the broken glass cut deeply into the palm of her hand. When I reached her side, the blood was gushing upward in a terrifying, irregular fountain. I used my fingers as a tourniquet and soon she lay quietly in my lap while we contacted the emergency hospital.

"I want to make a prayer," she told Grandma in a small voice. "But I haven't any words. You make the words, Grandma." But because Grandma's words were slow in coming, traveling as they must around a big grown-up lump of emotion, and because her need was urgent, Kristie patiently made her own prayer.

"God," she said, "you are my life. You love me. Even if all the blood runs out, you are my life. Even if I went in the den of lions with Daniel, you are my life. And," she sighed, "I love you."

In that confidence she rested.

At the hospital, the cool young doctor refused to perform the necessary surgery while I was in the room. My daughter lay there, very small in her bloody jeans, with her four freckles standing out on her little pug nose. I could not bear leaving her to face the ordeal alone.

"You just wait in the hall like the doctor says, Mommy," she advised.

For forty minutes I stood in that hallway and took strength from my small daughter's voice.

Once she yelped. Immediately she encouraged the doctor. "It's all right. I understand." But mostly she chatted with him about the everyday things in her life. How joyous she made it all sound . . . the triumph that her step-dad had "tooken my picture in Technicolor," the wonderful possibility of camp. Then she confessed a cherished secret.

She was not going to marry Hopalong Cassidy. She had seen a picture of Mrs. Hoppy in a magazine. Instead she was going to marry the tall Indian currently appearing in a color ad for a national railroad.

"Indians," I heard her inform the doctor, "are very close to God."

As I reentered the surgery, the young doctor put his arm on her shoulder. "Everything in her hand was laid wide open," he said gravely. "But your daughter has full use of all her fingers. No permanent damage. It was a miracle."

"It wasn't a miracle," said my little Indian firmly. "It was my Friend God."

The Widow's Son

by WALLACE F. BENNETT

One day in his early manhood, Heber J. Grant faced a career decision—the navy or the church. What happened is told here by his son-in-law, Senator Wallace Bennett of Utah.

HEBER J. GRANT, my father-in-law, was the seventh president of the Church of Jesus Christ of Latter-Day Saints, often called the "Mormon" church. He served in this capacity from 1918 until his death in 1945.

During his life he made and lost several comfortable fortunes, yet he never lost the simple faith in God and man which marked him with greatness.

Heber Grant's father, who was Brigham Young's counselor and the first mayor of Salt Lake, died nine days after Heber's birth, leaving the young mother, Rachel Ivins Grant, to earn a meager living for herself and her only child.

While her son was yet little more than an infant, Rachel was promised (in a prayer blessing offered by a beloved woman leader) that Heber would some day become one of the heads of the church. Rachel never told this to her son until after the prophecy was fulfilled, though its promise must have been a great sustaining force during the years she bent over her sewing machine.

Heber dreamed of having what they used to call "a higher education," but his mother's circumstances made that impossible. Then one day he met George Q. Cannon, the territorial representative in Congress, who offered him an appointment to either West Point or Annapolis without competitive examination. He chose Annapolis.

Next morning, chattering to his mother of his new dreams of the sea, he realized she had been weeping. He often told us that, in an instant, like the traditional drowning man, he saw himself an admiral and all the life he might have had passed before him.

Then, his decision made, he put his arms around his mother and said, "Mother, I don't want a naval education. I am going to stay home and take care of you, and have you quit keeping boarders for a living."

Then she broke down, and told him she had prayed all night that he give up his militaristic ambitions. The old promise of that prophetic prayer that he would become a church leader, was still strong in her heart.

His own prayers were a vital force in Heber J. Grant's life. He approached God with complete faith that if his request were reasonable and proper, it would be granted. He told us that twice during his long ministry he prayed to be appointed to a definite position in the church.

Once he asked the Lord to guide those in authority to appoint him as a leader of the young people's group. He felt he could make a real contribution, not only to the organization, but to the magazine it published, which was having a hard time. The very next day, he was called to the office of the then President of the church, Wilford Woodruff, and given the appointment, in which he served for long and well.

Later, he was sent to open a mission in Japan. After many discouraging months, he went out into the woods and, kneeling, prayed that he be allowed to serve, instead, as head of the European mission of the church. Within a week came a cable calling him home, and after a short stay in Salt Lake, he went on to Europe.

But prayer was only one of the twin powers of Heber J. Grant. The other was perseverance. When he determined on a goal, he would never rest until he achieved it.

Like all small boys, he loved to play marbles. One day someone with a little authority chided him for not working to help his widowed mother. This stung.

But characteristically he determined that he could help his

mother and still play marbles. He practiced every spare minute until he could beat anyone in the neighborhood. The marbles he won and sold back, as boys can, to their former owners, kept him in pocket money.

In his teens, he liked to play baseball. But he was not wanted because he was thin and frail. He promised himself he would one day play on the team that would win the territorial championship. He threw a baseball against the wall of his mother's barn, endlessly, as a target for accuracy. He developed enough skill to make his goal.

Someone called his handwriting "chicken tracks." It was the day of penmanship flourishes. He got writer's cramp, but eventually acquired enough grace to win prizes for handwriting.

But his real persistence was demonstrated in learning how to sing. He loved music always, but was almost monotone as a child. Several teachers began with him hopefully, only to end in a few weeks in despair, saying he could never learn to sing.

But after he was grown and in the service of the church he was determined to learn at least a few simple hymns. On the long wagon and carriage rides between the western settlements, he sang the same hymn a hundred times without pause.

Finally he mastered the unmistakable tone line. No triumph was ever greater to him. It's a famous and loving memory in Salt Lake that at a party of friends, he invited himself to sing. He offered his audience the choice of two hymns. His accompanist played what was called for, he sang the other, and didn't know the difference!

But even that was mastered by constant plugging and one of the prized possessions of every one of his descendants is a record of him singing "The Flag Without A Stain" on his eightieth birthday. To them, no one ever sang it better.

Prayer and perseverance—the twin forces of Heber J. Grant's success—are an unbeatable combination, and his finest bequest to us all.

40 Acres of Children

by LEAH E. YOUNG

Fourteen times throughout the years Mrs. Young breathed a special prayer, "Lord, bless this unborn child and help it to become a worthy citizen." Here is a family of sixteen you will remember. The story of how the biggest dreams can come true.

"IN THIS GOOD COUNTRY you can dream as big as you wish, and the Lord willing, make these dreams come true." I said this 42 years ago when my husband, John, and I stood looking at the rough farmhouse that was to be our home here in Virginia.

John is a good man and shared my faith and hopes. We wanted a big family, with education and careers for all. What better place could the son of a Negro slave and his wife find, to make those dreams come true, than this wonderful 40-acre farm?

As the years went by we began to pay for the farmhouse. John farmed well; I raised ducks, turkeys, geese and pigeons . . . corned fresh herring and canned all the food I could lay my hands on. We always had plenty to eat.

Nothing is more exciting than growing your own food. Every spring, when the earth was soft, rich and brown as we started planting, I would get down on my knees in thankfulness. "Bless these little seeds, Lord," I would say. "There are so many to feed."

Our family was growing. There were Flossie, Otis, Earlie, Rudolph, Hezekiah, Estrell, Josephine, Bernice. . . . As the children grew up they would bring in friends for dinner. But all were welcome and we always cooked for more than enough—even for the stranger who might drop by.

Because the nearest church was far away, and our family was growing fast, it became increasingly difficult to make the long trip each Sunday. So we decided to build our own church. John called together several of our neighbors: "What we need," he said, "is a church for everybody, one without denomination so we can all worship no matter what our different beliefs are."

That night we sang hymns and asked God to bless our work. The next day John, the children and neighbors began clearing the land. We constructed a beautiful church, inscribed thus today:

ST. JOHN'S CHAPEL
The Church of Christianity
Courtland, Virginia
Founded in 1920 by
John P. Young
Rebuilt 1948
Dedicated to the Glory of God

As the children grew up, our lives centered around the home and this church. In the evenings John tutored the children with their lessons and included a reading and explanation of the Scriptures. At mealtime everyone was prepared with a favorite Bible verse.

On several occasions when the preacher was absent on Sundays, one of us would step in and conduct the service. Eventually, every one of our family was able to handle the services.

I remember John in the pulpit once, telling the congregation, "Remember this always. You have got a man-part and a God-part and neither one must go hungry."

When the depression hit us, the bottom dropped out of cotton and it was hardly worth picking. A series of misfortunes followed. The chicken house burned, destroying 600 chickens. The bank went broke with all our savings. And to top it off—our farmhouse burned down and we weren't even able to save our own clothes.

The next day we began building a new house. To make up for low farm prices, Papa butchered, laid bricks, dug graves, built coffins and once even ran a wood yard while the boys ran the farm. I took in cleaning, sold peach pies, holly and mistletoe along the roadside and sewed coats, suits and dresses for the whole neighborhood.

Hard times and sickness drew our family closer together. I can remember when every child had the measles at the same time. I would walk from bed to bed saying a little prayer with each child. Once when I had a bad case of rheumatism, the whole family got on their knees around my bed. My pain cleared up soon after and has never returned.

But we always had fun no matter how hard times were. The children would label their hoes and race each other down the cornfield. In their enthusiasm some stalks would be cut down, too, and hastily buried. Papa would pretend not to see these. When work was done there were picnics in the woods and singing at the piano. The children even had their own orchestra, and somehow, we were able to find enough clothing and to grow enough food for all.

By this time, with the arrival of LaVerne, our fourteenth child, the family was complete. The oldest were finishing grade school and the real struggle for our dream of education began. Grammar school was just down the road and there my home-made feed-sack shirts and dresses had been adequate; shoes could be done without. But high school complicated this problem.

Five were now going to high school, which meant better clothes, shoes, and bus fares. It cost 25¢ a week to send one child on the bus, which meant $1.25 extra had to be found each week. We always managed somehow.

Sometime later, by dint of careful trading, we secured an old bus for ourselves and all the other children in the neighborhood.

Soon Flossie, the oldest, graduated and was ready for college. I sold my chickens to get a few dollar dresses for her. The night before she left for St. Phillips Medical College, we all knelt and prayed, as we did whenever anyone went away from home. We went with her the next morning, and discovered that she needed a registration fee to enter. John asked the superintendent if they could wait until crops came in for this money. They agreed.

Later Josephine left for Virginia State. She had only $2.50 to take with her, but, like Flossie, and the others after her, she got a job and earned her way through to a degree. As each graduated they helped the others through. The younger ones helped with the farm work and I taught the girls cooking and canning. Lillie later won in the 1950 Pillsbury baking contest.

Today most of our dreams have been fulfilled. They all finished high school and most of them college. Six were valedictorians, five won college scholarships. Josephine has her Master's degree in Home Economics and is working for her doctorate now at Cornell. Flossie is a registered nurse; Earlie, a contractor; Rudolph is in masonry and construction.

Margaret is a librarian, Joyce teaches mathematics and LaVerne teaches music; Hosea and Otis are carpenter and contractor. Maisy is a home economics teacher. Lillie and Bernice are also teachers in elementary and parochial schools; Hezekiah teaches agriculture and Estrell has become the farmer here at home. LaVerne is taking her fifth and final year in music at Virginia State College.

From the moment of conception, the children have been placed in God's hands. Fourteen different times I breathed a special prayer. "Lord, bless this unborn child and help it to become a worthy citizen." I am grateful that all births were normal.

It has been a good life and we are mighty thankful to the Lord for the dreams he sent us—and helped us to fulfill.

Beauty Is of The Spirit

by COLLEEN HUTCHINS

*Miss America of 1952 always thought of herself as too
tall, too skinny. Yet the philosophy of her mother,
and the quality of her family life, helped Colleen
Hutchins win the number one beauty achievement
in America. And the kidding from her brother, Basketball Star, Mel Hutchins, didn't hurt either.*

As soon as I heard about my brother's award several winters ago,
I called him in New York, where he was playing in the East-
West basketball game as a representative from Brigham Young
university.

"Mr. Mel Hutchins," the long distance operator said, "will you
accept a collect call from Miss Hutchins in Salt Lake City?"

Mel, you see, had won a cup as the most valuable player in this
game. Whenever he does something outstanding, it's sort of a
standing gag that I telephone him collect, no matter where he
happens to be.

"Congratulations!" I told him. We kidded around for a while,
he being offhand and modest about his new honor as usual. Then
he made this parting shot, "I'll get back at you in good time, just
wait."

Mel, I think gets real humility from mother. She is completely
calm and serene, at least on the surface, about the victories and
defeats of her seven children. She and my father together have a
deep religious philosophy that has laced our family tightly together over the years.

It is taken for granted that each member of our family plays an
active part in the church. All my brothers have had, or will have,
periods of training as missionaries—a general practice for young
men in our church.

I have taught Sunday School for years. It is work I love; teaching youngsters the importance of their own religion is, in my opinion, essential to our national health and vitality as well as to the children's own well being.

Our family ties mean even more now that some of us travel so widely. A prayer bond does a lot to knit us together. Mother, for example, is so concerned about the speed of travel these days that I think her prayer reaches out to us on wave lengths.

Not so long ago, my younger brother, Gene, was driving across the Great Salt Lake Desert in Utah. This road is so straight and smooth that it is very difficult to keep the speed down. There was a blow-out. Gene's convertible turned over three times.

The next thing Gene knew he was lying on a strange bed, having great trouble breathing. He felt no pain, but told us later, "I simply knew I was going to die. There wasn't any question about it."

So badly hurt was he that those attending him gave up hope. Gene heard one of them say, "Call the boy's family first, the doctor won't do him much good now."

Unable to get to Gene fast enough, we telephoned several young Mormon missionaries to rush ahead to him. They arrived and began a prayer vigil. Gene did pull out of it, making a remarkable recovery.

Several months ago when I went back to Utah for a visit, I drove over the same road with some friends. As we drew near the scene of Gene's accident, I told the others what had happened. For some reason I slowed down.

Then I began to hear a peculiar noise; it seemed to come from the engine.

I am no mechanic; a noise is just a noise to me, but I did stop at the side of the road. The front wheel was slanting away from the hub at close to a 45 degree angle, the only thing holding it to the wheel base being a small groove, worn into the metal itself. We were chilled at the thought of what might have happened.

Now, I have usually shied away from modern stories of prayer miracles, but these experiences convinced me that we should never underestimate what God can do for us, or through us, if we believe in prayer.

My entry as "Miss Utah" into the 1952 Miss America contest was the subject of conversation, and a lot of kidding in our family. So lightly did I take my chances that I acquired tickets to a Broadway play the night after the Atlantic City contest. It didn't occur to me I couldn't use the tickets if I won.

Many people perhaps don't realize that Miss America selections today are based on three separate tests: the girl's talent, physical appearance and general intelligence.

The first night was talent night. I was grateful that my family had encouraged all of us to develop one field in which we could perform better than average. With me it had always been dramatics.

The second night of the contest was the traditional bathing suit stroll. Now all members of our family are on the tall side; I am 5 feet 10 inches in stocking feet. Too much stature may seem to be a disadvantage to girls, but despite the kidding around in our family, we're all secretly proud of our height.

The most interesting, and most serious, part of the pageant was held on the third night. Questions were asked of contestants who then had to answer with impromptu speeches.

"What do you think is the most serious problem that faces America today?" I was asked.

My answer: "Our relationships with foreign countries." I then went on to explain my belief that any problem can be worked out on the basis of religious principles. William Penn's statement, "Those people who are not governed by God will be ruled by tyrants," makes my point for me.

While certainly no authority on foreign relations, I do believe that nations cannot rise higher than the standards by which their families live—certainly families with clear cut moral and spiritual codes have greater understanding, mutual respect and love.

When I called my mother to tell her that I was the new Miss America, I'll never forget her answer. I had to laugh, it was so typically mother.

"Well, goodness sakes, Colleen," she said, "What in the world did you win it on?"

Later, came the long distance call that I had been expecting. "Sit back and relax now, Miss America, for a nice long chat," Mel said. "This time you're paying for the call."

How To Guarantee
Our Free Way Of Life

I Am a Convert to Democracy

by INDUK PAHK

*A Korean mother, who rose from ignorance and pov-
erty, risks the life of her daughter in a Communist-
occupied city by broadcasting on the Voice of America. Mrs. Pahk has made 2,500 speeches in 35 countries, and her challenging message is important
reading for every freedom-loving American.*

I FIRST HEARD about America many years ago when a small girl
living with my family in North Korea. I heard about the wonderful American inventions, but what really impressed me was the
idea of God's love as brought home to us by a group of simple,
dedicated American missionaries.

My parents were ardent Buddhists, spiritualists and Confucian-
ists. No home had more idols than ours. When the dread cholera
came and took my father and brother, it left my mother and me
completely desolate. The idols were no comfort. In Korea, a family with no men is no family at all.

It was at this time that a cousin, who had recently become
Christian, tried to comfort us.

"Is your God sympathetic?" my mother asked.

"Not only does this God love everyone, and grieve with those
who have sorrow," our cousin said, "but this God has schools to
which women can go as well as men."

This was a startling new thought for my mother. It turned her
attention to me with new hope.

It was on Christmas day that mother and I walked three miles
over snowy country roads to the nearest Christian church. Missionaries in the crude building greeted us warmly and presented
me with a yellow pencil and a yellow writing pad. I was thrilled
speechless. My mother was so touched that when we returned
home that night, she burned all the idols in our home. Both of us

accepted this new Christianity, and I set about learning to read and write the Korean alphabet.

"I wonder if she has enough brains to learn it," my mother thought to herself, wavering between her new hope and the common Korean conception that all females were stupid. I showed her. I learned the alphabet in two weeks.

What few Christian schools there were in our country at that time started at high school level. Meanwhile, I needed elementary grounding, so we moved to another area where there was a regular Korean school—for boys only. From that moment on I was a boy!

In those days both sexes wore the same long braided hair, with black ribbons tied at the end for boys, red ribbons for girls. Only slight changes were needed in my other garments—my jacket had to be lengthened and mother converted a skirt into a pair of trousers. My feminine-sounding name, Imduk, became Induk.

Korean boys act like brats. The louder you read, the smarter you were. I shouted my head off. Boys were agile and athletic. I learned to climb trees, to play ball and to fish with the best of them. After two years I graduated without anyone knowing my real sex.

My mother, meanwhile, had saved enough money to buy me a railroad ticket to Seoul, home of Ewha Christian College for Korean women. Dressed now as a girl, I said goodbye to her, clutching my few articles of clothing and ninety cents. When I arrived at the college, Miss Iula Frey, the Principal, stared at me in dismay.

"But there's no money to feed you and no place for you to sleep," she said in answer to my request for admission. "I have fifty girls on the waiting list."

I looked around and saw an unused reception room. "I can sleep there," I pleaded. "I won't get in the way. I'll got to bed after the others and get up real early."

"But what will you eat?"

"I'll eat the scraps left by the others," I said desperately.

The kindly missionaries didn't have the heart to turn me away. An appeal was written to the United States, asking for additional funds to take care of just one more student. A man in Wilmington, Ill., Mr. C. G. Steinhard, who himself had just gone blind, heard of my situation.

"My physical light is gone," he said to his sister, "but I would like to share my spiritual light with this Korean girl." Together they managed to send $5 a month to Korea for seven years—the priceless sum needed to put a girl through school. (When I had a chance to thank this man in person many years later, he said: "You have caught the spiritual light, Induk. Share it with those who live in darkness.")

Upon my graduation from Ewha College, I became a school teacher and also took part in the Korean Independence movement. Then a calamity happened. A number of us were rounded up and thrown into jail as agitators. Some were beaten to death. In my cold, bare cell, illuminated only by a tiny light from one slit-like window, I prayed:

"If only I had a Bible to read and some rice to eat."

At that very same time Miss Frey at Ewha College was thinking:

"I wonder what Induk needs most—probably some rice."

So she began a systematic campaign to get some rice to me.

Meanwhile, two of my missionary friends, Dr. and Mrs. Billings, remembered me.

"What would be of most help to Induk?" they asked of each other.

"A Bible!" was their decision.

They began to exert steady pressure on a Judge they knew to have prison officials give me a Bible.

Several days later my prison door opened and guards handed me both a Bible and a container of rice!

How I pored over that book. Up to this time, Christianity had meant an education and a new world of opportunities to me, but I had never really known God. In this grimy prison I was suddenly able to feel the presence of God through that Bible. New strength and faith came. I read the Bible through twice, then began memorizing passages. Death lost its terror because God was there to steady and comfort me. After six months, officials set me free.

Strange how real and close God is to one in time of crisis, yet how easily we can let material interests and activities crowd Him into the background again. My great plans to help improve the conditions of Korean women were forgotten after my release from prison. For I met a young man and fell in love.

My husband-to-be was an innkeeper. We had furnished a home with many lovely possessions, when one night while we were away, the home burned to the ground. As we stared at the ashes, stunned and heartsick, a neighbor dashed up with a silver vase.

"I'm so very sorry," she sympathized, proffering me the silver vase. "You lent me that last week—at least something has been saved."

Accepting the vase numbly, I suddenly felt the great truth of a phrase I had learned: *That which I kept I lost, that which I shared I have.*

That experience made me resolve all over again to share the benefits of my Christian education, and live the kind of life that I knew God meant for me. Soon after, an opportunity arose for me to come to America and do some speaking. With the money earned, I was able to return and help my people. Other speaking invitations came, including one to the United Nations. Then I had an opportunity to bring a message to my people through the Voice of America.

During years of lecture trips, I have traveled 434,020 miles with over 2,500 speeches made in 4 continents and 35 countries. My husband, mother and first daughter are gone now and my daughter, Iris, is in danger, but I'll carry on my work as long as God gives me the strength. To American people who are disturbed over their responsibilities for world leadership, perhaps this message will help: *That which I kept I lost, that which I shared I have.*

And from my own experience, I know that the greatest thing Americans have to sell is not their wealth and comforts, but that America is a country founded on belief in God, where Man has freedom and opportunity to do, to think, to act and to become just what he chooses. Americans, although not without their faults, have shown that men and women of all races, colors and creeds can live together in harmony.

Our Troops Know It

by GENERAL MARK W. CLARK

> *The General's wife woke up in the night to find her husband on his knees, in prayer. "Nothing unusual about it" says General Clark in this personal account of divine guidance at work in the Armed Forces today. An encouraging message for parents of boys in service.*

ON A COLD BLEAK DAY in December, 1950, I stood on a platform at Camp Pickett when General of the Army Dwight Eisenhower told the members of the 43rd Infantry Division, "The United States, united in spirit, aware of its task and determined to do it, is the strongest force on earth."

The marshalling of the nation's material resources alone is not sufficient to secure the freedoms for which our ancestors fought and died. There must be a spiritual unity—a renewed recognition of the responsibilities of citizenship and belief in the basic factors which have enabled this country to achieve greatness.

The greatest of these is, of course, a belief in God and the teachings of Christianity.

One of the compelling reasons which brought our ancestors to this country was a desire for religious freedom. Thus, from the beginning, our freedom was based on a strong faith in God.

Spiritual influences constitute one of the greatest factors in the training of our youth, and the church and the clergy constitute a strong force for good. We must rely on the Church, home and school to instill in our youth an appreciation of his obligations of citizenship under a democratic system.

Our training job in the Army is much easier when these attributes have been acquired by our youth before they enter military service. Sending a child to Sunday School or church does not constitute the ultimate discharge of a parent's duty. The formation of character is a daily, an hourly task, and the training which results in good character must be accomplished by the parent in the home, by the teacher in the school, and by the pastor in the church, both simultaneously and continuously.

Spiritual welfare is a paramount factor in the training and military service of our soldiers. It is our constant aim to return soldiers to their home as good, or as better citizens, than they were when they came to us.

We in the Army recognize the need for character guidance in the development of our youth and have established a definite program designed to provide continuing training in subjects related to character building while our youth are in military service.

The Chaplain plays an important role in shaping and guiding the lives of America's soldiers. In recent years the scope of the Chaplain's responsibilities has been greatly increased. His duties are not limited to the religious welfare of our troops. He provides the necessary religious services and, in addition, he is with the troops in the field—sleeping and eating with them—in order that he may be constantly available to help in the solution of their personal problems and to guide them morally.

As I go about the country visiting our military installations I am greatly impressed by the interest in religion displayed by our soldiers. I think it is unfortunate that so many people's concept of a soldier is the very opposite of reverence. Last spring Mrs. Clark woke up in the middle of the night and found me on my knees praying for the safety of our son, Bill, whose company had been cut off in Korea. This was deemed to be so unusual as to deserve a comment in the newspaper. I see nothing unusual about it.

I know the American soldier well and I know that he has a basic belief in God, gained either or before, or after, he gets into the Army. And I know he is reverent and devout. It has been truthfully said that there are no atheists in the foxholes.

Since boyhood I have believed in prayer and, following a long standing custom, I daily ask guidance for my activities and God's mercy on the protection of our troops and loved ones.

During World War II, I gained mental strength for the difficult tasks of combat by reading each day a little prayer book, *the Daily Word,* a Unity publication.

On September 5, 1943, the day I went aboard a ship at Algiers to lead our Fifth Army to an invasion of the Italian mainland at Salerno, I picked up my little prayer book and read the following:

"Father, in Thy name I pray, let me know Thy will today. With Thee I am unafraid, for on Thee my mind is stayed. Though a thousand foes surround, safe in Thee I shall be found.

"I have a faith that Thou wilt be always guarding and directing me. In the air, on sea or land. Thy sure protection is at hand. Momently Thy love I share, Thy grace, and Thy protecting care. . . . Thou art with me all day long, showing me the way to go, helping me always to know Thou are justice, peace and life, healer of the nation's strife."

It seemed to have been written especially for the occasion. It helped immeasurably to allay my anxiety about this historic operation and to instill in me the confidence that God would see us through. There were many other times during the war when it was evident that divine guidance had been given us.

Faith has solved many momentous problems for me. I believe that our country's welfare depends on a return to old fashioned virtues and the development of the spiritual unity of our people.

Golden Rule at the Throttle

by ALLEN ROSE

> *The massive locomotive slowed to a stop at a small Texas town. The engineer climbed from his cab and presented a furry kitten, named Cinder II, to a little girl who had lost Cinder I under the wheels of this same locomotive several weeks before. The human side of a great railroad, the Texas & Pacific, and the story of its leader, William Vollmer.*

THE ENGINEER CLIMBED into a makeshift wagon seat aboard the first car of his three-car train. Ahead of him stretched 23 miles of track from Swanson's Landing to Marshall, Texas. Instead of a whistle cord, his right hand held a bull whip. His left hand gathered the reins of a team of six double-yoked oxen. The whip cracked and, in late January, 1858, a railroad was born.

There is no record of how long this odd caravan took to cover the 23 miles of pine dotted, East Texas countryside. The oxen pulled the cars over the flat ground and uphill. Downhill the "engine" rode on the flat car. And the train did reach Marshall.

The lurching oxen enabled the young railroad to fulfill the terms of its charter with a few days to spare. Fortunately, the charter had not specified the kind of power to be used. Otherwise, the delayed arrival of the wood-burning engine would have spelled disaster and the waste of many years of hard work.

This odd beginning marked the birth of what later became the Texas and Pacific Railroad; a vital 1900-mile link in one of our great transcontinental rail systems. To Bill Vollmer, the active, energetic president of the T&P, it typifies for him the resourcefulness, born of courage and faith, that built America, as well as great railroads.

At 65, President Vollmer is an old hand at railroading, with forty-nine years of service behind him. Forty were spent with the Missouri-Pacific lines where he rose to Senior Vice-President before moving on to the T&P.

He gets a kick out of his job. "There were always many things I wanted to try in this business," he tells you with a smile. "Now I'm in a spot where I can."

In the past eight crowded years, Bill Vollmer has done things on a scale that is large even for Texas and his adopted home town of Dallas. An Ohioan by birth, and by no stretch of imagination a native son, he was quickly accorded honors not usually given "foreigners."

Within a year he headed the Community Chest in Dallas, a tribute to his ability and leadership. Never a man to lend his name to something and let another do the work, his efforts on behalf of the Fund led him to take on other civic responsibilities.

In the meantime, the T&P has become a symbol of friendliness and service from New Orleans to El Paso. Vollmer's tall, husky figure is constantly out on the line, watching operations and lending wise counsel. Revenues have grown steadily under his hand.

Bill minimizes these accomplishments. He points out that he faced only tasks that "confront any executive in a new job. Furthermore, I inherited a good railroad. I had loyal employees and customers. I was working with a solid organization."

Nevertheless, when he took over back in 1945, the new President felt that something was missing. The road was making money, but Vollmer sensed that from a human standpoint his organization was cold and impersonal.

A feeling of unity and teamwork was lacking. To do something about that, he set out to meet each of his 8,000 employees. In eight years he has not only met most of them, but many of the road's customers in Texas and Louisiana as well. The T&P suddenly began to develop a reputation for being a very good neighbor.

One day, several years ago, a T&P train whistled its way

through the small town of Oxford, Louisiana. Somehow a little black cat got under the wheels. Probably no one aboard was even aware of the accident.

A little girl, by the name of Marlene Wendt, knew about it, however. It was her pet that had been run over.

She wrote the railroad a letter that tugged at the heart. "My cat was killed by one of your locomotives. He was a black cat named Cinder and had one white whisker. I loved my cat very much."

A few days later, the through train made an unprecedented stop at this small town. The engineer climbed down from his cab, holding in his arms a small furry object—Cinder II. When the train pulled out, Marlene Wendt was standing there, with big, wide shining eyes. In her arms she clutched a black cat with "one white whisker," given to her by the same engineer who ran over Cinder I.

In this and in other big and little ways, the T&P has assumed a "personality." It has come to stand for warmth and character.

Moving around as much as he does, Vollmer did discover, however, some things that bothered him and his associates. They noticed among all kinds of people a seeming lack of interest in individual freedom, and an indifference to the virtues of our forefathers: spiritual steadfastness, thrift, initiative, hard work ... the qualities that made America strong.

The problem was discussed often by Vollmer and his colleagues. How could a railroad help people to get back on the track? Out of their thinking grew an advertising program built on fundamental spiritual values and satisfying goals. It was to be not only a program of action, but a way of life. It was to be a pattern, not for individuals, but for a country faced with danger, within and without.

One day last May, readers of along-the-line newspapers in Louisiana, Texas and New Mexico opened their papers and found a large advertisement sponsored by the T&P. There was nothing unusual in that. Railroads, and all industry, have been making increasing use of institutional messages.

However, there was something unusual about this Texas & Pacific message. It said nothing about the T&P or about railroads in general. It made no attempt to bring in customers. It was selling the ideals and virtues embodied in four simple verbs—"*Work —Save—Vote—Pray.*"

The advertisement invited support for the program and suggested that interested people write in for a booklet written by Bill Vollmer. Entitled "The Four Pillars of Freedom," the booklet offered detailed information about the plan.

Those who sent for the booklet, and 200,000 copies were distributed in a little more than three months, were in for another surprise. For here was a corporation with a gross revenue of more than $70 million, annually, advocating prayer as one of the most important steps in a four-point program of *working, saving, voting* and *praying*.

It was a strong, earnest appeal for people to ask their God for help in a critical time. The booklet pointed out that without His help, no amount of hard work, thrift or good citizenship would work a lasting success. Perhaps the simplicity and earnestness of the message tapped the deep spiritual drive that lives in so many hearts and only waits for the right spark. Whatever the reason, T&P's neighbors, as well as people far away in Tacoma and Boston, were attracted to the program. A large department store used a portion of the article as its Independence Day advertisement. Newspapers reprinted the booklet verbatim, urging support.

"Your proper emphasis on prayer, and recognition of God, coming from the 'pulpit' of Big Business," wrote one young man, "is as refreshing as rain after a Texas sandstorm."

An interesting fact about the railroad's current campaign is that none of the persons involved, including Mr. Vollmer, wears his religion on his sleeve for all to see. Mr. Vollmer's guiding principle, which he follows faithfully, is the Golden Rule.

It is the bedrock of his nationally known employee relations work.

Eventually, the series of six advertisements, stressing work, thrift, citizenship and prayer, will be seen by nineteen million Americans. One of those messages, scheduled for Christmas, is a direct challenge to Americans of every walk and creed to let God into their lives; to let Him help work out our personal and national salvation.

No one can know now, of course, how far-reaching the effects of this crusade will be. Millions of people will have seen the advertisements before the formal campaign is ended. Perhaps as many as a half million copies of "The Four Pillars of Freedom" will have been distributed.

No matter what happens, Bill Vollmer is certain that, whether based on the T&P program or another, the time has come for Americans to show the world what we stand for and to demonstrate to others that we intend to support our beliefs.

Vollmer is surprised that people see anything unusual in his company's advocacy of prayer. He does admit that it is not customary, perhaps, for business to spend a lot of money to that end. But he points out that the country, which has made things like great railroads possible, was founded on a belief in God and justice.

The T&P president is disappointed that people apparently have forgotten that our country's great leaders were men of deep spiritual qualities. He can't imagine school children growing up without knowing this and understanding its influence and power.

"Our program," he insists, "is really a selfish one. I'm thinking of myself, my friends, our children and our country. What could be more selfish than to want to save the good things our way of life provides? What could be more selfish than to try to foster in others a belief in God's wisdom and trust in Him to the end that you and I and our country may be strong?"

The Flame of Great Venture

by MADAME CHIANG KAI-SHEK

Christianity can save China from Communism. This is the steadfast Christian belief in the hearts of the courageous couple who kept China alive during years of attacks by the Japanese Empire. Madame Chiang's inspiring story is of endless struggles against seemingly hopeless conditions.

I HAVE OFTEN been asked what faith means to me.

In my own life, faith is primarily the flame that illuminates any great venture. It lights up the path through the forest of despair and it gives us the courage, the strength and the gallantry to go on, undismayed and unbeaten, when conditions seem most hopeless. It is the dynamic spark which defies defeat.

In every life there are, inevitably, trials. But just as seeds need darkness in which to germinate, so must people who are vitally alive experience some of the gloom of misfortune if they are to realize the potential which is within them.

We grow by overcoming our disasters. Without faith we are constantly in danger of being overwhelmed by adversities. With faith we unite ourselves with the deep stream of the Eternal's purpose and meaning, and are thereby enabled to accomplish the impossible.

This does not mean that in our lives events and conditions can always be made to work out precisely as we would have them. It does mean that we have the power to direct our energies and will in furthering God's goal.

Recently I saw some photographs of children afflicted with poliomyelitis, demonstrating the Sister Kenny method. Just as the suffering children continue believingly to flex and exercise their atrophied muscles when they are prostrate and seemingly helpless, so individuals and nations must continue to strive, even in their blackest hours.

China's epic defiance of Japanese domination between 1937 and 1945 is a striking instance of the efficacy of faith. When Japan hurled its military machine upon us in 1937, opinion in the outside world gave China little more than a few weeks of possible resistance.

But the unshaken faith of my husband and his loyal co-workers galvanized China to achieve the unbelievable. The miracle of Chinese resistance was prolonged for eight years, four of them unaided and alone, and in the end, it was Japan that failed.

Faith points out to us that the one irretrievable attitude for men and for nations is the attitude of passivity and fatalism. If we accept defeat we become frustrated. Then we are indeed lost. But if we refuse to accept defeat by pressing onward in the face of external set-backs, then we develop an inner integrated wholeness of character which is invincible.

Thus, in the present awful struggle of my country with the evil forces of communism, the Christian attitude is not—as some Christians have mistakenly believed—one of submission and expedient compromise. One cannot compromise with evil and remain unsullied. In China today there are countless instances of unpublicized Christian martyrdom at the hands of communism. From the blood of such martyrdom will spring the seeds of the reborn China which will arise in the future.

Christian faith means that we must and can fight for our principles even at the risk of temporary defeat, and perhaps death. There can be no opportunistic bargaining, anytime, anywhere, between right and wrong.

Only this indomitable determination of man to make the supreme sacrifice for the substance of its faith has kept Christian right alive in this world through tortuous nights of human history. And because there are men and women ready to live and die for their convictions, the victories of communism will prove transient and ineffectual.

In this hour, all over the world there is a frenzied scramble for security. But when men speak of security they are only too often betrayed into a concept based on the material and the physical, whereas Christ taught us that real security emanates only from within. For peace of heart and serenity of mind cannot be attained when they are sought for themselves. They come as by-products and are the gifts of the spirit which performs each day's task day by day to the best of its ability according to God's guidance.

It is valuable therefore from time to time to detach ourselves mentally from the urgency of immediate events to reassess our relationship to God and to our fellowmen. Such a reassessment will reveal whether and how far short we have fallen in meeting the challenge of our convictions and principles, and bring into focus the actions necessary to right ourselves with God and men.

A living faith demands a continuous self-scrutiny.

A Stake in the Land

by WINFRED VAN ATTA

> *The young bride hated the unceasing wind, the bleak, treeless landscape of her new home in North Dakota. The farm was not what she had expected when she answered the newspaper advertisement of Peter Anderson, a young Swede who wanted to marry a good Lutheran girl from the Old Country. Winfred Van Atta, who knows the family, tells of pioneering courage that has made America strong.*

PETER ANDERSON was 21 when he arrived in New York from Sweden. His worldly possessions included a change of clothing, his mother's Swedish Bible and about $100.

Peter neither read nor spoke English, and knew only one person in America—a cousin who worked in a Minnesota lumber camp and whose address was stamped on a metal disc Peter wore on a chain around his neck.

Officials in New York helped Peter purchase an immigrant's ticket to St. Paul. He is not sure to this day what happened on the way. Thirty hours later, he stepped out into 30-below-zero weather. He was in Minot, North Dakota, 500 miles beyond his cousin. He had about $4 in his pocket.

In the restaurant across from the station, Peter met a young Swede named Christianson, who had arrived under similar circumstances a few months before.

"Labor is hard to get during the winter here," Christianson explained to him in Swedish. "It's no accident that we and other young immigrants arrived here by mistake."

But Peter shouldn't worry, Christianson went on to advise. The best opportunities in America were right here in North Dakota. He could have a job laying track for the St. Paul, Minneapolis and Manitoba Railroad, and there were millions of acres of good prairie land to be had free, if a man was willing to develop a homestead. The railroad would even sell a responsible homesteader stock and equipment on credit.

Peter worked for the railroad almost two years, and then filed claim for a 160-acre homestead at the edge of the Souris River Valley, 18 miles from Minot.

There was a flowing spring and pond on Peter's land and buffalo grass was abundant. After he had built a sod hut, and the railroad had sold him two carloads of imported Texas steers on credit, he would not have changed places with any man on earth. Drought in the Southwest sent beef prices sky high that fall, and Peter shipped his fat steers at a good profit. He purchased a team of horses and plow, and put in 20 acres of winter wheat.

By the end of his first five years, when he received title to his land, Peter had built a good barn and a two-room frame house. Only one thing was missing: a farmer needed a wife to keep his house and bear his sons. Unfortunately, there were few girls of marriageable age in North Dakota.

Peter solved his problem by placing an ad in a Swedish language newspaper published in New York: *Young Swedish man with North Dakota farm wants to marry good Lutheran girl from Old Country.*

Frieda Johnson had been in America less than a year when she answered Peter's ad from Providence, Rhode Island, where she worked as a domestic servant. "If you will tell me more about yourself and have a Lutheran minister vouch for your character, I might consider your proposition," she wrote.

Sixty years later, Peter's eyes would grow bright when he told about meeting his bride at the station. They had not exchanged photographs. When Frieda came down from the train, Peter could not believe she was the girl he had come to meet. "Ja, she vas beautiful," he said, "and yoost as sveet and good as she vas pretty."

An hour after they met, Peter and Frieda were married.

The marriage was to become one of those perfect unions. But there were adjustments to be made at first. For a time Frieda hated the unceasing wind, the bleak, treeless landscape, the scorching summer heat. And she feared the 40-below-zero winters. But after their two sons were born, Peter enlarged the house, and Frieda began to see a future for her sons in this rapidly developing frontier. In time, she also fell in love with the harsh, challenging country.

She worked alongside Peter in the fields, and tended large flocks of chickens and turkeys. Every penny was saved to buy more land, so that each of their boys might have a farm when they were old enough to marry.

There followed years of drought, years of panic, when banks closed, wiping out savings and credit; heart-breaking years when wheat prices were high, when crops were destroyed by hail, grasshoppers or wind. Yet there were always good years to offset the bad, and by 1914 the Andersons owned 360 acres of land.

This man was to become my uncle.

I met Peter Anderson for the first time in 1935. My bride was the daughter of a younger brother he had brought over from Sweden ten years after his own arrival. Uncle Peter was past 70 then. Driving the 18 miles from town to his farm, I found it hard to accept his optimism as normal. For times were then very bad.

Those who did not see it at first hand cannot possibly understand the meaning of the words, "dust bowl." On either side of the gravel road that led to Peter's farm, the huge, even-spaced fields lay barren and dead. Weatherbeaten farm buildings, deserted and lonely, protruded from dunes of dust. Farming equipment, almost buried, rusted in corners of fields.

Peter Anderson's neat red barns and white house, therefore, came as a surprise when they appeared on the road ahead. Even more surprising was the grove of stunted, but still colorful, evergreen trees that grew back of the house. After seeing the simple headstone that stood among the trees, I understood why Peter had kept them alive by carrying water to them from his spring.

FRIEDA EMMA ANDERSON

Born: 1868   Died: 1926

A Good and Faithful Wife

As I listened to Peter talk that blistering August afternoon, I knew why people had warned me that he was a little peculiar and queer. His original conception of his own little section of America had not changed.

"Ja, is bad now," he said, "but yoost come back next year. A little rain and this contray be yoost like garden again. Da Lord knows His business, I tal you, and He don't give up on good lan like dis. I see bad yar and I see dis lan go 40 bushels wheat to acre."

And Peter was disgusted with Swanson and Lindestrom, two neighbors. How could they give up and move to Illinois? This land had been good to them for 40 years. They had promised to work it and stick by it; otherwise the United States Government would not have given it to them free. They had special responsibility and should not give up so easily. The Lord was always finding ways to test men, and if men would only trust Him and wait, He always took care of those who had faith.

When there were no crops in the three years that followed, and things were at their very blackest in North Dakota, Peter Anderson took a step which his relatives thought was irrational. He withdrew his life's savings from the bank—the few thousands which could have kept him in comfort for his remaining years—and began to purchase for back taxes the farms which adjoined his. No amount of logic or persuasion could deter him from the course he had set. To protect him, his family petitioned the courts to have him declared incompetent to handle his affairs.

The judge was a kindly man—a man who also wanted to believe in a better tomorrow. "Is good lan," Peter told him, "and is good contray. Someone has got to have faith in da Lord and His lan."

The judge threw the case out of court. Peter continued to buy farms, spending most of his money, but getting much of his acreage for almost nothing.

And Peter was to have the satisfaction of knowing his faith in the Lord and the land was completely justified. For nine years running there has been rain, and his several farms have produced bumper crops, with prices the highest in history.

Aside from his responsibility to the land, which he accepted upon his promise to work and develop it, Peter Anderson has made an even greater contribution to America in his sons. One is now a farm advisor in North Dakota, directing crop planning and tree planting to avoid future dust bowls. The education Peter's land paid for, made this possible. The other is a government engineer, working on the nearby Garrison Dam, which is to help harness the unpredictable Missouri River and provide irrigation for the semidesert areas of North Dakota and Montana.

When I last saw Peter in July, 1951, he was still quite spry, directing a crew of men who were building waterproof walls in the cellar of his house.

One night a year later, Peter, then in his 90th year, came home from the fields. Friends are convinced he had no plans to go out that evening. So it was perhaps the same divine sixth sense people say he has always been blessed with that prompted Peter to shave carefully, put on his Sunday suit and lie down for the final time on his old-fashioned four-poster bed.

My Personal Job

by ROBERT A. MILLIKAN

> *Dr. Millikan, one of America's greatest scientists and a Nobel prize winner, stated, "it is my personal opinion that no atheist can be a very good scientist." Here are some of his personal convictions about science and religion.*

"WHAT CAN I do to help make a better world?" is a question asked by every conscientious person.

To me, the answer lies in the cultivation and the dissemination throughout mankind of two great influences: (1) the spirit of science or knowledge, and (2) the spirit of religion.

Those are the two pillars on which rest all human progress and human well-being. The collapse of either one of these pillars will bring down the whole structure.

I shall not dwell here upon the accomplishments of science for everyone knows that within a hundred years science has created here in the U.S.A. the greatest abundance that has ever existed at any time or place on earth.

But I must make crystal clear what I mean by the spirit of religion. For this is the influence which has spread our abundance into the highest standard of living the common man has ever known . . . and has linked our abundance with personal and spiritual freedom.

In the long sweep of evolution, what we call spirit, or soul, was the latest and certainly the most important element in the whole evolutionary process. Breasted calls the moment at which it first appeared "The Dawn of Conscience." I shall call it also the dawn of religion. For conscience implies responsibility—a consciousness that I ought or I ought not. That is what I mean when I talk about the essence or spirit of religion. For I am interested, not in creeds, but in human life and conduct.

Jesus put the essence of his teaching into the Golden Rule: "Whatsoever ye would that men should do to you, do ye even so to them."

That says clearly you are the sole judge of what you ought to do. For man alone, of all creation, has been given this power of choice between good and evil, and it is in the exercise of that choice that man develops a soul. It is in choosing the good, instead of the evil way that man is able to fulfill his great mission on earth.

Montesquieu, the great philosopher, made an answer to the question—what can I do to help make a better world?

"If I knew something beneficial to myself but harmful to my family, I would drive it out of my mind. If I knew something advantageous to my family, but injurious to my country, I would try to forget it. If I knew something profitable to my country, but detrimental to the human race, I would consider it a crime."

To me, the supreme opportunity and responsibility of each of us is still just as Montesquieu stated it 200 years ago. In other words, my personal job is to shape my conduct so that it would promote the well-being of mankind as a whole if everyone followed my example. That is what choosing the good, instead of the evil, way means. That is my fundamental freedom, my fundamental responsibility.

Here in America we have plenty of statistics that show how well freedom works in economics. The following statistics show how freedom works in religion:

In 1789 the new Constitution of the United States first divorced church and state. The Constitution guaranteed religious freedom. Since 1789, there has never been any compulsion on the religious beliefs of Americans. Today, church membership in this country totals more than 86,000,000; 55.9% of the population of the United States of America, including Protestants, Catholics and Jews.

This figure alone makes the United States the world's foremost exponent of a Christian civilization, a way of life based on a fundamental belief in God and in the teachings of Jesus . . . as distinct from a materialistic, godless type of civilization.

Religion and science, then, are, as I see it, the two great sister forces that have pulled, and are still pulling, mankind continually onward and upward.

The Court of Last Resort

by RAYMOND SCHINDLER

> *What could you do if you were wrongly convicted
> of murder? Viewing reports that there were unjustly
> convicted men in American prisons, a group of
> prominent leaders called on Raymond Schindler, a
> man whom many consider the country's number one
> detective. This is the story of the creation of a needed
> Court of public opinion.*

VANCE HARDY was imprisoned 27 years for a murder he did not
commit.

For a while, he held out hope. Hardy's sister wrote each week
that she was saving money . . . $97 . . . $107 . . . $200 towards an
appeal. It took her 15 years to put aside enough for the lawyer,
and court expenses. So sure was Miss Hardy of her brother's innocence that she spent some of the precious money to buy Vance a
fine suit and some new shirts.

But the appeal was defeated.

The judge reaffirmed the verdict of guilt; the lawyer pocketed
his fee and forgot the case. For 12 years more, Miss Hardy stored
Vance's new clothes. And Vance, despairing of ever proving his
innocence while in prison, tried to escape. As the result of this attempt, he spent eight years in solitary. The cell had no windows;
air and light came in through a slit near the ceiling. On the floor
were two boards and two blankets for a bed. Once a week, he was
allowed to leave his cell for an hour and a half, and to take a bath.

Through the prison chaplain, Vance Hardy's case came to our
attention at the *Court of Last Resort*. Erle Stanley Gardner, creator of Perry Mason detective stories, together with Harry Steeger,
the publisher of *Argosy* magazine, had started the Court for just
such cases as this. Erle wrote histories of the men and women be-

lieved to be wrongly imprisoned and *Argosy* would print the stories.

I was asked to assist in these investigations. Others devoting their time to assist us were: Dr. LeMoyne Snyder, lawyer, physician and pathologist; Alex Gregory, investigator and operator of the Lie Detector and our permanent paid agent, ex-warden Tom Smith of Walla Walla prison. Those of us who work on the Court donate our time and our effort, of course. This is, after all, the "something" we can contribute to what we believe in. Already this Court has been, indeed, the Last Resort *of twelve innocent people since it was founded early in 1948.*

In the case of Vance Hardy, once we had the complete dossier of his history, we had enough evidence to question whether or not a gross miscarriage of justice had been done. Then we began investigation. Months of dreary work followed; interviews, travel, reviewing musty court records, tracking down witnesses, seeking new evidence on a trail, cold years before, initiating lengthy legal processes, and incurring great expense.

But the results were rewarding. We found a witness who had perjured himself, and with this new evidence, we approached G. Mennen Williams, Governor of Michigan. A short time ago, we were able to phone Hardy's sister:

"Get out that suit; Vance is coming home."

Particularly for me, I think, this side of an investigator's work has been a pleasant one. Because often, of course, under different circumstances, the truth which I have uncovered has meant that a man was sent to prison. I grew up in a poor but very happy family. My father, an inspired Unitarian minister—until his death at 93, two years ago, was a great-hearted humanitarian.

But it was my Mother, even more than Dad, who taught me to look upon the convict, as well as on other unfortunates, as a man in trouble rather than as an evil person. Mother was a Sunday School teacher who practiced the letter of what she taught. Our home, furnished in the old manner by the generosity of Dad's parish, was always open house to those poorer than we.

Looking back on our childhood, I remember Mother's peculiar genius for seeking out the despairing and troubled and asking them into her heart. Later, she was one of the first women to interest herself in the lot of prison inmates and to work for what is now widely accepted as rehabilitation rather than punishment.

Remembering her, I have several times hired the very men, whom I was responsible for sending to prison, to work for me when they had served their terms. Only once have I been sorry that I believed in them.

This faith in the basic goodness of most men who cross the line of the law makes it particularly difficult for us on the Court to choose which cases we will champion.

To investigate and appeal every case where there is a question as to the guilt of the prisoner would, of course, be a job too vast for any one organization. We have had to limit ourselves as to the kind of cases we would undertake. The limitations we have chosen have been that the prisoner must have been convicted of murder, be penniless, without counsel, and have exhausted all other remedies.

We chose murder because the stamp of "killer" must be the hardest for an innocent man to bear. Clarence Boggie served thirteen and a half years in Walla Walla Prison on the charge of murdering an old man.

When we succeeded in proving his innocence and having him freed, he wrote us, "The charge of *murder* is almost more than any normal person can stand, but, to be accused of killing a poor old man over 80 years of age was a nightmare experience from which I'll never fully recover. I had guards come by my cell with many visitors and stop and point me out and say, 'There is a murderer who killed an old man!' . . . that hurts, and I still hurt over it."

In Boggie's case, as in Vance Hardy's our first contact was through the prison chaplain. That we have been largely successful in selecting the truly innocent is due, in my opinion, to the work of these prison chaplains. They know the prisoners best, and it is rarely that they are deceived as to the guilt or innocence of the men under their care.

The prison chaplain does more for the innocent man, though, than help to secure his release from prison. He helps him to become really free, free from bitterness at the wrong done him, free from a grudge against society which might send him back behind bars, this time for a crime of his own. The chaplain touches these men's lives with a vision so Christ-like that they are able to say, as Clarence Boggie said, "I hold no malice nor hate against anyone," and mean even the real murderer who let him take his punishment.

This is the aspect of the work of the Court which is closest to my heart. All my life I have been concerned with the problem of the rehabilitation of the criminal, but the psychological crisis facing the innocent man trying to make the step back into his old life after long imprisonment is one that tears at the soul.

How can you say to a man, "We're sorry about these 18 years that were taken from you. Your house, your car, your savings are gone. Your wife is a stranger, your children are grown. Here's a new suit of clothes and ten dollars. Good luck!"

When the $10.00 are gone, where will he find work, without a social security number or a record of steady employment? Whom does he know but other ex-convicts? . . . men little prepared to give him the right kind of help.

Aware of these adjustments facing the men we have helped to free, I have headed a rehabilitation committee as part of the job of the Court. Our first duty is to find work for them, so they can live in dignity, and security, from the despair which might otherwise overcome them. We have never made a direct appeal for money, yet a week never passes without the mail bringing contributions from *Argosy* readers, from the audiences of radio and television shows where we appear with these men and from people who have read the story of their release.

The expressions of sympathy and interest from people of small incomes all over the country mean the most, of course, to the men themselves. Boggie, after his release, wrote, not just to the officials of the Court, but also to all the friends whose names he did not know. "To speak of you as dear friends is not enough. You have not only taken me out of prison, you have proven to me that there are still some who live by the Golden Rule."

Often the insufficiencies of what we can do loom large. Louis Gross contracted tuberculosis while he was in prison. After proving his innocence we could have arranged permanent sanitarium care for him, but that was not what he wanted. Although he will never be able to work, he wanted to go home; to keep, for what life was left to him, a vestige of normalcy.

Clarence Boggie's heart was weakened by the years of inactivity. He had boasted, in prison, that he could move more lumber in a day than any man under him. After his release he went back to the mills. He died a few months later. All we could say of this man whom all of us had come to love, was:

"Thank God he died a free man!"